SketchUp 2014 for Architectural Visualization

Second Edition

Create stunning photorealistic and artistic visuals
of your SketchUp models

Thomas Bleicher

Robin de Jongh

BIRMINGHAM - MUMBAI

SketchUp 2014 for Architectural Visualization

Second Edition

First published: April 2010

Second edition: May 2014

Production Reference: 1200514

Published by Packt Publishing Ltd.
Livery Place
35 Livery Street
Birmingham B3 2PB, UK.

ISBN 978-1-78355-841-4

www.packtpub.com

Cover Image by Aniket Sawant (aniket_sawant_photography@hotmail.com)

Credits

Authors

Thomas Bleicher

Robin de Jongh

Reviewers

Ricky Mujica

Atulit Kumar

Francis Perea

Orlando Toro

Commissioning Editor

Martin Bell

Acquisition Editors

Rebecca Youé

David Barnes

Content Development Editor

Azharuddin Sheikh

Copy Editors

Alisha Aranha

Janbal Dharmaraj

Mradula Hegde

Insiya Morbiwala

Karuna Narayanan

Laxmi Subramanian

Technical Editors

Kunal Anil Gaikwad

Pramod Kumavat

Mukul Pawar

Siddhi Rane

Project Coordinator

Kranti Berde

Proofreaders

Ameesha Green

Linda Morris

Bernadette Watkins

Indexer

Tejal Soni

Graphics

Abhinash Sahu

Production Coordinator

Nitesh Thakur

Cover Work

Nitesh Thakur

About the Authors

Thomas Bleicher has graduated as an architect in Germany and worked as an architect, lighting designer, and daylight consultant in the UK. SketchUp is a central part in his work. He is now working as a design coordinator in the Cayman Islands.

To Jacqueline, for everything.

Robin de Jongh is the author of several books on professional workflows with SketchUp, GIMP, and Unity3D. He has worked for many years in the construction industry as a CAD designer and at one time ran his own architectural visualization company using SketchUp as the main presentation tool. He now works as an acquisitions editor for Manning Publications where he mentors new authors, and publishes books on Open Source technology topics.

You can find him blogging at www.robindejongh.com.

I would like to thank my co-author Thomas Bleicher, for an amazing job with the update and for working so hard to make the second edition of this book even more valuable for the readers. Thanks to our Acquisition Editor Rebecca Youé who ably guided the project from start to finish. Also, special thanks to Kim Frederik and Patrick Nieborg who have selflessly guided a generation of would-be digital artists on various SketchUp rendering forums, to Ioannis Pantazopoulos — creator of Thea Render, and the still great (and still free) Kerkythea. Thanks to the entire team at SketchUp HQ for their continued superb work on SketchUp, the software that didn't just lower the entry barrier for 3D modeling and visualization... but destroyed it!

About the Reviewers

Ricky Mujica is a New York City born illustrator and alumni of High School of Art and Design, Parsons School of Design, and Parsons in Paris. He specializes in book cover illustration using digital media, and fine art using traditional media.

He started his illustration career in 1983 using traditional oil paints and made his first digital illustrations in 1997. He has hundreds of illustrations to his credit and has collaborated in beta testing and the creation of several user manuals for projects involving specialized, industry-specific CG software packages.

His clients include Harper Collins, Harlequin Books, Bantam, Dell, Little Brown Books, New York Times, Daily News, Ebony Magazine, US Tennis, 7UP, Scholastic Books, among others.

He has been included in the Society of Illustrators' annual shows on several occasions and has won several awards including "Best in Show" at the New York City Art Expo.

> I would like to thank Packt Publishing for giving me the opportunity to review this fantastic book.

Atulit Kumar is a graduate student at Carnegie Mellon University's Entertainment Technology Center. His primary interests are computer graphics and specifically physically based rendering and animation. Over the course of his undergraduate and graduate studies, he has interned at Intel Labs and Disney Research where he researched on high performance computing and physically based character animation, respectively.

He is also a technical reviewer of *3D Printing with SketchUp*, *Packt Publishing*.

Francis Perea is a Professional Education Professor at Consejería de Educación de la Junta de Andalucía with more than 14 years of experience. He has specialized in System Administration, Web Development, and Content Management Systems. In his spare time, he works as a freelancer and collaborates, among others, with ñ multimedia, a little design studio in Córdoba working as a system administrator and main web developer.

When not sitting in front of a computer, he can be found running or ridding his bike through the tracks and hills in Axarquía County where he lives.

I would like to thank my wife, Salomé, and our three kids, Paula, Álvaro, and Javi, for all the support they give me, even when we all are busy. There are no words enough to express my gratitude.

I would also thank my colleagues in ñ multimedia and patient students. The need to be at the level you demand is what keeps me going forward.

Orlando Toro is a visualization artist and freelance designer based in Barquisimeto, Venezuela. His background is Computer Science with extensive experience with PC and Network Support. After discovering the world of Computer Graphics, he specialized in 2D and 3D graphic arts, which has allowed him to produce visuals for a wide range of projects, in and out his country. He also works as a photographer and session drummer. He is the CEO and Owner of Atenax Project (visual art) and bbluestudios (photography and film), 3D partner at Mytoslab in Greece, Technical Reviewer at Packt Publishing, and contributor of Semeruco Films, Unidad Metrica and Aporta Comunicación Integral in Venezuela. Outside CG, Orlando is a partner at Odontospa (dental clinic and spa) and CEO and founder of Tamborire.org (Online Musicians Academic). When he is not doing 3D, he is busy with photography, training workshops, playing drums, or just hanging out with his wife and son, which he really loves to do.

I want to first of all thank God for all the blessings, to my family, my wife, and my son for always being there for me at all times and being my light on the road. Thanks to Packt Publishing crew for the opportunity, support, confidence, and such a fabulous time creating this book. It was an amazing experience!

www.PacktPub.com

Support files, eBooks, discount offers, and more

You might want to visit www.PacktPub.com for support files and downloads related to your book.

Did you know that Packt offers eBook versions of every book published, with PDF and ePub files available? You can upgrade to the eBook version at www.PacktPub.com and as a print book customer, you are entitled to a discount on the eBook copy. Get in touch with us at service@packtpub.com for more details.

At www.PacktPub.com, you can also read a collection of free technical articles, sign up for a range of free newsletters, and receive exclusive discounts and offers on Packt books and eBooks.

http://PacktLib.PacktPub.com

Do you need instant solutions to your IT questions? PacktLib is Packt's online digital book library. Here, you can access, read, and search across Packt's entire library of books.

Why subscribe?

- Fully searchable across every book published by Packt
- Copy and paste, print, and bookmark content
- On demand and accessible via web browser

Free access for Packt account holders

If you have an account with Packt at www.PacktPub.com, you can use this to access PacktLib today and view nine entirely free books. Simply use your login credentials for immediate access.

Table of Contents

Preface

SketchUp 2014 for Architectural Visualization Second Edition shows you how to master SketchUp's unique tools to create architectural visuals using professional rendering and image editing techniques in a clear and friendly way. You will be able to get started immediately using SketchUp 2014 (Pro or Maker), professional rendering, and image processing software.

The book shows you how to create watercolor and pencil-style sketchy visuals. You will also create composites of real and rendered images, creating digital and paper presentations to wow clients. If you are impatient, you will find a "quickstart" tutorial in the first chapter to get you rendering a photorealistic scene immediately. The rest of the book builds on this knowledge by introducing you gradually to in-depth concepts, tricks, and insights in an easy-to-follow format through quick tutorials.

Using easy step-by-step explanations, this book opens the door to the world of architectural visualization. With no prior visualization experience, you will quickly get to grips with materials, texturing, composition, photo-compositing, lighting setup, rendering, and postprocessing. You will be able to take SketchUp's "sketchy" output and add the artistic touch to create pencil and watercolor scenes.

What this book covers

Chapter 1, Quick Start Tutorial, provides an immediate fix if you're impatient to get photorealistic rendered SketchUp scenes. Straight away, you will learn how to model the gallery scene, set up lighting, add materials, and finally render in Thea Render.

Chapter 2, Collecting a Toolset, helps you select the right SketchUp 2014 edition. Did you know that by downloading a few free plugins or other software, you can turn SketchUp into a fully functional 3D visualization and animation suite, similar to high-end commercial software? Follow this chapter to obtain all the goodies.

Chapter 3, Composing the Scene, discusses how to take the hard work out of modeling by setting up your scenes prior to starting modeling work. You will learn how to start from CAD plans or site images and build the scene optimized for quick rendering or animation later.

Chapter 4, Modeling for Visualization, discusses a number of techniques specific to SketchUp. SketchUp is so easy that we are tempted to jump right in and model everything. But this can lead to an ineffective model, which will slow down your computer and your progress. This chapter will lead you through some advanced modeling methods that will save you time and hassle and will allow you to produce large and complex models.

Chapter 5, Applying Textures and Materials for Photorealistic Rendering, is concerned with applying materials and textures for added realism, as the name suggests. Now that we all have digital cameras and easy access to online image resources, we have an effective way of "dressing" the model. The tutorials in this chapter show you how to use SketchUp's unique photo and material handling tools to create intricately textured models.

Chapter 6, Entourage the SketchUp Way, shows the challenges and solutions for using entourage. After you've created the scene, modeled the building, and applied materials, you'll want to add life to the scene with entourage. Learn how to find the best people, foliage, vehicles, and furniture online or create your own personal collection. With the methods in this chapter, you will be able to build up a comprehensive library to use, give, or sell to others.

Chapter 7, Non-photoreal Visuals with SketchUp, discusses all the basics you need to create artistic visual styles using GIMP. Exporting images from SketchUp is not the only way to produce sketchy visuals. By combining several image layers in GIMP or Photoshop, you will learn how to simulate sketchy pencil and watercolor styles. Fans of this style will be pleased to know that the famous *Dennis Technique* is presented in this chapter along with Dennis's own creations.

Chapter 8, Photorealistic Rendering, lets you explore our rendering software in more detail, giving you the skills and confidence to tackle any rendering project. A hassle-free method of working is introduced along with proven settings for outdoor and indoor scenes.

Chapter 9, Postproduction in GIMP, lets you double your skills as a rendering artist. The rendering process isn't the end of the line, because there are lots of subtle but important after-effects you can apply to make the image even more effective. This chapter covers how to add reflections without rendering, creating depth of field effects from a depth render, adjusting levels for realistic daylight scenes, and composing real and rendered images.

Chapter 10, Animations, discusses the basics for producing animated walkthroughs and flyovers. The crowning glory of your visualization project is likely to be a rendered or artistic-style animation. The tutorials in this chapter will take you through this step-by-step process, showing you how to create storyboards, set up cameras and paths in SketchUp with extra plugin functionality, export test animations and final renders. Photoreal animations are then combined to make a simple show reel.

Chapter 11, Presenting Visuals in LayOut, lets you experience the capabilities of the LayOut tool. LayOut is bundled as part of SketchUp Pro and is introduced in this chapter for those who wish to explore the free trial before committing to Pro. You will learn how to bring together SketchUp models and artistic or rendered output into a screen presentation or printed portfolio, adding borders, text, and dimensions.

Chapter 12, Interactive Visualization, takes you beyond the limits of classic architectural visualization and explores options of interactive 3D presentations. We will show you how to use new technologies to create a first-hand experience of the SketchUp design for your clients.

Appendix, Choosing a Rendering Software, gives you a few pointers towards choosing a rendering software that will fit your requirements and lists a few representative and popular choices.

What you need for this book

To run the examples in the book, you will need the following software:

- SketchUp 2014 (Maker or Pro)
- Thea Render (the trial version will do if you just want to try the waters)
- GIMP or Photoshop for editing and combining images
- VirtualDub (Windows) or Zeitraffer (Mac)
- MovieMaker (Windows) or iMovie (Mac) to create movies

An Internet connection is needed for some sections of the book.

Who this book is for

This book is suitable for all levels of SketchUp users, from amateurs right through to architectural technicians, professional architects, and designers who want to take their 3D designs to the next level of presentation. *SketchUp 2014 for Architectural Visualization* is also particularly suitable as a companion to any architectural design or multimedia course and is accessible to anyone who has familiarized themselves with the basics of SketchUp through online videos.

Conventions

In this book, you will find a number of styles of text that distinguish between different kinds of information. Here are some examples of these styles, and an explanation of their meaning:

Code words in text, database table names, folder names, filenames, file extensions, pathnames, dummy URLs, user input, and Twitter handles are shown as follows: "Save in the My Documents folder."

New terms and **important words** are shown in bold. Words that you see on the screen, in menus or dialog boxes for example, appear in the text like this: "Select the image you want to use and click on **Open**".

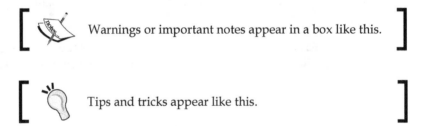

[Warnings or important notes appear in a box like this.   ]

[Tips and tricks appear like this.   ]

Reader feedback

Feedback from our readers is always welcome. Let us know what you think about this book—what you liked or may have disliked. Reader feedback is important for us to develop titles that you really get the most out of.

To send us general feedback, simply send an e-mail to feedback@packtpub.com, and mention the book title via the subject of your message.

If there is a book that you need and would like to see us publish, please send us a note in the **SUGGEST A TITLE** form on www.packtpub.com or e-mail suggest@packtpub.com.

If there is a topic that you have expertise in and you are interested in either writing or contributing to a book on, see our author guide on www.packtpub.com/authors.

Customer support

Now that you are the proud owner of a Packt book, we have a number of things to help you to get the most from your purchase.

Downloading the color images of this book

We also provide you a PDF file that has color images of the screenshots/diagrams used in this book. The color images will help you better understand the changes in the output. You can download this file from: https://www.packtpub.com/sites/default/files/downloads/8414OT_ColoredImages.pdf

Downloading the example code

You can download the example code files for all Packt books you have purchased from your account at http://www.packtpub.com. If you purchased this book elsewhere, you can visit http://www.packtpub.com/support and register to have the files e-mailed directly to you.

Errata

Although we have taken every care to ensure the accuracy of our content, mistakes to happen. If you find a mistake in our books – maybe a mistake in the text or the code – we would be grateful if you would report this to us. By doing so you can save other readers from frustration and help us improve subsequent version of the book. If you find any errata, please report them by visiting http://www.packtpub.com/support, selecting your book, clicking on the let us know link, and entering the details of your errata. Once your errata are verified, your submission will be accepted and the errata added to any list of existing errata. Any existing errata can be viewed by selecting your title from http://www.packtpub.com/support.

Piracy

Piracy of copyright material on the Internet is an ongoing problem across all media. At Packt, we take the protection of our copyright and licenses very seriously. If you come across any illegal copies of our works, in any form, on the Internet, please provide us with the location address or web site name immediately so that we can pursue a remedy.

Please contact us at `copyright@packtpub.com` with a link to the suspected pirated material.

We appreciate your help in protecting our authors, and our ability to bring you valuable content.

Questions

You can contact us at `questions@packtpub.com` if you are having a problem with any aspect of the book, and we will do our best to address it.

1
Quick Start Tutorial

So, you've decided to learn how to use SketchUp for architectural visualization? Maybe a friend told you how easy it is, and you decided to give it a go yourself? Or you heard all the hype about it on the Internet? Well, whatever your reason for picking up this book, you've come to the right place! SketchUp is the easiest, most powerful, effective, and fun-to-use application you will ever come across for 3D work. This book shows you how to use SketchUp and other software to achieve great architectural visuals in no time.

This chapter shows you all you need to get up and running immediately, and it will give you a flavor of what is in the rest of the book. In this chapter, you will learn how to produce the following:

- A photorealistic rendering of a scene modeled in SketchUp
- Real-world shadows and lighting using a physically accurate light simulator
- Materials that reflect or absorb light

When you have followed the tutorial and seen how easy it is to produce great results with SketchUp, you will be able to go on and refine your skills and techniques in the subsequent chapters. The rendering software you'll be using is **Thea Render**, which is a professional visualization software. Rendering is the process that generates an image from the 3D-scene geometry you prepare in SketchUp. To find out more about Thea and how to install it, jump to *Chapter 2, Collecting a Toolset*, but come back again!

Here's what you can expect from just 20 minutes of modeling and rendering:

- Reflection, highlights, and surface texture even with simple materials
- Soft shadows and indirectly lit surfaces
- Physically accurate lighting from the Sun and sky

If all that's achieved with just a few minutes in SketchUp and a bit of rendering, what do you think you could do after reading the whole book? Have you ever achieved such great results as quickly in any other software package?

This chapter is as much about expelling the myths about SketchUp as it is an introduction to photorealistic architectural visualization. I hope you will be enthused by it when you see the quality of your own results.

 If you don't have SketchUp installed already, you should now skip ahead to *Chapter 2, Collecting a Toolset*, where you will find the download and installation instructions for SketchUp and Thea Render.

The SketchUp interface

To make sure that you know at least a bit about SketchUp, we will give you an ultra-short overview of the main interface elements and drawing tools. If you already know how to use it, you can skip this section and start with the *Modeling the room* section.

The main window and pallets

The SketchUp user interface consists of the main 3D window with tool bars and a number of pallets that can be switched on and off as required.

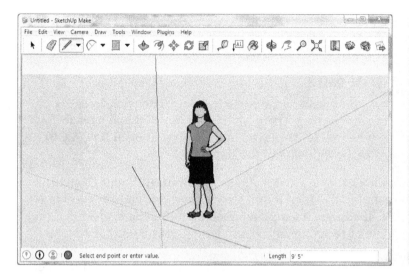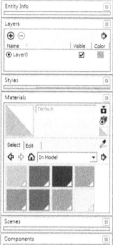

The main window along the top edge has a menu bar with several entries (on Mac, this will appear at the top of the screen) and a number of toolbars. When you start SketchUp with a new empty scene, you will find a stylized person near the coordinate origin. This person can give you a bit of reference about the size of your scene until you have added your own geometry.

Toolbars

Toolbars behave differently on Windows and Macs: In Windows, you can enable and disable individual toolbars by navigating to **View | Toolbars**. For a start, you should have at least the **Getting Started** toolbar enabled. As in other Windows applications, toolbars can be disconnected from the main window and left floating on the screen or aligned along the vertical edge of the main window.
Just click on the small grey dots at the left edge of a toolbar and drag it around.

On Mac, you only get one toolbar, but it is easy to customize its content.
Just right-click and select **Customize Toolbar** from the context menu. You can enable additional floating toolbars by navigating to **View | Tool Pallets**. These tool pallets can't be docked to the main window, though.

Some plugins also add new toolbars to your screen when they are installed. You can enable and disable these like any other toolbar.

The status bar

Along the bottom of the main window, you can see the status bar. You should always keep an eye on the text displayed here, because it gives you a clue about the options that are possible with your currently selected tool. For example, in the previous screenshot, the line tool is active, and SketchUp expects the input of the endpoint or a numeric length for the line.

The Value Control Box

Anytime SketchUp allows you to enter a value such as the dimensions of a rectangle, you can just type the values. There is no input box that you have to click first. Whatever you type will be displayed in the **Value Control Box (VCB)**. This is the small text area at the right end of the status bar.

SketchUp is very accommodating in what it allows for input. Although SketchUp uses inches as its internal unit, the default unit size for numeric values is set via the file-specific template. If you use a template based on millimeters and enter 500, SketchUp will create a line or rectangle of 500 mm length. If you use a template based on inches, it will instead create a 500 inch long element. However, you can add a common unit indicator such as 500mm (for 500 millimeter) or 5'6" (for 5 feet and 6 inches) to enter a dimension regardless of the current template.

Other possible inputs are the number of elements for an array or the number of sides for a circle or polygon. Just remember to look at the status bar for a hint.

Pallet windows

The dialog boxes or pallet windows are not integrated in the main window. These are individual windows that float on top of the main SketchUp window and usually contain lists of materials or styles to choose from. You can enable and disable the dialog boxes via the **Window** menu. Some tools (such as the **Paint Bucket** tool) also show the associated dialog box when they are selected. Some dialogs are universally useful, and you should keep them around any time. These are as follows:

- **Entity Info**
- **Layers**
- **Materials**
- **Outliner**

Other dialog boxes are only useful for specific models (such as **Component Attributes**) or at a later stage in the modeling process. We will introduce each window later when we need its functionality.

You can organize your dialog windows in a stack and move them around the screen as one unit. The stack also snaps to the top or side of your screen and the side of the main SketchUp window. In the stack, all windows will take the same width, but you can still change the height. You can also double-click on the title bar of a window to collapse or expand its main content. You can keep many dialogs in the stack if you keep the windows that you are not using at that moment collapsed.

In the rest of the book, we usually refer to the dialog windows as **pallets** to avoid confusion with other dialogs that occasionally pop up in SketchUp. This is also consistent with other applications such as GIMP.

The Getting Started toolbar

Without any modifications, SketchUp's default toolbar contains a selection of tools that are frequently used and are important to know. This selection is called the **Getting Started** toolbar. The following screenshot shows the **Getting Started** toolbar:

Navigation

To move around in the 3D scene, you use the navigation tools. You can also find these in the **Camera** toolbar and the **Camera** drop-down menu. The following screenshot shows the navigation tools:

Orbit

The **Orbit** tool (the icon with the red and green arrows) is what you will mostly use to move your viewpoint. When you click on the tool button, your cursor changes to the tool icon, and you can change your perspective viewpoint up, down, left, or right by left-clicking on the scene and moving the mouse while you keep the button pressed. Note that your view also rotates so that you are still looking at the same object, only from another direction.

You can quickly activate the **Orbit** tool via the *O* key on your keyboard, but the best way to switch to **Orbit** is via the middle mouse button or scroll wheel. Just pressing and holding the button will activate the **Orbit** tool without interrupting any other tool that you are using.

Pan

Next in line is the **Pan** tool (hand icon); it is also accessible via the *H* key. This tool translates your viewpoint relative to the scene. Again, select the tool and keep the left-mouse button pressed while you move your mouse over the screen. You can see how the scene "moves" in the 3D window according to your mouse movements. In reality, it's not the scene that moves, but it is your viewpoint (or camera if you like) that moves in the opposite direction.

Zoom

Finally, there are the **Zoom** and **Zoom Extents** tools that will move your viewpoint in and out of the scene, thus showing you a smaller or larger part of the model. The **Zoom** tool works again via the left-mouse button, but it is far easier to zoom in and out with a scroll wheel on your mouse. The **Zoom Extents** tool moves and centers the camera to show the whole model. This is very useful whenever you get lost in your scene or something obstructs your view of the part that you want to work on.

Keyboard shortcuts

Frequently used tools are accessible via keyboard shortcuts. Mastering these can speed up your SketchUp work significantly. Check the SketchUp quick reference cards available at www.sketchup.com/content/quick-reference-cards-0 for details.

Select and Erase

The **Select** tool (arrow) and **Eraser** tool are not actually drawing tools, but you should know how to remove elements when you have created them. The following screenshot shows the **Select** and **Erase** tools:

The **Select** tool works as expected. Just select the tool (the keyboard shortcut is *Space bar*) and click on any element in the scene. If you hold down the *Shift* key, you can add and remove elements from the selection. If you double-click on an element, the elements that are immediately connected are also selected and triple-clicking will select all the elements that are in contact with it. For example, if you click on one side of a cube, only the polygon will be selected. Double-click on the cube, and you select the polygon and the four surrounding edges. Triple-click and the entire cube will be selected.

To use the **Eraser** tool, you don't need to select an element; you just use the tool and click on the element you want to delete. Intuitively, the *Delete* key on your keyboard works as well when the item is selected.

Drawing tools

To create new elements, you use the drawing tools. You can also find them in the **Drawing** toolbar or via the **Draw** drop-down menu. In SketchUp 2014, the **Getting Started** toolbar shows a collapsed view of the main drawing tools. To access the hidden functions, click on the arrow next to each icon and select the specific feature from the drop-down list. In the following image, you can see the default tool icons and the functions that they access:

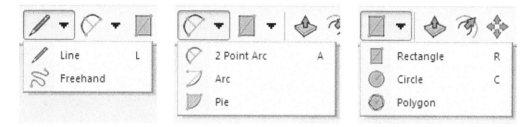

The **Line** tool draws a straight line between two points. A line in SketchUp is also called an *edge*. Three or more lines can form the boundary of a polygon. When you create a closed line loop out of coplanar lines, a 3D surface is created between them.

The **Rectangle** tool creates a rectangular polygon and the four edges surrounding it. If you delete the polygon afterwards, the edges will still remain. You can use the numeric input option to specify an exact width and height after you have placed the first point of the rectangle.

For the **Circle** and **Polygon** tools, you first place the center point and specify a second point on the circumference. Alternatively, you can specify the radius numerically. If you type a number before you place the center point, you set the number of sides (in SketchUp, even a circle is made out of short straight segments, but you usually don't see them).

You can also specify the sides of a circle segment created with the **2 Point Arc** tool, but to place it, you pick the start and end points and then indicate the bulge of the arc (numerically or by picking a third point). SketchUp 2014 also introduced two new arc tools: **Arc** and **Pie**. You use these by picking the center of the arc first and then the start and end of the segment.

Edit tools

In SketchUp, the drawing elements only create flat surfaces. To create volumetric 3D objects, you have to extrude one of these polygons using the **Push/Pull** tool. You can see the icon in the following screenshot (first icon from the left):

The **Push/Pull** tool is probably the quintessential SketchUp tool. To use it, select the tool and then move the cursor over an existing surface. Surfaces that can be extruded will be shown in a darker shade while the cursor is above them. Click anywhere inside the surface and move the mouse up or down along the surface normal. You will see that the polygon will be extruded to a box or prism shape along its surface normal. To set the endpoint for the extrusion, type the desired height of the object or click somewhere in the scene to set the height via reference.

The next modification tool is the **Offset** tool. The workflow of this tool is similar to that of the **Push/Pull** tool, but the edges of the surface will be offset in the plane of the surface, not orthogonal to it. Again, you can specify the offset distance via keyboard inputs or reference points.

The **Move** tool (four-way arrow) is a universal tool in SketchUp. You can use it to move an object as well as rotate or copy it or create a linear array. To simply move something, select the object (or objects) and then activate the **Move** tool. Click somewhere in the scene to set a reference point and move the cursor in the direction that you want the object to move. You can set the distance via keyboard inputs or by clicking again to set the end point for the move.

To create a copy, you follow the same steps mentioned earlier, but you have to hold down the *Ctrl* key (or the *Option* key on Mac) before you click to set the start point. A useful variation of this is the creation of an array instead of a single copy: After you have placed your first copy, you can type an asterisk (*) followed by the number of copies you want to create. For example, type *5 if you want to create five copies of the object, each with the same distance from the previous copy. You can also move the first copy to the end of the array and then type /5 to create four further copies, which are evenly spaced between the first and the last ones.

The **Rotate** tool (two round arrows) works like the **Move** tool but rotates the object around a center. It can also be used to create polar arrays of objects.

The **Scale** tool is the last of the standard modification tools. When you select it, you will see green boxes around the object that you want to scale. Select one of the corner boxes to scale the object in two (or three) dimensions, or select a box in the middle to scale in one dimension only. You can also type in a number such as 2.0 for a fixed scaling factor to double the size of the object.

To mirror an object in SketchUp, use the **Scale** tool, scale the object along a single axis, and use a scaling factor of -1.

Core concepts

The tools we have introduced so far should be familiar to you if you have used 3D or CAD software before. The following sections highlight a few of the drawing concepts that make SketchUp such a unique tool. It is essential to understand these ideas to achieve a productive workflow and get the most out of the SketchUp tool set.

Splitting and healing

Lines and other edges that are part of a new element do interact with existing geometry: a line crossing another line or 3D surface will split this other element in two (two independent lines or two surfaces). On the other hand, if you remove a line between coplanar surfaces, the surfaces will merge into one. This is sometimes called "healing" of an edge or face. The endpoints of lines will also merge with the existing geometry. If you draw a line from one corner of a rectangle and then try to move the line, it will take the corner point along and distort the rectangle.

Groups

To avoid the interaction of geometry with each other, you can place elements into groups. Elements in a group will only interact with elements in the same group but not with anything outside. You will use groups a lot when you build complex models. **Components** are a special type of group; they all share one common definition, and so any change applied to one instance of a component is visible in all the other copies. You may know this concept from blocks in AutoCAD.

To create a component, select all the edges and faces you want to have in the group and then right-click on it and select **Make Group** from the context menu. A group also provides a bit of protection for its elements. You have to double-click on the group first before you can modify any of the geometric elements in it. You can still snap to the edges and corners, though.

If you find that you left out some elements after you created the group, you can select them and navigate to **Edit | Cut** to move them to the clipboard. Then, double-click on the group to allow changes and navigate to **Edit | Paste in Place**. The elements will be inserted in the same location, but now, they are part of the group.

Inferencing

For precise drawing, you can snap to the end and midpoints of a line or an edge. You will also see the appearance of colored guidelines while you are drawing, and your cursor will have a tendency to follow these guides. This is known as **inferencing**, and it allows you to draw elements that are precisely aligned with the current coordinate system or other existing geometry.

The simplest inferencing takes place when you draw a line close to the cardinal axes of the scene. If you try to draw a line that is roughly parallel to the y axis (green axis), you will see that the unfinished line segment will suddenly align itself with the y axis and turn green. If you move the cursor a bit, this will only change the length of the line but not the direction. Only when you move the cursor far away enough from the y axis, the unfinished line will snap back to the pencil tool. This works for all three axes and with any tool in SketchUp. Sometimes, you may want to switch it off, but unfortunately, there is no way to do this. You can only zoom in closer to your scene to make the inferencing less sensitive.

Layers and visibility

One last feature you should know about before we model a room is **layers**. Like in a CAD application, you can assign elements to a specific layer and turn the visibility of layers on and off. Note that the geometry will still interact with each other even if it's on a hidden layer. It is a good practice to create all geometric elements on the default layer (**Layer0**) and only assign a group or component to a different layer. We will discuss the use of layers in more detail later in the book.

You can also temporarily hide specific objects if they are getting in the way. For example, if you want to see the inside of a room, just select all the elements and then right-click and select **Hide** from the context menu. To make them visible again, navigate to **Edit | Unhide | All**.

Further resources

There are many useful resources available online to help you improve your SketchUp skills. They are as follows:

- The SketchUp Concepts Guide page (`help.sketchup.com/en/article/115426`) for a quick overview

- The SketchUp User's Guide page (`help.sketchup.com/en/article/116174`) for a detailed description of the tools and their use

- YouTube channels, `harwoodpodcast` and `4sketchupgo2school`, for many detailed video tutorials to introduce various modeling techniques

After this quick introduction, we can now continue with a hands-on tutorial. We will create a simple interior scene and use the Thea Render plugin to create a photorealistic rendering.

Downloading the example code

You can download the example code files for this book from your account at `http://www.packtpub.com`. If you purchased this book elsewhere, you can visit `http://www.packtpub.com/support` and register to have the files e-mailed directly to you.

Modeling the room

One of the common misconceptions about photorealistic modeling and rendering is that it requires very detailed models before the rendering is effective. This simply is not true with today's software sophistication. The gallery scene you'll be modeling here is simple and easy to produce in SketchUp, just like the majority of rooms in the real world:

1. Start by firing up SketchUp; then select **Model Info** from the **Window** menu.

2. **Select Units** from the list on the left.

3. Set the units to the values shown in the following screenshot. You can use inches if you like, but you may find it easier to follow if you use millimeters:

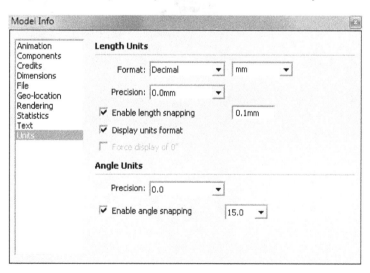

4. Close the **Model Info** dialog window by clicking on the red X button.

5. Start modeling by selecting the **Rectangle** function from the **Draw** menu.

6. Click on the origin and draw a rectangle of any size. Click on the left-mouse button to place the opposite corner and create the rectangle.

7. Now, type in 4000,10000. This appears in the little text box at the bottom-right corner of the screen (VCB). Hit *Enter*, and your rectangle will resize to 4,000 mm by 10,000 mm (4 x 10 meters).

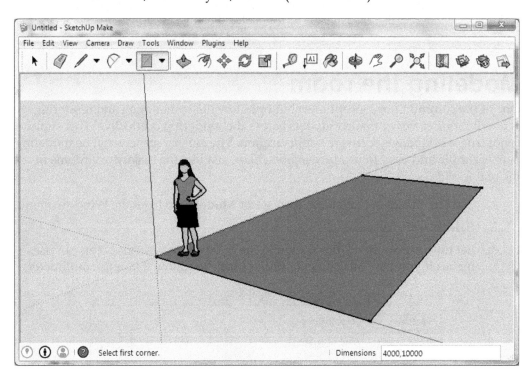

8. Rotate the view by pressing the middle-mouse button (MMB or scroll wheel) and moving the mouse. Now, select the **Push/Pull** tool and click on the rectangle, moving the mouse to extrude the rectangle into a box, as seen in the following screenshot:

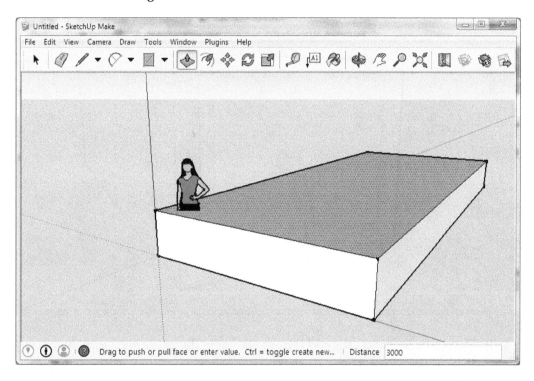

9. Type 3000 and hit *Enter*.

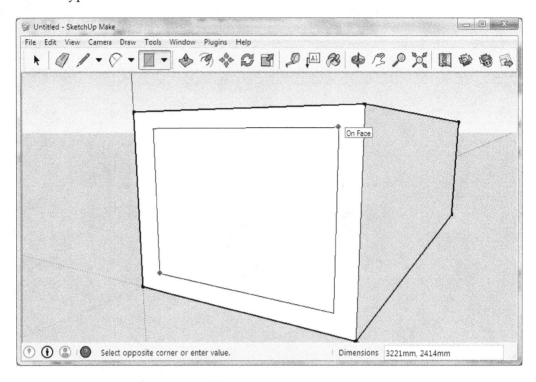

10. Draw a rectangle on the end face, as shown in the previous screenshot.

11. Now, select and delete the face (hit the *Delete* key or right-click and select **Erase** from the context menu).

12. Triple-click on the geometry. Notice how all the connected faces are now selected.

13. Right-click and select **Reverse Faces**. The *outside* faces will now be drawn in a darker shade. We need to do this because we're going to place the camera inside the room you've just created.

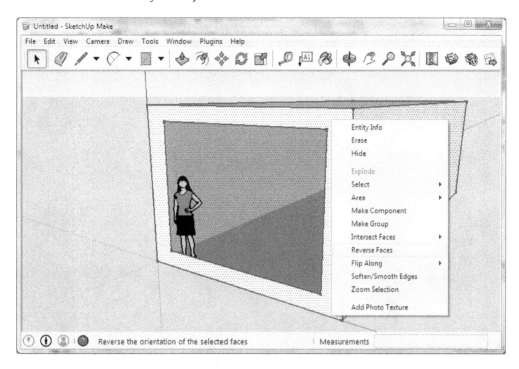

Setting up the view

You're now going to set up the camera view and sun lighting. You might have noticed that there are very few actual camera buttons in SketchUp. This is because SketchUp is all about "what you see is what you get". If you see it on the screen, this is what you'll see in your render. All the complex camera stuff is taken care of in the background, and the right settings will be exported to the renderer without you or me having to worry about it. We will look at how to set up scenes for maximum impact in *Chapter 3, Composing the Scene*.

Setting up the camera view

The following are the steps to set up a view interactively:

1. Rotate and zoom in on the view so that you're more or less looking at the scene, as shown in the following screenshot.

2. Navigate to **Camera | Walk**.

3. Type in your eye height in mm (say, 1200). The camera changes to a view from this eye level. A lower viewpoint will make the room look a bit bigger.

4. Navigate to **Camera | Look Around** to move your head around and compose the view you want, and use **Walk** to move in or out of the scene by holding the left-mouse button and moving the mouse up or down.

Saving the camera view

Now that you're happy with the view you have created, you need to save it so that it can't be changed by accident or while doing further modeling tasks. You do this by creating a scene that will be imported into the rendering software as a camera view:

1. Navigate to **Window | Scenes**.

2. Press the "Plus" icon in the pop-up window. A new scene is created, and a tab called **Scene 1** will appear at the top of the main viewing window.

Rotate your view now with the middle-mouse button, then click on the tab. You are taken back to the view that was used when you created the scene. Scenes retain their view settings as part of their options.

Setting up the sun

We want to get some direct sunlight in through the window to bounce off the wall and floor. Within SketchUp, the "sun" only lights up areas that are not obstructed, and there is a sharp contrast between light and dark. In the renderer, the sunlight will bounce into the whole room. There is more on lighting in *Chapter 8, Photorealistic Rendering*. You can change the lighting and shadows in a scene by changing the Sun's position via date and time as explained in the following steps:

1. Navigate to **Window | Shadows** to activate the **Shadow Settings** panel, as shown in the following screenshot:

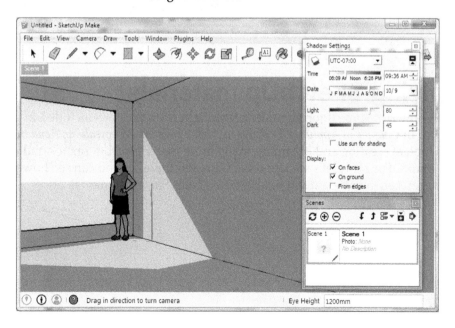

2. Click the icon in the top-left corner of the panel to switch on the display of shadows.

3. Move the sliders around for **Time** and **Date** until you get the effect that is similar to the previous screenshot.

4. When you have found a nice setting, click on the **Update** icon from the **Scenes** panel and confirm to update all the settings in the popup window. Shadow settings are part of the scene information, and by updating the scene now, you can return to your settings later just by clicking on the scene tab.

You now have all the lighting you need for a daytime indoor scene. The following screenshot is what you would get if you did a quick test render in Thea Render. As you can see, the whole room is lit by the sun, just as it would be in real life:

Applying SketchUp materials

You will now add some flooring materials straight from the ones included in SketchUp. In *Chapter 5, Applying Textures and Materials for Photorealistic Rendering*, we will look at creating and obtaining many more materials from photos and online texture banks. For now, let's stick to what's already there, so you can see how good a render you can get straight out of a basic, no frills, SketchUp model.

Timber flooring material

In SketchUp, materials are applied with the **paint bucket** tool. You only need to select the right material or color and "pour" it onto a surface:

1. If the **Materials** pallet is not visible, navigate to **Window | Materials** to enable it.

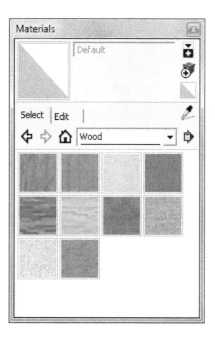

2. Select **Wood** from the drop-down box.

3. Select a wood material by clicking on one of the thumbnail images. Your cursor will change to a **Paint Bucket** symbol.

4. Click on the floor to apply the material. Try a few different wood patterns until you find the one that you like best.

5. Now, draw a rectangle on the floor for a carpet, as shown in the following screenshot:

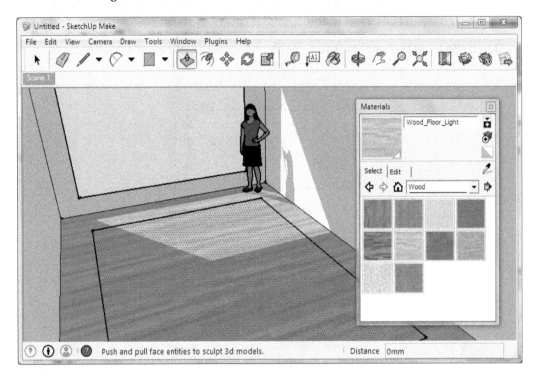

6. Use the **Push/Pull** tool to slightly elevate the rectangle.

7. Select a carpet texture and paint it onto the raised surface, as shown in the following screenshot:

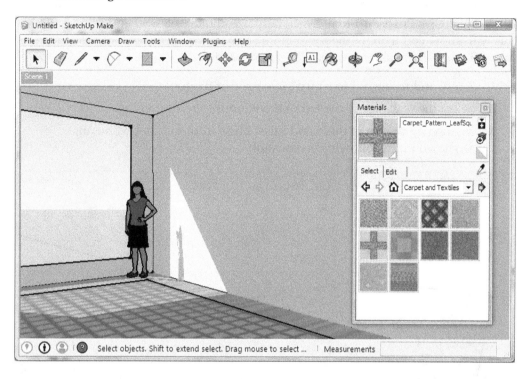

You've now got two textures in the scene that you'll be able to modify in Thea to add shininess, highlights, or reflections. The matt will stay as it is. You will learn how to add surface details such as the ones in *Chapter 8, Photorealistic Rendering*. We will look at creating and applying SketchUp materials in more detail in *Chapter 5, Applying Textures and Materials for Photorealistic Rendering*.

Modeling the window

The scene doesn't look realistic with just a hole in the wall. Let's make a window using SketchUp's **Push/Pull** tool. It will help if you hide the wall and ceiling now. This will allow you to view the room more easily as you progress with the tutorial. You will reinstate them later when they are needed again.

1. Zoom and rotate out to a bird's eye view of the room.

2. Select the wall face to the left of the window and the ceiling.

3. Right-click on one of them and select **Hide** from the context menu, as shown in the following screenshot:

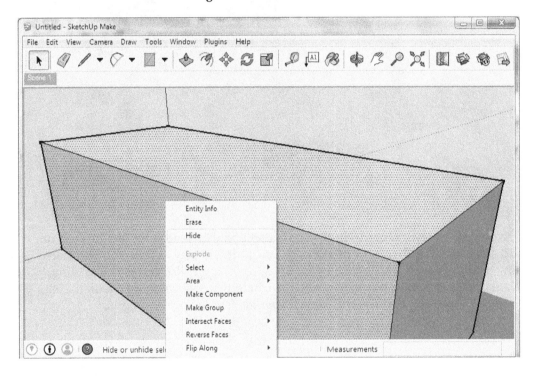

To create a window reveal efficiently, we have to be a bit creative with the tools that SketchUp offers:

1. First, use the **Line** tool (**Draw | Line**) to draw along the edge of the existing window opening. Make sure that you snap to the endpoints (corners) at the beginning and end of the line.

2. As soon as the line is completed, SketchUp will close the opening with a new rectangle. Use the **Push/Pull** tool to push the new rectangle outwards by about 200 mm. This will create a reveal for the window.

3. Delete the window rectangle again. As you see, the fastest way to create the four sides for the reveal is to create and extrude an extra rectangle that we do not need.

4. With the **Line** tool, draw a line out from the edge of the bottom window along the green axis, then down along the blue axis, back to the wall, and back to the start, as shown at the left in the following image.

5. Select the **Arc** tool from the **Draw** menu. Draw an arc as shown in the following image; then, delete the corners with the **Erase** tool (middle of the following image).

6. Use the **Push/Pull** tool to extrude the shape along the bottom of the window in the first part of the image and then from the other direction to form a windowsill, as shown in the following image:

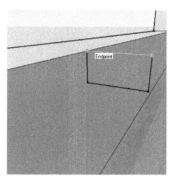  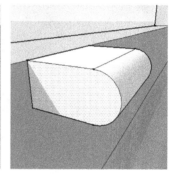

7. Select the **Rectangle** tool and move the cursor along the top corner of the window. When you see a **Tooltip** saying **Midpoint**, click and draw a rectangle across the lintel.

8. Use the **Arc** tool to round off the front and delete the corners as you did earlier.

9. Use the **Push/Pull** tool again to extrude the shape down to span the whole window frame.

10. Create the glass pane by selecting the midpoint of one corner and then the opposite corner with the **Rectangle** tool, as shown at the right of the following image:

11. Select this rectangle and apply the **Translucent_Glass_Blue** material from the **Translucent** collection with the **Paint Bucket** tool on both sides of the rectangle (inside and outside). Your scene should now look similar to the following screenshot:

12. If any wall faces have turned blue, select them now. Right-click on them and select **Reverse Faces** from the context menu.

13. Reinstate the hidden faces by navigating to **Edit | Unhide | All**.

14. Check if these faces also need reversing.

15. Double-click on the **Scene 1** tab to reset the view to the interior of the room.

Painting with digital photos

For the artwork on the wall, you can simply grab some images of your own or browse the Web. For this tutorial, it doesn't matter where you get them from. However, if you have some art of your own, why not scan or photograph it and use it here? It can be your own 3D portfolio!

1. Select **Import** from the **File** menu.

2. Change the **Files of type:** option to **All Supported Image Types**.

3. Choose an image you want to use for your artwork.

4. Now, move the cursor to the wall and click on it to set the bottom-left corner of the image. Stretch the image to the size you want and click on the wall again, as shown in the following screenshot:

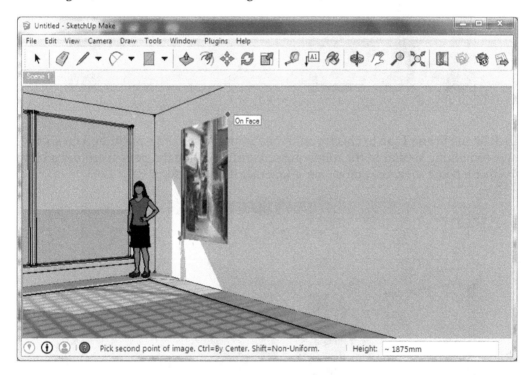

5. Repeat this for more images. Remember to click on the **Scene 1** tab from time to time so that you can see what will or will not be in the frame when you render.

6. Trace a rectangle around each image. You can snap to the corners of the images to draw accurately.

7. Finally use the **Push/Pull** tool to give each canvas some depth. You can see the canvas edge in the following image:

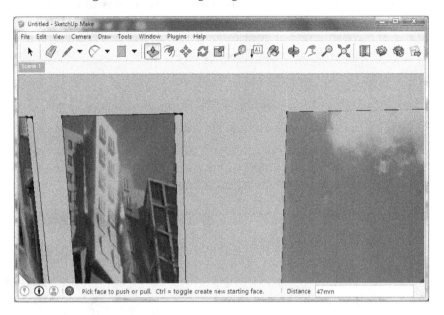

Click on the **Scene 1** tab to check your scene from the camera's position. You should have something similar to the following screenshot. Move the person around a bit to give her a better view or remove her altogether if you prefer:

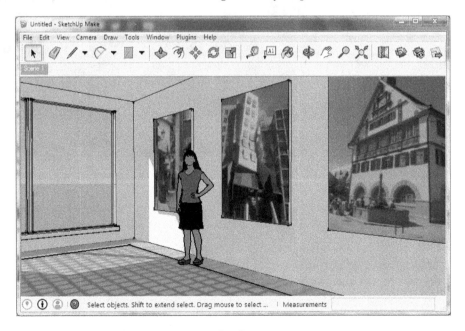

Doing a test rendering

We are already in good shape with our scene. So, the first thing we should do is a test rendering:

1. Navigate to **Plugins | Thea Render | Thea Rendering Window** to open the main rendering window within SketchUp.

2. Below the main window area, you will find the rendering controls. Check if the **Mode** is set to **Unbiased (TR1)** on the **Rendering** tab.

3. Now, just click on the **Start** button in the middle (the triangle pointing to the right) to export the scene and get the rendering started.

After a short time, the rendering will appear and will improve gradually. Most likely, it is going to be too dark to see anything, though. While the rendering is still continuing, you can adjust the brightness of the image:

1. Switch to the **Display** tab.

2. Adjust the setting for **ISO** to 800 or 1600.

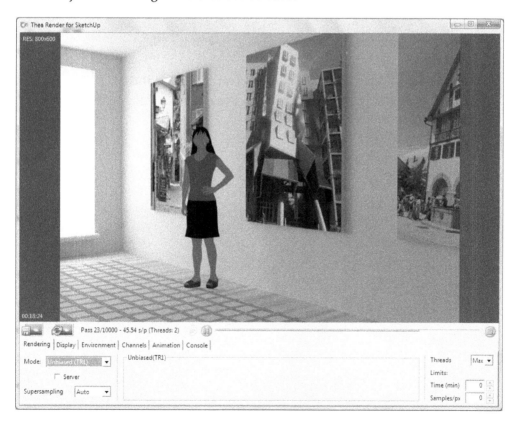

Give it a bit of time to render until you have a good idea of the light and reflections; then hit the **Stop** button at the far right. You should notice the following:

- The image aspect ratio is different from the SketchUp view
- The floor is not as reflective as we would expect from a polished laminate
- The light is diffused near the window, and the shadows are not sharp as we see in SketchUp

This is not too surprising since at the moment, all materials have the same properties (except for the window that is translucent). To improve the image, we have to define some additional properties for the materials.

Enhancing SketchUp materials

In order to produce photorealistic images, we need to improve the optical characteristics of the SketchUp materials. Without any special assignment, SketchUp materials get translated into a default material that only maintains the color and texture from SketchUp. To define advanced properties, we can use the **Thea Tool** window:

1. Open the **Thea Tool** window by navigating to the **Plugins | Thea Render** menu.
2. On the **Camera** tab, change the **Aspect ratio** to **SU Window**.
3. Click on the **Materials** tab. You will see the materials dialog shown in the following screenshot:

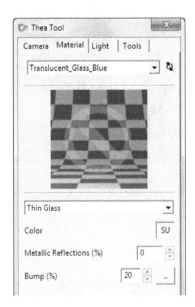

4. In the drop-down menu at the top, select the **Translucent_Glass_Blue** material. This is the material we used for the window.

5. In the drop-down menu below the preview area, select **Thin Glass**.

6. Click on the **SU** button to the right of the **Color** label. A new (blue) button will appear next to it.

7. Click on it to open a color selector.

8. Pick a white color from the palette and click on **OK** to close the selector.

9. You can leave the remaining options for the glass material as they are.

10. Next, select the material you used for the floor (**Wood_Floor_Light** in our case).

11. In the second drop-down, pick **Thea Material (Mat-Lab)**.

The **Thea Material Lab** window will open and show a preview of the material as it is. You can see this in the following screenshot:

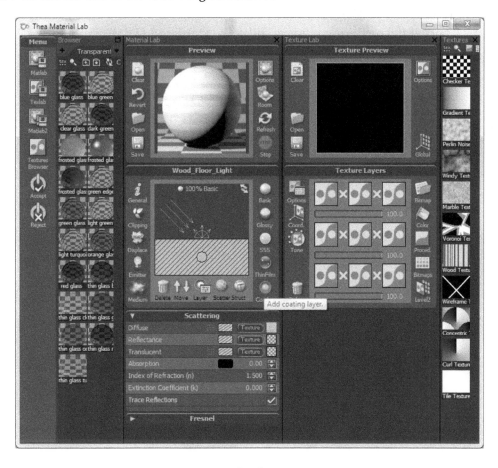

1. Below the **Preview** panel, you will find the material properties panel. Find the **Coating** button in the bottom-right corner of the window and click on it (only once!).

2. A new layer will be added to the material built up, and the preview window should update in a short time. You can see the change in specular highlights in the preview.

3. Click on the **Accept** button to the left of the **Material Lab** window to apply your changes and close the window.

4. Finally select the carpet material (**Carpet_Pattern_LeafSpares_Tan**).

5. Select **Matte** as Thea material type.

6. Increase the **Bump** value to 50%.

With these changes, we have addressed the issues we noticed in our first test render. We are ready to give it another go!

1. Open the **Thea Rendering Window** again.

2. Check if the rendering mode is still set to **Unbiased (TR1)**.

3. Press the **Start** button. The scene will be exported again, and a new rendering process starts.

4. Let the rendering continue for a while until you can make out a few more details.

5. If you find that the rendering is too bright or too dark, switch to the **Display** tab.

6. Adjust the **ISO, Shutter**, and **f-number** settings until the image is reasonably lit. You can see a possible combination in the following screenshot:

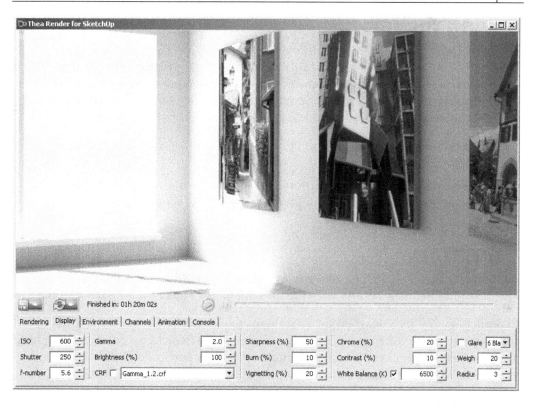

When the image quality has progressed sufficiently, you can check the issues we noted earlier. You see that the sunlight through the window is now clearly defined; there is a bit of specular reflection visible on the floor, and the carpet does not seem to reflect the light anymore.

Saving the image

The rendered image will progress in the render window. With each new pass, the image will look a bit better. The **unbiased rendering process** will continue like this but it will never finish. You can set **Limits** for **Time** or **Samples** on the **Rendering** tab to terminate the rendering after a specific time, but you can also just stop the calculations when you think that the quality of the image is sufficient:

1. Either wait for your **Limit** to be reached, or click on the **Stop** button to interrupt the rendering.

2. Click on the **Save Image** button at the far left of the screen, and choose a name and file type for the rendered image. PNG is usually ok.

Summary

This chapter was designed to give you a taste of how easily and quickly you can get great photorealistic results with the SketchUp and Thea Render combination.

In particular, you have learned the basic steps towards modeling a simple indoor studio scene and setting up a daylight environment in SketchUp. You have also used the Thea Render plugin to assign advanced optical properties to SketchUp materials and created a photorealistic rendering without leaving the SketchUp interface.

This is the basic framework for achieving successful renderings of most interior and outdoor scenes. You're now able to immediately apply what you've learned in your own projects. The remaining chapters in this book provide additional information when you want to take your skills a step or two further. You can dip in whenever you need some specific guidance or follow the chapters in a course format.

In the next chapter, you'll find out how to create your own visualization and animation studio setup to create even better architectural visuals!

2
Collecting a Toolset

"As an artist, all I need is my paints and brushes - and someone to drag me away when the canvas is done."

– Pablo Picasso

SketchUp is a great tool for editing 3D content. It has a simple interface, is easy to understand, and very powerful for architectural modeling. No wonder it became one of the standard tools that you can find in every design studio.

Part of its success is the focus on simple modeling tasks and the fact that it was available for free, while it was owned by Google. However, this means that we have to look for other programs and utilities to assist us in the creation of rich and realistic architectural visuals and use a number of tools to manipulate and postprocess the generated images.

In this chapter, you will learn to perform the following tasks:

- Select the right SketchUp 2014 edition for you
- Discover plugins to improve the SketchUp workflow
- Set up a postprocessing studio for our renderings
- Install Thea Render and integrate it into SketchUp
- Get ready to produce animations from our images

Free, libre, or what?

One of the biggest changes for the end user that came out of the acquisition of SketchUp by Trimble affects the licensing of SketchUp. Google saw SketchUp as a tool to enable everyone to produce content for Google Earth, and Google being Google, they could also afford to give it away for free to everyone.

Unfortunately, Trimble had other ideas, and one of the first changes was to discontinue the free SketchUp edition for professional users. You can still download and use a free version (since 2013, it is called *SketchUp Make*), but you are not allowed to use it for commercial projects. This is good because it still allows everyone access to a fantastic tool to realize their dream projects and to learn and test the software without the need to pay for a license. It also pushes SketchUp as a professional tool back among all the other commercial software that promises quality and efficiency for a price.

In the previous edition of this book, good arguments were made for the use of free software in our visualization workflow. These arguments still stand, and we still encourage you to use free and open source software wherever it makes sense. However, when you work for money, the time you spend on training and learning several tools also has to be considered as an investment. It can be more effective to choose a commercial software package that you or your colleagues already know, over a free tool that does a similar job. For the rest of the book, we try to present both options when possible but will demonstrate the techniques only for the tools that are available to everyone.

Trimble SketchUp

Before you can go off and download SketchUp, you have to choose the type of work you are going to do with it. The following three options are available:

- **Professional Work** will lead you to *SketchUp Pro 2014*.
- **Personal Projects** will lead you to download *SketchUp Make*.
- **Educational Use** lets you decide which one you want. You will get discounts if you choose SketchUp Pro.

The following screenshot shows the options that you can select as per your requirement when you go on to http://www.sketchup.com/download:

SketchUp Pro, LayOut, and Style Builder

Every download also includes LayOut and Style Builder, but these will stop working after a trial period of 8 hours, unless you buy and register a license. In these 8 hours, you can explore if the features it offers are really what you are looking for and decide if SketchUp is the right tool for you. Since you are reading this book, you obviously have made the right decision. A word of warning: SketchUp Pro will stop working altogether after 8 hours of use if you do not purchase and enter a license. In the previous editions, you could still use it with a limited feature set.

LayOut is a standalone program and is explained in more detail in *Chapter 11, Presenting Visuals in LayOut*. With LayOut, you can easily import your SketchUp models and create slideshow pages for print or onscreen presentations rather like PowerPoint or Keynote. Style Builder is an external tool for the creation of new visual styles that can be used in SketchUp.

SketchUp Pro also enables you to import and export CAD data, which is a must when using SketchUp within a professional workflow. You also gain the privilege of creating dynamic components, which work a little like dynamic blocks in AutoCAD.

An additional import format with SketchUp Pro:

- AutoCAD (.dwg, .dxf)

Additional 2D-export formats with SketchUp Pro:

- Portable Document Format (`.pdf`)
- Encapsulated Postscript (`.eps`)
- Epix (`.epx`)
- AutoCAD (`.dwg`, `.dxf`)

Additional 3D-export formats with SketchUp Pro:

- 3DS (`.3ds`)
- Collada (`.dae`)
- AutoCAD DWG (`.dwg`)
- AutoCAD DXF (`.dxf`)
- FBX (`.fbx`)
- IFC (`.ifc`)
- Google Earth (`.kmz`)
- OBJ (`.obj`)
- XSI (`.xsi`)
- VRML (`.vrml`)

The 3D Warehouse

Google has established the 3D Warehouse as a platform for SketchUp users to easily share their models with the rest of the world. Trimble also took over the Warehouse from Google when it acquired SketchUp. Thanks to the large and active user group that SketchUp has gained over the last few years, the Warehouse is an invaluable resource for all sorts of 3D models that you can use to enrich your own designs.

In SketchUp 2014, the 3D Warehouse browser received a web technology based face lift:

1. Open SketchUp 2014 with a new scene.

2. Navigate to **File** | **3D Warehouse** | **Get Models** ....

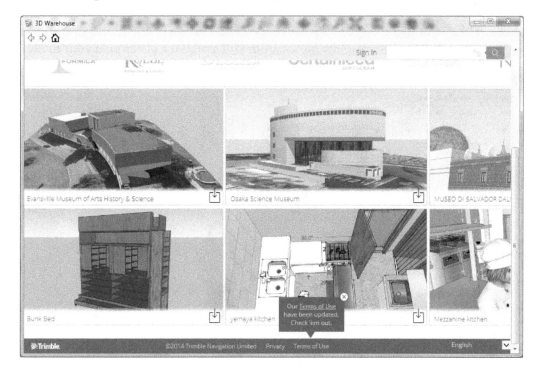

3. A browser window will open. This window allows you to search for key words in the models.

 Use the search key, author:Google, to focus on components that were distributed as bonus packs in the earlier versions of SketchUp.

4. Use the navigation buttons or enter different key words to refine your search.

5. When you have found a component you like, click on its tile. The component details will be displayed.

6. Hit the **Download** button, and you will be prompted if you want to load the component directly into your SketchUp model.

7. Select **Yes**, and the component will be downloaded ready to be placed into the model.

8. The cursor will change to the **Move** tool, and the newly downloaded component will stick to the mouse until you assign it a position in your model. You will see a window similar to the one in the following screenshot:

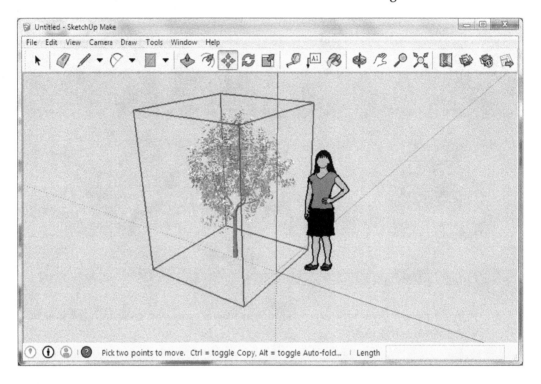

If you choose not to insert the component directly into the scene, you can still download and save it to your hard drive. Using this method, you can find and collect all the bonus pack components from the 3D Warehouse. Of course, you only need to download components you are likely to use.

The main collections that you should look for include the following:

- **construction**
- **film and stage**
- **architecture**
- **landscape architecture**

- mechanical
- 2D People
- transportation
- shapes

Unlimited upgrades – Ruby plugins

If you've ever looked over the shoulder of someone who has been using SketchUp for a long time, you'll see lots of buttons you never came across earlier. If you wait until they've gone for a break and secretly check out what's in their menus, there'll be twice as many menu items as yours.

These additional tools are due to the SketchUp **Ruby API** (*Application Programming Interface*) that allows anyone with a bit of knowledge of the Ruby programming language to create new functions that can be used in SketchUp. The plugins can extend SketchUp with simple tools that help you to do an ordinary task in a slightly different way or can automate complex procedures that can even generate entire cities.

 With SketchUp 2014, Trimble also updated the Ruby API to a new version. The changes are small, but there are some scripts that cause problems with the new version of SketchUp. Most actively maintained scripts should be updated in a short time, though.

In SketchUp 2014, the installation of plugins is fully integrated via the **Extension Warehouse**, **Extension Preferences**, and finally via the `Plugins` folder for older Ruby scripts that do not offer the full functionality of extensions.

The Extension Warehouse

The most convenient way to download and install Ruby scripts is via the Extension Warehouse menu entry:

1. You can find it in the **Extension Warehouse** browser in the **Window** menu.
2. Locate the search entry box in the top-right corner and enter your search term (for example `canvas`).
3. A list of related plugins is displayed (or in the case of canvas, only one plugin is displayed).

4. Select the plugin you are interested in, and you will be shown the details page. Usually, there is a short video presentation of the tool at the top of the page.

5. If you want to download the plugin, select the red **Install** button in the top-right corner of the details page and confirm that you really want the plugin to be installed.

6. The plugin will now be downloaded and installed. Afterwards, the label of the button will have changed to **Uninstall**. This tells you that the plugin is successfully installed.

Take a few moments to browse the categories and plugins in the Extension Warehouse. You may not see the benefit of many of the available tools yet, but once you have some experience with SketchUp modeling and the type of 3D scenes you are frequently working with, you may remember that there was a tool in the Warehouse that could help you perform your task more efficiently.

The Extension Manager

Extensions that are available as a direct download, but not within the Extension Warehouse, can be installed via the built-in Extension Manager. Ruby scripts that can be installed via the manager have a `*.rbz` file extension (they are, in fact, common `*.zip` files with a bit of extra programming sauce). As a demonstration for this type of extension, we will install the SketchUcation Plugin Store:

1. Open a web browser and go to `http://sketchucation.com/resources/plugin-store-download`. You will get to a page that is shown in the following screenshot.

2. Download the extension archive, `SketchUcationTools.rbz`, via the **Download Now** button and save it to your hard drive.

3. Open SketchUp and navigate to **Window | Preferences** (on Windows) or **SketchUp | Preferences ...**(on Mac).

4. The **System Preferences** window opens, as shown in the following screenshot:

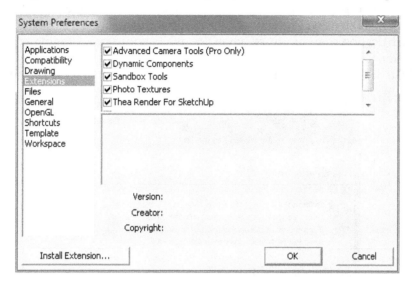

5. In the list box to the left, highlight the entry, **Extensions**. You will now see a list of extensions that are already installed on the right.

6. You can enable and disable the extensions with the checkbox next to the extension names.

7. Click on the **Install Extension...** button at the bottom of the window.

8. A file browser pops up. Navigate to your download location and select the `SketchUcationTools.rbz` file.

9. Click on **Open** and wait for the confirmation that the installation was successful.

10. Check that the new tool is now listed among your other extensions.

11. Close the **System Preferences** window.

You will find a new submenu called **SketchUcation** under the **Plugins** menu (the **Plugins** menu only appears after you install a plugin). The **SketchUcation Plugin Store** entry starts the store browser window, but you have to register on the SketchUcation website before you can use the store (the other tools work without registration).

The Plugin Store is great, because it gives you access to a much larger number of plugins than the Extension Warehouse. The plugins are mostly developed by members of the SketchUcation community, so when you read about a new plugin in one of the SketchUcation forums, chances are that you can just go and download it right away. Version 2.0.0 of **SketchUcation Plugin Store** is shown in the following screenshot:

Old style Ruby scripts

Now and then, you will come across an older Ruby script that cannot be installed via the methods discussed earlier. These are either single Ruby files or a file and a folder with additional resources. In both cases, you just need to copy the file(s) into the SketchUp Plugins folder and restart SketchUp.

Since SketchUp 2014, the `Plugins` folder is located in the Windows user profile, and you first have to make the `AppData` folder visible before you can access its content:

1. Open a Windows Explorer window.
2. Navigate to **Tools | Folder options...**.
3. In the new window, select the **View** tab.
4. Under **Advanced settings**, select the **Show hidden files and folders** option.
5. Check that you can now see a folder called `AppData` in your home folder (`C:\Users\<username>`).

On a recent Mac (OS X 10.7 and later), you also have to unhide your personal `Library` folder. On older Macs this folder is visible by default. Perform the following steps on your Mac machine:

1. Open `Terminal.app` and type the following command:

   ```
   chflags nohidden ~/Library
   ```

2. Check in **Finder** that you can see a folder called `Library` in your user folder.

You are now ready to install the Ruby script using the following steps:

1. Download the script file to your computer.
2. If it is a `*.zip` archive, unpack it to a temporary folder and locate the `*.rb` and other necessary files and folders.
3. If there is some documentation, such as a `README.txt` file, read it now!
4. On Windows, just open the `C:\Users\<username>\AppData\Roaming\SketchUp\SketchUp 2014\SketchUp\Plugins` folder.
5. On a Mac, the folder is in your home directory under `Library/Application Support/SketchUp 2014/SketchUp/Plugins`.
6. Copy the necessary file (or files) into the `Plugins` folder.
7. Restart SketchUp.

The plugin will now execute when SketchUp starts up and create the necessary toolbar buttons, menu, or context menu entries.

Now you know all the options to install Ruby plugins in SketchUp. You'll discover several of these as we progress through the book. Just go ahead and install them.

Thea Render

There are an incredible number of rendering applications and plugins out there that range from professional high-end renderers to small experimental one-man projects. Technologies range from physically based radiosity engines to gaming platforms, and then, you have to decide how tightly you want your renderer integrated into SketchUp. A strong integration usually means sacrifices in render options or quality.

To help you choose the perfect renderer for your requirements, we have prepared a short and noncomprehensive list of the currently available renderers at the end of the book. By the time you have read the rendering chapters in this book, the entire technobabble will make complete sense; we promise.

Why use Thea Render?

Although it is relatively new among the SketchUp render extensions, we have chosen Thea Render for this book for several reasons:

- It is a mid-priced product but also has a free trial version available. If you decide to buy it (after testing), you won't have to apply for a bank loan to get the full version.

- It has a biased and unbiased render engine for the fast rendering of animation frames and simple high-quality photo-real still images.

- It comes as an integrated plugin as well as a fully featured standalone studio application.

- It is under active development and is constantly evolving.

- There are plenty of other features that will keep you busy experimenting, long after you have mastered the basics of image rendering.

- Last but not least, Thea is written by the same developer team that created Kerkythea. These guys know what they are doing.

Installing Thea Studio

Begin by downloading the Thea Studio installer from the Thea Render website at `http://www.thearender.com`.

On Windows, just double-click the installer and follow the steps of the setup wizard. Make a note of the data location folder. This folder will contain the materials and resources that we will need later on in the book.

On a Mac, double-click on the disk image (`*.dmg`) file. **Finder** will show the contents of the file. Select `Thea.app` and drag it into your `Applications` folder. Open **Applications** and double-click on the new `Thea.app` file. Now, you will be prompted to choose or confirm the data location folder. Afterwards, the Thea Studio application will start.

Installing the Thea for SketchUp plugin

The Thea for SketchUp plugin installer is provided as a setup wizard that does not require the usual extension installation method, as shown in the following steps:

1. Download the plugin from the website's download section. Look for the **SketchUp Plugin** link in the sidebar to the right, and download the installer.

2. Close SketchUp if you have it open.

3. Double-click on the installer file to start the setup wizard.

4. Follow the steps through.

5. If you have more than one edition of SketchUp installed, you can install the plugin for all the versions at the same time.

6. Open SketchUp and confirm that the **Plugins** menu now shows a submenu for Thea Render.

Downloading bonus content

As a licensed user, you have the opportunity to download additional materials to use in your renderings. To gain access to the content, you need a user account for the Thea Render forums:

1. Sign up for a user ID at `http://www.thearender.com/forum`. Sign up with the same e-mail address you used to buy your Thea license.

2. Send an e-mail to `license@thearender.com` (again, from the same e-mail account). Add your forum nickname, and ask to be added to the Licensed User Club.

3. When your club membership is confirmed, you can access the forum with links to the additional downloads.

4. On the Thea website, navigate to **Resources | Libraries**.

5. Follow the **Download** link for each library to the forum post. From the links in the post, you can download a compressed archive of the library.

6. Extract the library after the download. You will get a `*.lib.thea` file.

7. Double-click on the `*.lib.thea` file to start the Thea library installer.

8. The **Install Library** dialog will prompt you to confirm the data folder and accept the license. Click on the check button to complete the installation.

9. Repeat steps 5 to 8 for each library you want to install. The **Install Library** dialog that appears while installing the **Brick Walls** library is shown in the following screenshot:

To make your new Thea materials available in SketchUp, perform the following steps:

1. Download the **Material Libraries in SKM format** item from the libraries.

2. Extract the `*.zip` file.

3. On Windows, copy the individual material folders into the `C:\Program Files\SketchUp\SketchUp 2014\Materials\Thea Materials` application folder. You will already find folders for the Thea standard materials that have been created by the Thea installation.

4. On Mac, you can copy the folders either in your user specific library path, `Library/Application Support/SketchUp 2014/SketchUp/Materials`, or in the system-wide folder, `/Applications/SketchUp 2014/SketchUp.app/Contents/Resources/Content/Materials`. In this second location, the materials will also be available for other users on your computer.

Now, you have all the first-class materials available in SketchUp. These materials will translate to high-quality materials in Thea.

Image-processing studio with GIMP

If you already have Photoshop (the commercial equivalent of GIMP), lucky you! All of the instructions for GIMP in this book should work for Photoshop too, so you don't need to install GIMP (unless you have trouble following the GIMP instructions in this book). Photoshop Elements or similar software won't do, because they don't have layer masks.

Why do I need a professional-level image processor?

Creating great architectural visuals in SketchUp requires a large amount of digital image processing. This is a good thing, because it makes our lives easy, as we will see later. Every digital image we use greatly diminishes the need for creating complex geometry in SketchUp. So, we need to have tools at our disposal that will quickly and easily manipulate all the different photos and textures that will go into SketchUp, and all the images that come out. We will also be combining the output from SketchUp with rendered images later on.

Should I buy a pen tablet?

The answer to this is yes. If you're going to spend a lot of time doing architectural visuals, you will find that the finer control and comfort of a tablet over a mouse is well worth the investment. Some small and mid-sized tablets receive excellent reviews and should be sufficient for most people. They also start at a price of less than $100, so you don't have to make too much of an investment.

Learning what GIMP/Photoshop can do will be one of the Eureka moments in this book. Until you learn about layers and masks, the door to digital graphics will remain firmly closed to you. Layers will allow you to composite multiple takes of the same scene together so that you get the best out of SketchUp's native output.

Grabbing a copy of GIMP

Although the GIMP project does not provide official installers, contributed precompiled binary setup files are linked on their web page for the Windows and Mac platforms.

1. Open `http://www.gimp.org/downloads/` in your browser.

2. Click on the download link for the most recent version and save the installer file to your hard drive. For Mac users, we recommend that you download GIMP from `http://gimp.lisanet.de/Website/Download.html`, because it comes with all the filters and extensions we will need.

3. Double-click on the installer file to start the installation routine on Windows, or open the disk image file (`*.dmg`) and drag the `GIMP.app` package into the `Applications` folder if you are on a Mac.

4. The first time you start GIMP, it will prepare some files for later use. This may take a few moments.

5. If you are on Windows and used a download link from `gimp.org`, you should also download the gimp extensions from `https://code.google.com/p/gimp-extensions`. This download contains all the filters we will use in this book.

Becoming a movie-making genius... almost!

Alright, we're not going to turn you into a fully clued-up movie producer just yet. However, you don't have to be one with the following video-editing tools. One of the most painful experiences we had while researching this book was navigating through the maze of compression codecs, frame rates, aspect ratios, and other thorny issues that make digital moving-image production such a nightmare.

In this book, we will produce animations that are suitable for upload to popular video streaming sites such as YouTube or Vimeo. For this, we will use the following two dedicated tools:

- **VirtualDub** (Windows) to create an animation out of our rendered images
- **HandBrake** (Windows and Mac) to convert the video into a streaming version with H.264 compression

We will look at the details of the process of making a movie in *Chapter 10, Animations*, and also introduce a few other tools to make our lives as movie producers easier.

Why can't I just use the output from SketchUp?

The raw animated output from SketchUp will invariably be one of the following:

- Strongly compressed with visual artifacts and noise
- Impractically large in size
- Limited to the artificial SketchUp styles

Following the easy steps in *Chapter 10, Animations*, with the software you're about to download will sort out all three problems. You will be completely amazed at how much the file size can be reduced with no perceivable reduction in quality.

VirtualDub

VirtualDub is the answer to most of our moving image woes on Windows. It's free; this is unbelievable as the next best available software is Adobe After Effects or Autodesk Combustion, both retailing at around $1000. VirtualDub will allow you to composite still images together to form a video, with the use of a whole host of filters thrown into the bargain. The GUI of VirtualDub Version 1.8.6 is similar to the one shown in the following screenshot:

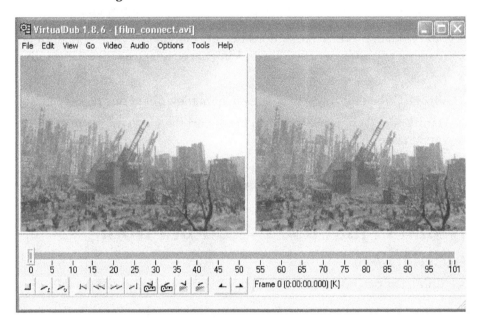

VirtualDub doesn't have an install program, so you will have to save it somewhere and create a desktop shortcut to it manually. Here's how to do it:

1. Get the latest stable release of VirtualDub from
   http://www.virtualdub.org. Just follow the links to the
   download mirror. Do not download the 64-bit version even
   if you are on a 64-bit system!
2. Save the ZIP file to your hard drive.
3. Extract the VirtualDub folder from the archive.
4. Move the entire VirtualDub folder to a permanent location on
   your hard drive (for example, C:\Program Files).
5. Open the folder and right-click on the VirtualDub.exe file.
6. Select **Send to | Desktop (create shortcut)**.
7. A new icon will be created on your desktop.

Mac alternatives

If you work on a Mac, chances are that you already have an application that can convert a set of images into a video. QuickTime Pro can be used for this and is very popular on Mac. If you don't have suitable software and also don't want to spend any money on new software just to create videos, you will still be able to generate animations with the free app Zeitraffer from the Apple App Store. Just type `zeitraffer` in the search field in the App Store, and download it to your Mac.

HandBrake

We will use HandBrake to convert the animation from VirtualDub into a compressed streaming video format that is suitable for websites such as YouTube. HandBrake is available for both Windows and Mac OS X platforms. Just head to `http://handbrake.fr`, and download and install the latest version.

Summary

So now, you're all set! In this chapter, you were introduced to the following concepts that will be at the core of your arch-viz activities:

- How to find and install unlimited 3D content from the 3D Warehouse
- Upgrade and extend SketchUp via the extension system
- Why a professional-level graphics tool like GIMP is so important
- Becoming a movie-making genius (almost) overnight
- Using a fully functional pro renderer integrated with SketchUp

Congratulations! You now have a fully functional visualization studio. This setup will save you an enormous amount of time later. It sets you up with a seamless workflow that works and works.

Now, go to the next chapter to get started with visualization in SketchUp, or return to *Chapter 1, Quick Start Tutorial*, if you were skipping ahead for the software!

3

Composing the Scene

Imagine you're a wildlife photographer. You're stalking a rare, brightly plumaged bird through the undergrowth. You lie in the grass for hours, centipedes and large spiders crawling over your face and neck. Then, when your body is stiff and aching, sun baked and drenched in sweat, the bird alights on a log with a fish in its mouth, the sun glimmering delightfully from the scales. You squeeze the shutter and success is yours.

Now, imagine yourself, instead, in a vast empty film studio. It's bare. Everything is lit in the same uniform, bright, diffused boring light. There's nothing to photograph except a skip full of plywood and canvas sheets. You'll have to make up your own scene.

In this chapter, you will learn how to plan out and set up a scene so that success is guaranteed later. You will discover the following:

- The main ways to start your scene
- Framing the scene using carefully chosen entourage place markers
- Using virtual plywood props and painted backdrops
- How to set up the sky, sun, and shadows
- How to set up lively camera angles to add interest

The importance of planning

The lack of subject matter is the reality for architectural visualizers. While a photographer creates art from what's available in nature, the architectural visualizer is faced with having to create everything from scratch, just like a film or stage designer. So, what will you show when you can show whatever you like?

- Close-ups of the building facade or views of the whole site?
- Worm's-eye view, a person's eye level, or aerial view?
- Photorealistic or artistic watercolor?
- Animation or stills?
- Flyovers or walkthroughs?
- Shadow studies?
- Sections through the building, individual wings, or phases?

It's a bewildering array of possibilities, and the temptation is always just to launch in and start building.

How to begin with the end in mind

Many people (often including me) start right out, modeling everything they see in as much detail as possible and simply run out of time. Their presentation is unfocused and patchy, because having modeled everything, they sure as anything want to include it all in the presentation!

The better way to go about it—the vital ingredient to success—is to begin with the end in mind. Sketch each still. Storyboard each moving sequence. Then, model only what you need to get these shots done. This way, you conserve energy in the areas that don't need your time and divert it to the areas that do.

There's much more detail on planning for animations or stills in *Chapter 10, Animations*. If you're designing a scene for animation of any kind, you should definitely read that chapter before you start modeling. If you're just doing stills, that chapter will help, but it isn't essential.

Sketch out your visuals

Take a few sheets of paper and a thick pencil or marker and sketch each visual
you wish to create. Sketch quickly, and don't worry at all about making it look good.
If you want to, include written information here about how you will achieve each
item in the scene; here's one as an example:

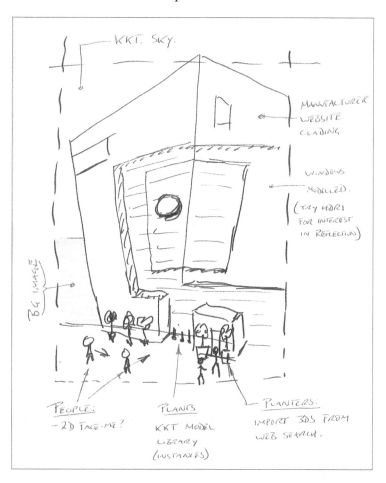

I've included positions of people and plants (entourage), notes on whether details will be modeled or textured, and information on where the background and the sky will come from (in this case, an image for the background and a basic sky will be chosen from within the rendering software). Draw a frame to help you compose the view.

Now that you've sketched your main visual, how about some extra views? It's often good to give an idea of the building's context and maybe a close-up, to show some neat features, as shown in the following image:

These will help focus your mind on what you want to show and what you can leave out. You can refer to these images when you need them. You can see how we progress with this visual later on in the chapter.

Think like a film set designer

Successful film and stage designers save time with the following visual tricks:

- Painted scenery backdrops
- 2D cardboard cutouts swapped for 3D items
- Modeling highly detailed images only for close-up shots

In this chapter, we will introduce the use of a backdrop image for whatever stays in the background and never enters into a close shot. We will also use 2D cutouts for peripheral elements rather than 3D geometry, which eats up our modeling time. Once you have mastered these simple time-saving principles, you'll be a top arch-viz artist.

Setting up an arch-viz scene

There are several ways to begin setting up our scene. All of these will help anchor your scene in the existing surroundings and give the model a context and scale that our audience needs to relate to the project.

The following are the main scene setup methods:

- Import a satellite image and terrain data via geolocation
- Use a site photograph with the Match Photo tool
- Import a scanned site map, image, or pencil sketch
- Build on data from an imported CAD file

Any of these can be used in combination, and it is this flexibility that makes SketchUp so unique. SketchUp is equally at home with accurate CAD, as it is with pencil concept art. We're going to look at each of these starting points individually so that you can choose the best combination for your particular way of working.

Of course, you can also just start sketching away and build up a complete scene with context from scratch. However, there is nothing special about this, is there?

Importing terrain data

Thanks to its history with **Google Earth**, SketchUp offers an easy way to import a 2D site image from Google Earth. Often, this is the quickest way to get context information on a site, especially in the early stages of a concept design or projects in faraway places, where detailed survey maps are hard to come by or do not exist at all.

1. Open the tool by navigating to **File** | **Geo-location** | **Add Location...**.

A slimmed down Google Earth browser window, as shown in the following screenshot, will appear, and as a seasoned Google Maps user, you should feel right at home:

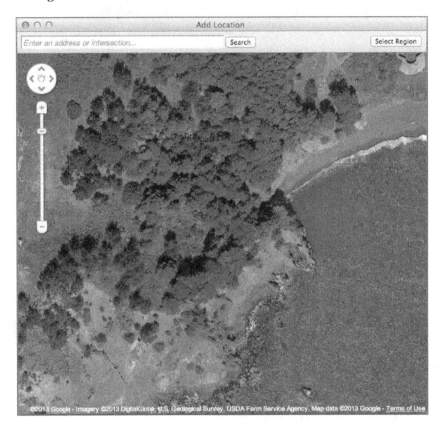

2. Use the search bar at the top of the window or the zoom and navigation controls to focus on a piece of land you want to use for the model.

3. Click on the **Select Region** button in the top-right corner of the screen, when you have found the right place.

4. A frame with a pin in each corner appears.

5. Adjust the frame so that the center shows the area you want to import into your model.

6. When you are done, click on the **Grab** button in the top-right corner of the screen.

7. The image will be imported and centered into your model.

8. However, that's not all. Navigate to **File | Geo-Location | Show Terrain**.

9. The image turns into a textured 3D landscape with true elevation
    information, as seen in the following screenshot:

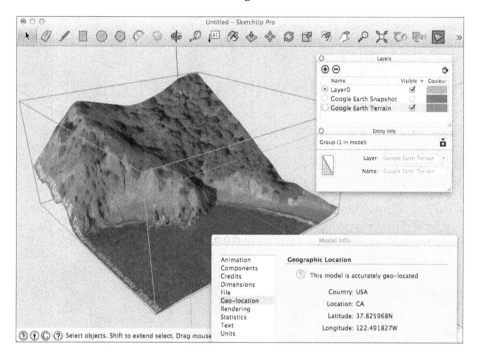

Let's inspect what we have just imported into our model. Open your **Layers** dialog.
You will find two new layers in the model: one called **Google Earth Snapshot** and
the other called **Google Earth Terrain**. On the snapshot layer, you can find the
flat 2D image of the site that was displayed first. The terrain layer contains the **3D
topographic mesh** as a component. Switching between the two via the **Show Terrain**
option toggles the visibility of the layers, so that only one is present in the scene.

The import also gave our model the correct coordinates of the location that we
picked. In the **Geo-location** section of the **Model Info** dialog, you can see the name
of the new **Location** and information about the **Latitude** and **Longitude**.

To modify the imported terrain to fit your new design, do the following:

1. Right-click on the component and select **unlock**.
2. Right-click again and select **explode**.
3. Show the hidden elements by navigating to **View | Hidden Geometry**.
4. Navigate to **View | Face Style** to disable **textures** and, maybe, even switch
    to a **Wireframe** view of the model. You will now see the individual lines that
    make up the imported terrain.

There are a number of plugins and extensions out there that can help you with editing free form geometry such as terrain meshes. The **Sandbox Tools** are already included in SketchUp, and several others are available via the **Extension Warehouse** and **Plugin Store**. If you are planning to do this type of modeling a lot, it is worth checking them out.

Using a site photo with Match Photo

One of the best ways to bring across the concept of a new building is to put it into its existing setting. We can do this with a photo of the site as it is now, before the building commences. It's also one of the easiest ways of producing great architectural visuals because you don't have to worry about all the extra bits of the entourage that need to be selected and arranged. They're already in the photo.

If you can get your hands on a decent camera and the site is relatively uncluttered, this may be the best way to go. The following is an example image of a home that is about to undergo renovation:

What you need from a Match Photo image

You're going to use the tool **Match Photo** to set up the SketchUp camera, so that it matches the position and focal distance of the camera you used to take your photo. Before SketchUp Version 6, we used to do this by trial and error, but since Version 6, SketchUp includes Match Photo, which automates the whole task for you. Using this feature, you can create "before" and "after" photos that are very useful for renovation projects, such as the home extension shown in the following image. The realism that the architect has achieved here wouldn't have been possible without exactly matching the camera view:

First, some points about the kind of photographs you need to take:

- The image needs to show strong vertical and horizontal corners or lines
- Horizontal lines need to form a true right angle, such as the corners of a 90-degree building
- The picture should be taken with a horizontal line of sight (don't tilt the camera up or down)

- Sunny days with defined shadows work best when you are planning to use the scene for photorealistic rendering
- The image can't be cropped or changed in proportions by an image-editing program
- Use a digital SLR with good lenses if possible. Failing this, a high-resolution compact camera or even a good smartphone camera will do

For a before and after scene, it is important to make a note of the following important details:

- The date and time of day
- The site map or location sketch (to work out the North location)
- Take a reference photo of the sky
- Include some right angles in the frame (like the corner of a building)

These allow SketchUp to recreate the position of the camera and sun. You might wish to use the sky's photo to select similar sky settings in your rendering application or to pick a similar HDR sky for rendering (for example, clear, cloudy, or overcast).

Setting up a Match Photo scene

Match Photo works by recognizing **perspective foreshortening** in the frame. In order to do this, there have to be some buildings or walls or other items with right angles. All you have to do, is open the photo in SketchUp and line up some colored lines with these features.

1. Select a suitable site image.
2. From the drop-down menu, navigate to **Camera | Match New Photo**.
3. Navigate to your photo and select **Open**.
4. The image will be imported and red, green, and blue lines will be displayed on top.

5. Move the origin point (the yellow square) to a corner of a building (or other architectural feature of the building) at ground level, as shown in the following screenshot:

6. Click and hold the left-mouse button to move the grips.

7. Align one of the green dotted lines along an edge going off to the right.

8. Align the second green line in the same plain but higher up the blue line (the *z* axis), as shown in the following screenshot:

9. Do the same with the two red lines to the left.

10. Click on **Done**, as shown in the following screenshot:

SketchUp has now created a new scene (see the tab at the top of the 3D window), which you can click on whenever you want to come back to this view. You will see the image only in this scene. If you move the viewpoint away from the viewpoint of the image, the backdrop will disappear.

You have now set up the blue, green, and red axes to correspond to the up/down, forward/backward and left/right directions that you have captured in the photograph. Having done this, you can now happily draw away in the scene, knowing that the model you create will always look as if it is right within the photograph. The depth of the field, focal length, and eye height have all been taken care of. This is a big deal, because doing this by trial and error would have taken far more time and probably caused a lot of frustration!

3D drawing in a 2D photo

You can now test your new perspective setup by drawing a simple box into the scene. If this looks right in relation to the photo, you know you've done the Match Photo process correctly.

1. Select the **pencil** tool.

2. Click on the **origin** (where the blue, red, and green axes meet).

3. Move up the *blue* axis and click on the blue axis to set the end point of the line at the height of the eaves or gutters of the building.

4. Move along the *green* axis and click on a point along the axis to define the width of the facade.

5. Move down the blue axis, hold the *Shift* key to activate the constraint to the blue axis and click on the origin.

6. Release the *Shift* key and click on the **origin** again to complete the face, as you can see in the following screenshot:

7. Select the **Push/Pull** tool.

8. Push the face along the **red** axis to form a 3D box, as shown in the following screenshot:

The perspective of this box should be in keeping with the house, wall, or any other right-angled item that you included in your photo. If it isn't, just click on the photo match pallet, click on the cogs symbol to edit the Match Photo setup, and tweak the dotted lines. The best indication that you're right is when the blue axis lines up perfectly with the corner.

You have just created a 3D box to represent the existing building. Rotate the view with the mouse to view it. Notice that the photo disappears. Don't worry; you can bring it back at any time by clicking on the scene tab that the Match Photo tool created at the start.

You can now draw or add anything onto this scene, and it will look correct if you place items into the scene in relation to the 3D box, as you can see in the following screenshot:

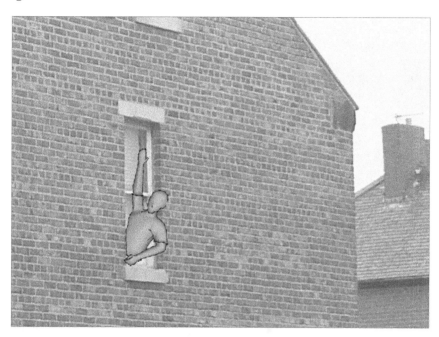

Setting up a real-world location and the Sun's position

Before we can create renderings of the new geometry that blend in with the rest of our photo, we have to set the **location** and **orientation** of our scene. Once this is set, the shadows on the model will match up with the shadows in the picture.

For scenes created with the Match Photo tool, setting the orientation is important, because the lines you set as your x and y axes are most likely not aligned with East and North, respectively. Unfortunately, the simple controls for the location and orientation settings have been removed since SketchUp 2013.

Luckily, you can still download a plugin by Jim Foltz. This plugin recreates the necessary controls. He has kindly allowed us to provide a copy of the Ruby files on the Packt support website. Go to `http://www.packtpub.com/support` and select the title of the book from the drop-down list. Then, download the files `model_location.rb` and `inputbox.rb` from the `Chapter 3` folder and copy them both into your plugins folder (refer *Chapter 2, Collecting a Toolset*, for details). Restart SketchUp, and you will find a new **Model Location** entry under the **Plugins** menu, as shown in the following screenshot:

With this simple tool, you can set the location, time zone, and North orientation of your scene. A simple way of going about this is to set up the location, date, and time of day using the **Shadow Setting** menu in SketchUp. If you have previously noted down the time and date when you took the photo, you can set this up now too.

1. Open the plugin from the menu by navigating to **Plugins | Model Location**.

2. Set the **Latitude** and **Longitude** of your site.

3. You can also give a name for the **Location** and **Country**, but this has no influence on the **Shadow Setting**.

4. Change the **Time Zone** to the right offset for your country. If you want to simulate **Daylight Saving Time**, also set the **Daylight** option to **true**.

5. Set **Show North?** to **true**. The North direction will now be displayed in the model as an orange line. Adjust the **North Angle** until the line points to the geographic North in the model.

Setting up the time and date for shadows

All that remains is to tell SketchUp what time of day and date the photo was taken. You can do this with the **Shadow Settings** dialog box, as shown in the following screenshot:

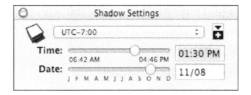

1. Navigate to **Window | Shadows**.
2. Use the sliders or type in the date and time.
3. You can adjust the time zone here as well. Notice that the setting will also update in the **Model Location** plugin.
4. If you don't see the shadows in the model yet, open the **View** menu and click on **Shadows**. A check mark indicates that shadows are displayed in the model.

 Use this function to set up accurate shadow studies for all your projects. For example, you can now check the sunlight that each room will receive at any day of the year.

You have now set the location, orientation, time, and date of your site. This means that the Sun and shadows will behave just as they would if you were really there.

Check the shadow cast by the box. Does it match with the photo? If not, you may have got the North orientation mixed up or forgotten to set the correct location. You can go back and change this now. You can also use trial and error on the sliders for the date and time to match the shadows in the photo as closely as possible.

Now that you've learned everything you need to know about setting up a physically accurate environment, let's look at the other great methods you can use to set up a site in SketchUp. Don't forget; even though shadows and shading look quite cartoony now, these settings will be used to define the physically accurate Sun and sky conditions when you export them to a renderer.

Sketch plan

SketchUp works surprisingly well with sketchy details. So, even importing a rough sketch plan or a scan of an old hard copy drawing you might have found lying around still works well as basis for your 3D scene.

1. Scan the map image. Don't go crazy with the scan resolution (DPI). Use just enough quality to clearly see the lines you are going to use in the model.

2. Save it as a **JPEG** or **PNG** image.

3. In SketchUp, navigate to **File | Import...**.

4. Navigate to the image and click on **Open**.

5. Click where you want it and drag it to a size about as big as the site.

6. If your image contains a **drawing scale**, measure the size of the scale in the scene and scale the image.

7. Now, you can start creating your geometry right on top of the image and build up the footprint and floor plans of the building.

As long as you use the image lines as guides, you will produce a proportional model. It is surprising how little detail you need to start drawing meaningful 3D visuals.

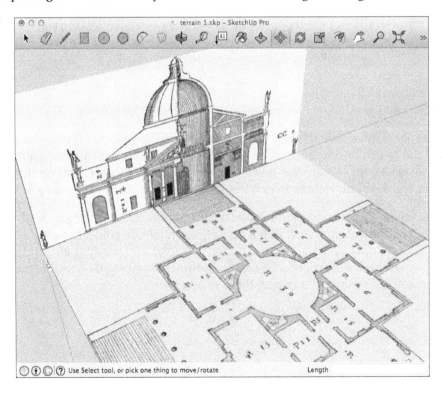

Now, just try to draw a very basic (or pretentious) house and garden plan or look for one in an architectural or DIY magazine. Scan this into the computer, or alternatively, find one on Google Image Search and use that. Can you see how easy it is to construct from sketches? The important thing here is that you've used a proportional sketch or drawing as guideline rather than just starting to draw in 3D from scratch.

Starting with a 2D CAD site plan

If you have an existing CAD drawing, either a proposed or existing site plan, you can easily import it into SketchUp and build up the 3D site from there. The benefit of a CAD drawing over an image is the precision that CAD data provides. Also, CAD lines will be imported as SketchUp **edges**, which you can snap to when creating the 3D elements.

You should have a CAD application such as AutoCAD LT or a free alternative such as DoubleCAD XT (`www.doublecad.com`) or DraftSight (`www.3ds.com/products-services/draftsight/`) available to do some cleanup work. Usually, CAD drawings are not optimized for rough SketchUp work but contain a lot more information than necessary. Here are a few things you should look out for before you import a CAD drawing into SketchUp:

- Remove unnecessary elements such as text, grid lines, or sheet layout elements
- Remove pattern fills and hatches, especially if they are individual lines and not complex drawing elements
- Use the `explode` command to convert 2D polylines to normal lines
- Remove geometric details you will not use in your model (such as crown molding)
- Identify the layers you do need for your model (walls, doors, windows, and hard landscape) and delete all the others

In *Chapter 4*, *Modeling for Visualization*, you will also learn how to import and use CAD elevations (side and front views) to build up the detail.

 You need SketchUp 2014 Pro to import DWG or DXF files into your scene.

Setting up a CAD site plan

Follow these basic steps to clean up your CAD drawing for use in SketchUp:

1. Open the CAD plan in your CAD drawing application.

2. Save a copy of the file and rename it `cadplan_xref.dwg` or similar.

3. Delete all the lines, hatchings, xrefs, dimensions, text, and blocks you don't need.

4. You can keep the 2D blocks representing the elements that you do want to replace with 3D geometry (such as plants) in your drawing, but make sure that the blocks do not contain too many lines.

5. You should be left with clear outlines of buildings, roads, and landscaping.

6. Select everything and move it near to the absolute origin (0,0) of the drawing.

7. **Zoom to extents** to verify that no stray lines are left at a great distance from the center.

8. In AutoCAD, you can use the `purge` command to clean up the drawing structure and remove unused elements and layers.

9. Hit **Save**.

You now have a basic plan from which you can begin modeling the environment around your building and the building itself. Now, you need to import it into SketchUp at the correct scale.

1. Open up SketchUp.

2. Start the import tool by navigating to **File | import**.

3. Change the **Format** drop-down box to **AutoCAD Files**.

4. Hit the **Options...** button and verify the import settings, as follows:

   ° Adjust the **Scale** to fit to your CAD drawing scale

   ° **Preserve drawing origin** is useful if you have split your CAD drawing in multiple files (such as floor levels) and want to import them at the same position in the model

- ° **Merge coplanar faces** and **Orient faces consistently** are relevant if you import 3D elements. You can always have them checked, as seen in the following screenshot:

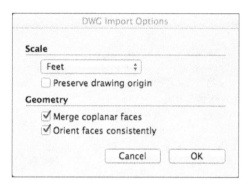

5. Select your drawing file and click on **Open**.

6. You will see a **progress window** displaying the elements that are being processed. At the end, a **summary** of imported drawing elements is displayed.

7. Hit **Zoom Extents**. If the view zooms out so far that you can't identify any of your drawing elements, you will see that there were some stray lines left in the drawing that were not deleted. You can try and hunt them down in SketchUp or return to the CAD drawing to delete these lines and repeat the import. Either way, you should remove these extra lines.

8. If your scene already contained an element (such as the default *Sophie* component), all lines will be combined in a component. If the scene was completely empty, the lines will be independent. If this is the case, select all the lines now and turn them into a component.

9. Use the **Tape Measure** tool to verify the size of the imported lines. Measure the length of an element with a known dimension (such as a wall) and make sure you snap to the end points of the line.

10. If the scale is not correct, just type the correct length right after you took the measurement and hit *Enter*.

11. SketchUp will ask: **Do you want to resize the model?**

12. Confirm that you want to resize the model, and all drawing elements will be scaled to the correct size. Measure the new size again to confirm.

In the following screenshot, you can see an imported CAD plan scaled to the right size. You can compare the size of the person with the size of the door opening or a chair to confirm the correct scale.

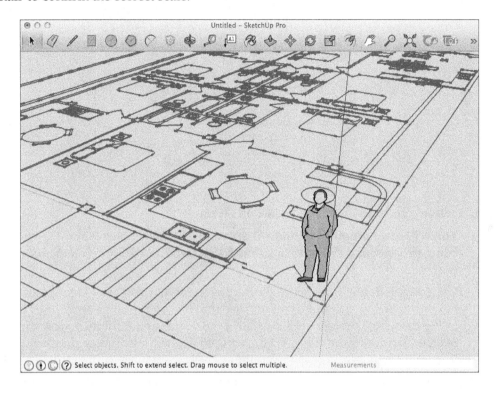

You now have the plan within SketchUp and scaled to real-world dimensions. This is important, because SketchUp is built for real-world architectural models, and every component you will add to your model (such as persons or plants) will come in at a realistic size.

Cleaning up the imported CAD data

If you only have a few layers in your CAD file, you can leave it at that. However, if there are dozens of layers in the file, these have now been replicated in SketchUp. It's time to do a bit of cleanup work:

1. Open the **Layer** dialog by navigating to **Window | Layers**.
2. Activate **Layer0**.
3. Select all the CAD layers by holding down the *Shift* key.
4. Select the minus icon at the top to delete all the layers.

5. A popup will give you a choice about what to do with the content of the layers. Select **Move to Default Layer**.

6. Click on **Delete**.

7. The layers will vanish, and all content will be placed on **Layer0**.

8. Create a new layer called CAD drawing.

9. Select the component of the drawing and assign it to the newly created layer. Now, you can switch off the layer when you don't want to see it in your model.

CAD applications use layers to separate elements. In SketchUp, all the basic elements should be drawn on **Layer0**, and only the containers (groups and components) should be assigned to a different layer to control the visibility of the object. We have created this structure in SketchUp and at the same time, got rid of a number of imported layers that are not useful to us.

Importing 3D data from CAD

If you are lucky and can get a ready-made 3D model for your visualization project, you can also import the entire 3D model into SketchUp. The supported formats are as follows:

- DWG/DXF
- 3DS
- DAE (Collada)
- OBJ (via plugin only)

When you import 3D content from another application, you have to be careful with the complexity and level of detail. CAD and BIM models can be large in dimensions but still model every detail down to the doorknob in very high resolution. If you actually succeed with the import, the performance of SketchUp will certainly suffer.

Most CAD applications will create triangle surfaces when exporting 3D objects, because these are the most basic objects that every application can handle. In SketchUp, we would prefer to have complex polygonal faces to make use of the native surface tools. Luckily, there is a plugin that can combine triangles to polygons for us. It is **Cleanup** by Thomthom. You can download it from the Plugin Store.

Although importing a finished 3D model may look like a big time saver, you will find that you will have to spend a lot of effort on cleaning up, restructuring, and converting the triangular surfaces into something that can be easily handled and modified with SketchUp. Therefore, directly importing CAD or 3D data is most useful for objects that you are not going to edit a lot, such as a car or a surrounding urban block. If you are going to make a lot of modifications to the geometry, it may be faster to recreate the model from scratch with all the tools and the correct structure of a SketchUp model.

Fleshing out your site plan

Now that you've set up your site base using one of the methods introduced in the preceding section, you can flesh out the volumes in no time. This process is called **massing**. The idea here is to give an overall impression of the 3D space that buildings occupy. Details can be modeled later on, provided they will be visible in the frame.

Massing the buildings

To begin massing your context, perform the following steps:

1. Make sure that your base plan is turned into a group.
2. Right-click and select **Lock**. Now, you can't inadvertently change anything.
3. With the **pencil** tool, retrace the outline of a building.
4. Notice how the rubber band turns magenta to lock to the perpendicular (right angle) of an existing line. In this way, you can draw all walls at right angles to the first wall.
5. Complete the outline by returning to your starting point. SketchUp will fill the outline with a surface.
6. Push-pull the surface up to the height of the building.

You can turn the building now into a component to use elsewhere:

1. Triple-click on a surface of the new building.

2. Check that all the lines and polygons that belong to the building are now selected.

3. Right-click and select **Make Component**.

4. Assign a recognizable name to the new component. If you don't have anything else to go by, use the street name and building number.

5. Repeat the previous steps to create boxes for all the buildings on your site.

Stick to adding simple blocks quickly to your site, so that you can get a good idea of how your new building fits in. You can create more details or add textures to these buildings later if you need to. The following image shows a few street blocks with the buildings as rough 3D shapes. It's already enough detail to give you the overall idea of a city blocks and connecting streets.

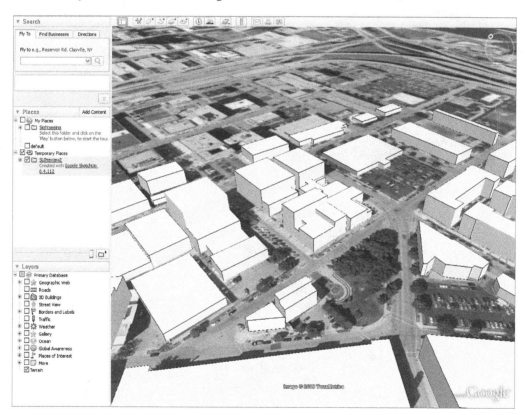

Setting up the camera to challenge and impress

Take a look at the following two examples. Which of the two do you find more stimulating?

The SketchUp camera view can be set up to simulate the human eye, a long-range camera, or even a fisheye lens. To you and me, this means that we get great flexibility in the effects we can achieve when composing our scene. The two images here demonstrate that the same model need not convey the same impression. Here, the first image is rather mundane and ordinary, but the second one is aggressive and challenging. When setting up the view, experiment with the field of view and different angles until you have the striking image that will wow your clients.

Alternatively, depending on what you're trying to convey, you may like to go safe and conventional. The choice is yours.

Changing the field of view

Carry out the following steps to change the field of view:

1. Navigate to **Camera** | **Zoom** or click on the **Zoom** icon (represented by a magnifying glass).

2. Hold down *Shift* and move the mouse up or down to increase or decrease the field of view. Notice how the background changes in relation to the foreground.

3. Notice that the **Value Control Box** (bottom right) changes to show the value of the current field of view in degrees.

4. Now, try typing in some values and hit *Enter* each time.

The beauty of SketchUp is that the view changes in real time letting you experiment to your heart's content. The field of view isn't the only tool you can use to break away from the mundane!

Think like a pigeon

Have you ever found yourself wondering what the world looks like to a pigeon walking around in the street? No? Well, I must admit neither have I until now, but let me assure you that the pigeon's view on the world is a very interesting one! Take a look at this sequence of three images, again starting with a standard SketchUp view of our model and then how a pigeon would see it on the ground and in flight.

Which of these gives the best impression of height?

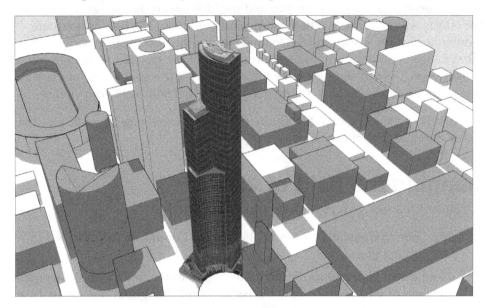

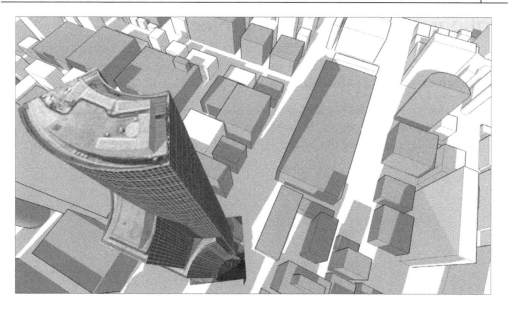

This just demonstrates how easy it is to surprise people by showing them buildings from a perspective they have never considered before. People want to be challenged in this way. Experimenting a little with viewing angles will pay off in the end with a gripping rather than a mundane image.

Of course, sometimes they just want to see how a building will look like to them. It all depends on knowing the audience and purpose of the visualization.

Here are some other things to try:

- Banking
- Tilting (hold *Ctrl* (for Windows) or *Option* (for Mac) while using the Orbit tool)
- Flying right in close on detail (usually, with the loss of feathers)
- Top-down views
- Panoramas

Orthographic and parallel projection

The **perspective projection** mimics the human visual perception, where far away objects look smaller and objects close up look larger. This is our natural experience, and we can easily relate to these images.

However, for architectural presentation, we also use **parallel projection**. This method of projection preserves the aspect ratio of vertical and horizontal lines and so, it is valuable to estimate the proportions of a building façade or other details.

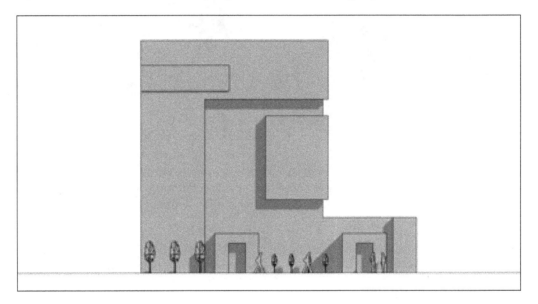

Turning perspective view off is necessary for modeling when you need to see orthographic views (top, left, front, and so on). It's also good when you want to output these views to create 2D drawings for construction documentation. If you are used to 3D CAD drawing, you may even prefer this look over perspective views.

To change between the projection modes, navigate to **Camera | Parallel Projection** or **Camera | Perspective**. By navigating to **Camera | Standard Views...**, you can set up presets for orthographic views. If you are going to refer to a specific view frequently during the modeling, you can also save all the settings in a scene tab.

Saving days of toil with ready-made scenery

Robin once spent four days modeling scenery, people, trees, and streets full of buildings in order to finish off a view. The new building itself had only taken a day to model! In order to avoid this, most professional architectural visualizers make heavy use of paid-for entourage (trees, people, cars, buildings, and such) to liven up a view.

Of all the important developments that have made 3D computer visualization what it is now, the availability of digital cameras must be the most important factor. You will already have come across the basic techniques you need. The rest will be discussed in more detail in *Chapter 5*, *Applying Textures and Materials for Photorealistic Rendering*, and *Chapter 6*, *Entourage the SketchUp Way*.

Billboard scenery elements

Virtually, any photo you take or find on the Internet can be turned into a scenery element. Take this one of wild horses, for example. Would you have ever thought of using an image like this in an arch-viz scene?

However, horse lovers need a home too! The rendered-up version made it to the finals of a rendering competition, which was designed to show off the capabilities of **IRender** without doing any postprocessing in Photoshop. All I did was to cut out the foreground, mid-ground, and background from the same image and set them up, as you can see in the following screenshot:

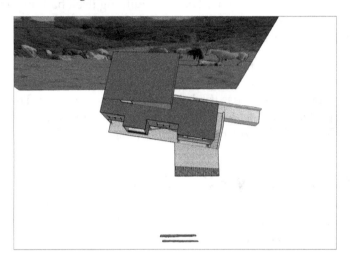

All you need to remember when doing this is that the further away from the camera the billboard image is, the larger it will have to be, so the individual cutouts will need to be resized by eye. Here's how it came together. This is purely a SketchUp output without any rendering. You can see the cutout edges in black, in the following screenshot:

Harnessing the plethora of online images

In *Chapter 6, Entourage the SketchUp Way,* we will look at the best place to obtain images on the Internet, to turn them into entourage. However, don't forget to use them here too.

Creating billboard elements

We create billboard elements as follows:

1. Insert your image into SketchUp somewhere out of the way.
2. Right-click and select **Explode**.
3. Double-click to select and then turn the selection into a component.
4. Copy it using the **Move** tool with the *Ctrl* key pressed (*Option* on Mac).
5. Rotate the copy upright (90 degrees).
6. Place it where you need it. Scale as necessary.
7. Now, go back to the first copy. Double-click on it to edit it.
8. Select a plan view by navigating to **Camera | Standard Views | Top**.
9. Draw over areas to be clipped and deleted. The in-place component automatically changes too.

You can download this SketchUp scene from the download section of this book at www.packtpub.com/support.

When you import and explode images in SketchUp, they behave in just the same way as any rectangle surface with a texture applied to it. So, you can draw on it and erase sections. This can however be difficult when your image is in position, because it might be at a weird angle or obstructed by other items. Using this technique, you have the image lying horizontally in the plan view, so you can draw over it in a flat 2D view.

The following image is what the horses looked like when they were clipped. As you can see, you could create whole scenes just with photos and no other modeling at all!

However, usually, you would use this technique to insert a foreground image of foliage or people and a background image of, say, a city or country scene:

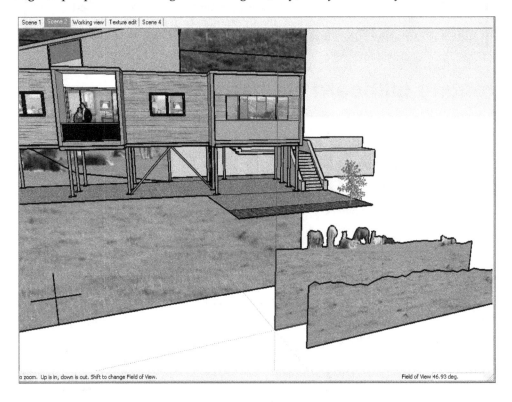

Framing the scene with entourage

Having set up your scene, your choice of entourage is now the most important decision you will have to make in the visualization process. Clever use of the entourage will frame the picture, enhance it, and distract the viewer from the details that you don't want them to see. More than this, choosing the right kind of entourage can increase or reduce the render time by an order of magnitude.

Choosing your final entourage will be covered in more detail in *Chapter 6, Entourage the SketchUp Way*, and you really don't want to have to worry about specifics until then. Choices on what trees to use, whether they will be 3D or 2D, downloaded from a website or created yourself will all be decided later, and we will discover together what the best options for creating great looking architectural renders are. However, for now, what you need the most, is creative flexibility.

The specifity trap

What is the *specifity trap*? Well, I actually made up the term, so you won't find it in any dictionary. The *specifity trap* is when you bog yourself down in specifics far too early on in the design process. Using a specific finished entourage at this early stage will force your creative brain to focus on it rather than the building. Worse, it will take lots of computing power away from SketchUp, particularly, if you insert lots of 3D trees or people. It's like looking around for a house to buy and then arguing with your partner about the shrubs next to the front lawn or rejecting the house because you don't like the color of the living room wall. It really doesn't matter for now.

High Polygon Count means highly detailed 3D geometry. It refers to the number of faces (polygons) used to create a shape or geometry. The higher the number of polygons, the longer SketchUp takes to process what's there and the more computing power it needs. This means that if you add a lot of detailed 3D entourage to your scene, you might find moving the view around extremely slow and jumpy. You'll learn how to model scenes with a low polygon count in *Chapter 4, Modeling for Visualization*.

Rough placeholders

So, the answer to all your problems here is to insert basic, rough, sketch-like entourage just to indicate, more or less, where a tree, person, or car will go. You will change these placeholders to something nicer later. This is really easy. Here are the benefits of this way of working:

- Uncluttered workspace
- No high polygon 3D people/trees/cars to slow SketchUp down
- Creativity isn't stifled by concentrating on what doesn't really matter at this stage
- You retain flexibility to swap entourage later depending on what kind of output you go for (photoreal, sketchy, watercolor, and so on)

If your composition doesn't look right with basic entourage, it won't look right with highly polished stuff either. However, at least, you can spot this early on and make adjustments before you've put in too much effort.

Inserting entourage placeholders

If you haven't done so already, frame your scene exactly how you want it and save the view as you have it now, so that you can keep going back to it.

Based on the composition you're aiming to achieve, insert any trees and people as follows.

1. Open the **Components** browser by navigating to **Window | Components**.
2. Select **People** from the drop-down menu. The basic collection will be loaded.
3. Pick the **2D People** collection.
4. In the **3D Warehouse** window, select a basic person (don't worry about anything else for now — you'll replace them later).
5. Move the cursor into the view area and place the person somewhere near where you'd like them.
6. Click on the scene tab at the top of the view window and check whether the composition looks right.
7. Move the person around (watching the axis color as necessary).
8. Repeat steps 4 to 7 until you have populated your scene.
9. Choose a different collection of entourage components such as plants, but remember to use the most basic items for now. When you insert plants, you can also use the scale tool to introduce a bit of variety.

You will now have a fully composed scene: a sketched-out canvas ready for you to fill in the boxes. Remember to save the model!

Printing a test view

At this stage, it's a good idea to print a black-and-white version of the scene for you to sketch over with any ideas:

1. Navigate to **Window | Styles** to open the **Styles** dialog.
2. Select a black-and-white style from the default styles.
3. Navigate to **File | Print** from the menu.
4. Adjust the print option to fill the page.
5. Click on **Print**.

The following image is the massing model of the sketch we started with, complete with basic entourage and billboard backgrounds:

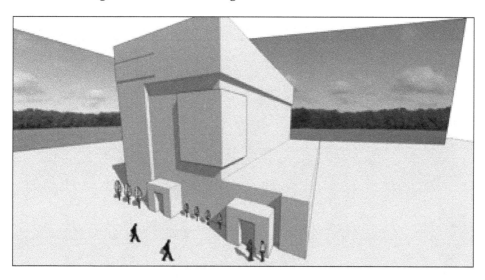

You can download the .skp file in the code download pack at www.packtpub.com/support.

Summary

You have now completed the most important stage in creating great architectural visuals using SketchUp! It wasn't hard, was it? The piece of paper in your hand is proof that a great visual is on the way. If you completed the quick start tutorial in *Chapter 1, Quick Start Tutorial*, you will know how easy the rest can be.

In this chapter, you learned how to think like a film set designer when setting up your scene and anchor your scene in the surrounding context. Then, you created camera perspectives with an extra wow factor. You have simulated accurate sunlight with location, orientation, time, and date in SketchUp. Finally, you used photos for billboard scenery and placed marker entourage to quickly view and make adjustments to your surroundings.

In the next chapter, you will learn how to model within SketchUp for great results quickly and easily. Remember that all you need to do is follow the tried and tested methods step by step. These individual steps are all baby steps, but at the end of the journey, you will be amazed at how far you have travelled. By setting up your scene just like you have done in this chapter, you have ensured that the rest of the process will be quick and easy.

4

Modeling for Visualization

No doubt, you're already a dab hand at creating models with SketchUp's easy-to-use but powerful toolset. But what precisely is modeling anyway? Simply put, it is the process of creating the basic geometry — polygons and other surfaces — used in a 3D scene. In this chapter, you will learn the modeling techniques specifically required for architectural visualization. We will look at the following topics:

- Setting up a file structure for your project
- Modeling details from CAD elevations or photos
- Low polygon modeling to increase computer speed
- Harnessing the power of components
- Modeling main building features for visualization

If you've already completed *Chapter 3, Composing the Scene*, you will have started your scene using one of the following four methods, or a combination of these:

- Importing Google Earth terrain data or other online mapping images
- Using a site photograph with Match Photo
- Using a scanned 2D sketch or drawing
- Using an existing CAD drawing

Using any of these methods will instantly give your model focus and context. If you haven't done so already, flesh out your main scene by replacing all the buildings that give context but are not the main focus, with boxes.

Project file layout

When starting a SketchUp project, it is a good idea to set up your file structure first. Start with a main folder for the project, and create subfolders inside this main folder for site components, images, entourage, output drawings, and whatever else you need. This will help you when you need to transport your main model to another computer or when you do your daily backups. You just grab the whole folder hierarchy to keep the scene dependencies intact.

Creating the basic building shape

We are going to create a dummy building within our context scene, save it as a separate model file, and then open it individually to start modeling the details. This is a good modeling technique, especially for large or intricate scenes, and will also keep you away from being distracted as you work on it. To create the basic building shape, perform the following steps:

1. Draw the basic outline of the building you will be modeling.
2. Push-pull it to the maximum height (usually the **ridge** height).
3. Triple-click on it to select all the faces and edges.
4. Right-click on it and select **Make Component** from the context menu.
5. The **Create Component** dialog box appears.

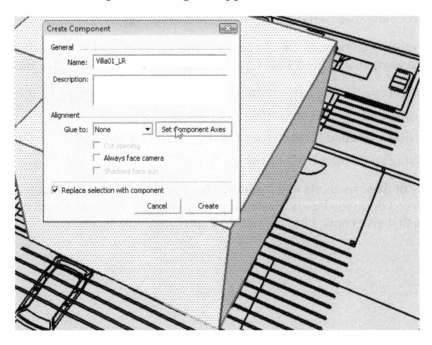

6. Click on the **Set Component Axes** button.

7. Set the origin at a corner of your building and align the main axis (in red) with the main facade of your building; then set the green axis to the back of the building.

8. Enter a name to identify the component in the **Name** field.

9. Click on the **Create** button. Your faces are now part of a component in the main scene.

10. Now right-click on the new component and choose **Save As**.

11. A file browser window opens that lets you save the component as a new `*.skp` file.

12. Navigate to the `Components` folder in your project and save it with an easy-to-identify name and append `_LR` to the filename, for example, `Main_Street_96_LR.skp`.

13. Repeat these steps but now replace the `_LR` file with `_HR`.

You have now created a low-resolution (`_LR`) and a high-resolution (`_HR`) SketchUp file from your component. You can keep the `_LR` file version more or less as you see it now, and model the `_HR` file version to perfection (or near enough!).

The reason for creating two versions of everything is simple: we want to stay as focused and unencumbered with detail as possible while we are modeling, and throughout the design process. When the time comes to produce some great visuals, we will bring all the detailed elements back in. The rest of the time, we will have the `_LR` file versions in place to give us a sense of context and scale.

This also helps us with the limitations of SketchUp. The lower the amount of polygons in the scene, the quicker we can maneuver around the SketchUp environment (also explained in the *Low polygon modeling techniques* section of this chapter). Components also have some other useful aspects that we will explore further in this chapter.

Swapping _LR with _HR resolution versions

Now here comes the clever bit! If you now double-click on the newly created `*_HR.skp` file, a second instance of SketchUp will start that contains only the content of the component. Now with the `_HR` component open in the second SketchUp window, perform the following steps:

1. Modify the `_HR` component geometry to add more details.

2. Save your changes.

3. Go back to the original SketchUp window that contains the main scene.

4. Right-click on the still _LR component in the main scene.

5. Click on **Reload**.

6. If the last thing you did was to save the *_HR.skp file, the content will update immediately because SketchUp recognizes that the file with the component definition has changed.

7. Otherwise, you will get prompted if you want to replace the existing component with a different file. Select **Yes** in this case.

8. Navigate to the updated component file and select **Open**. The scene updates with the changes you just made.

9. Repeat the steps from 4 to 8, but this time swap the _HR component with the _LR component.

10. Check your scene again and see how the simple component is back in place.

As you move along, you will use this method to swap all the scene placeholders that you've set up in *Chapter 3, Composing the Scene*, with final items of entourage (which will be covered in *Chapter 6, Entourage the SketchUp Way*) and other scenery.

Let's think of an everyday example; you have a large housing site with 40 house plots. Each of these has 20 bushes in the garden, made of the same component but scaled and rotated differently to give an impression of variety. Each bush may have 3,000 faces, giving a total of 2.4 million faces just for garden shrubs! Replacing just one of these component definitions with a simplified version (say a box) will update them all in one go and allow you to navigate your scene smoothly again.

When importing AutoCAD files, blocks import into SketchUp as components. If you have trees in your 2D CAD plan, you can swap them out for 3D versions in SketchUp using the preceding method of swapping. What's particularly good about this is that all copies of the AutoCAD block will update with the same SketchUp component so that you can instantly turn all 2D trees in to 3D objects in one stroke!

Carving out the detail

When visualizing with SketchUp, the great benefit is that most of the detail can be introduced easily with textures and photographs. So, we don't need to be a 3D CAD virtuoso to create great looking architectural visuals. In fact, the general rule of thumb when deciding whether to model more detail is: if in doubt, don't bother!

The following are some reasons to be lazy:

- You can always model more details later if you really need to, but you can never retrieve the time you spent if you did too much too soon

- Applying images and textures will work much better on simple flat surfaces

- The more complex your model is initially, the harder it is to change details later on

 Modeling buildings in SketchUp is really easy. That's because SketchUp has been developed with the architectural market specifically in mind. You will already have picked up lots of useful tips from the training videos on www.sketchup.com/learn/videos or on YouTube.

Modeling buildings in SketchUp

Open up your main building file (that's the *_HR.skp component file created). We are now going to start modifying this simplified building to resemble the finished design.

At this stage, we really just need to focus on the major shape of the building. Often just walls and roof will suffice. There are several main ways of doing this:

- From CAD elevations

- From a photograph

- By eye or measurements

Modeling detail from CAD elevations

When your design architect can provide you with CAD drawings, this is the best way to start your project. Import and scale your **CAD elevation** using the methods you learned in *Chapter 3, Composing the Scene*. Because there is already some geometry in the SketchUp scene, the CAD elements will automatically turn into a group. To align the 2D drawing with your model, do the following steps:

1. Select the **Move** tool.

2. Hover over the CAD drawing edge a short bit in from the corner. The rotation grips appear as shown in the following screenshot:

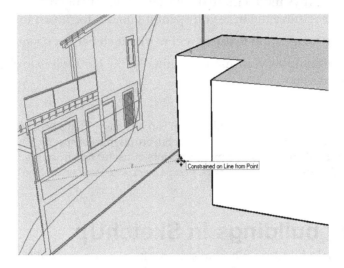

3. Click on a grip and rotate the elevation by 90 degrees.

4. Move the ground level of the CAD elevation to a corresponding point in your model (bottom corner). Make sure you snap to the reference points.

5. Align the elevation with the front facade of your building (parallel or orthogonal as required). Use the axis constraints (by holding down the *Shift* key) to limit movement of the component to only one direction and then move the mouse to a corner of the building to snap to it.

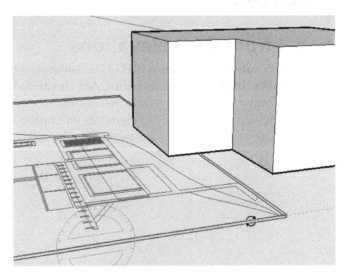

Set up two or three elevations using this method so that you can model all sides of the building. Now, start creating 3D geometry using the elevations as reference points, as given in the following steps:

1. Select the **Pencil** tool.

2. Hover over the building face. Hold the *Shift* key to constrain the pencil line to this face.

3. Click wherever you need to on the CAD elevation as illustrated in the following screenshot. Can you see how the line on the face (right) follows wherever you move and click the pencil?

4. Continue to draw outlines of the main features and push-pull, inferencing to another elevation or plan.

5. Remember to create a component or group the main elements together when necessary.

The following figure shows a finished building done with this method, showing the CAD elevations set up at front and sides:

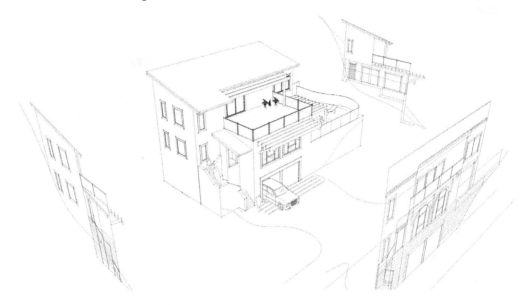

Modeling from a photograph

Use this method when you need to model an existing building that needs modifications, create building elements that already exist to include in your new building, or just model for fun, computer-game levels, and so on. You can use any photos you have taken. The perspective should be more perpendicular to the building to avoid any obstructions by protruding building elements. To use this method, perform the following steps:

1. Start with your basic building block.

2. Navigate to **File | Import** and then click on **All Supported Image Types** in the drop-down box.

3. Select the **Use as texture** option.

4. Select the image you want to use and click on **Open**.

5. Click on the bottom-left corner of the side of the building that matches the photo.

6. The bottom-left corner of the image will be anchored to the corner.

7. Now drag the mouse across until the image fills the face.

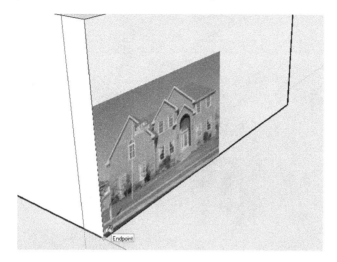

8. Right-click on the image, and then choose **Texture | Position**.

9. The image now shows pins of different colors in the corners.

10. Click once on a pin to lift it up.

11. Zoom in to the corner of the building image and click to place the pin there as shown in the preceding screenshot.

12. Repeat for the other three corners of the facade. Usually, you will need the two bottom corners and the upper corners just below the roof.

13. Now drag each pin to the right-hand side corner of your 3D placeholder box.

14. Repeat for the other corners. You will now see the image stretched more or less to fit to the face.

15. Right-click on the image and select **Done**.

16. You can now push-pull to increase the building to ridge height to match the real building size.

17. Draw over the geometry along the features in the image and push-pull as necessary to give them some depth.

You just created the main shape of a building using only a digital photo. This is an excellent and easy method for creating simple buildings. The big benefit is that textures are retained on the model, making the texturing process easier later on. The following is the finished model with no more than some roof textures and windows added:

Modeling by eye or measurements

The third way to go is to draw by eye or using basic measurements. For visualization purposes, nothing needs to be very accurate anyway. Just open up the _HR version of your building and start modeling. This method is the reason why SketchUp took off so quickly amongst architects. They just wanted a 3D sketchpad!

So have a go at this if you haven't done so already. Use the rectangle tool and enter the basic x and y dimensions on the keyboard, then use SketchUp's modeling tools to experiment creating basic building shapes. Review the training videos on http://sketchup.com/learn/videos or YouTube or use the menu entry **Help | Help Center | Online Tutorials** to find what you need.

Use construction lines

Make use of the tape measure tool to set up basic grids or construction lines when modeling by eye. Select the tape measure, click on a line, and then type in the offset dimension to create a parallel construction line.

Low polygon modeling techniques

In this section, we will look at the low polygon modeling techniques that are especially relevant for visualization, animation, and game design uses.

What is low polygon?

In SketchUp, everything you create is formed from a wire frame over which a skin is stretched. You can see this process happening when you draw any shape with the pencil tool. The lines are the frame and when a shape (polygon) is complete, the frame receives a skin (surface). Even complex objects are made up of flat polygons, but their edges are hidden so you cannot see them. Go to **View | Hidden Geometry** to see what I mean. Low polygon modeling is where you create things in SketchUp while constantly striving to keep the amount of polygons to a minimum.

The following screenshot shows how to set this up:

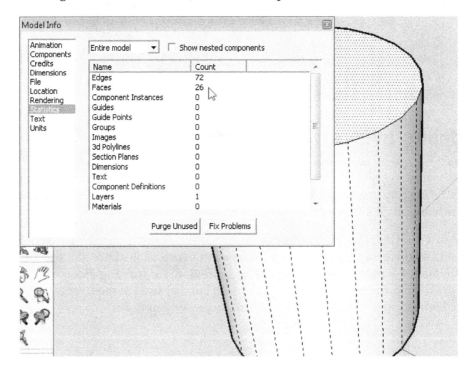

So what's the big deal about low polygon modeling?

Have you ever downloaded a huge model from the 3D Warehouse and found that SketchUp becomes unresponsive? Low polygon modeling makes the difference between smooth and easy navigation around large scenes and a slow jumpy nightmare. That's because SketchUp has to calculate where all these polygons are many times per second when rotating/orbiting a view. This is even more difficult once shadows are switched on because SketchUp also has to work out where shadows hit each polygon. Take a look at the following model. It has 80,000 faces! This can really lock up SketchUp or at least make it hard to use:

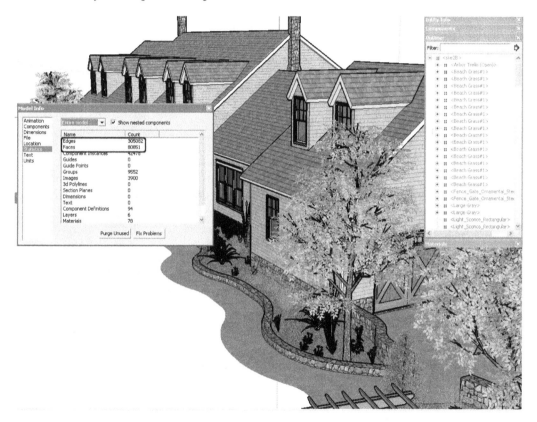

Removing the foliage shows us where most of the polygons were used. The model now shows 70,000 less faces as you can see in the following screenshot. Foliage is often the biggest problem when downloading 3D Warehouse models. We'll look at cleaning up large 3D Warehouse models further in this chapter.

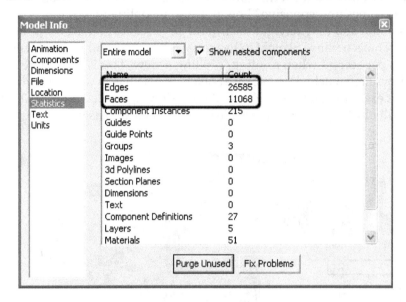

But things get worse. When rendering a photoreal scene, physically accurate light, shadows, and reflections have to be calculated by the computer for each and every polygon you've modeled. If you don't take polygons into account, this can add hours to your rendering time.

Having said all that, you really don't need to worry. With SketchUp, low polygon modeling is easy when you keep in mind a few simple rules; they are as follows:

1. Will I see it?
2. Can I replace it with 2D?
3. Can I reduce the number of segments in an arc or circle?

Will I see it?

The first and most important question we have to ask ourselves when we start modeling is, "Will this be seen in the final image?" We have already set up the scene and viewpoints in *Chapter 3, Composing the Scene*, so we know what will be visible.

Ask yourself this; if you only need one view, does this house need to have a back to it at all? Will the interior of this building be seen when the windows are only a few millimeters in size in the final image? The trick here is to constantly click on the scene tab you have set up and check how much detail is necessary for a particular object in this specific view.

Can I replace it with 2D?

SketchUp has a most amazing 2D billboard capability called **face-me**, which we have already touched on in *Chapter 3, Composing the Scene*. You can create a 2D component and set it to always face the camera. This is incredibly useful for keeping the polygon count down, because a flat item has so few polygons compared to 3D. Face-me components will be covered in more detail in *Chapter 6, Entourage the SketchUp Way*.

As well as face-me components, simple 2D billboards can be created. You've already learned this skill in *Chapter 3, Composing the Scene*!

Another way of replacing real geometry details with 2D images is called **bump mapping**. SketchUp does not use it directly but all external renderers will offer this option. With bump mapping, you can modify the surface normal of a polygon based on an applied texture image. This adds perceived depth to a surface and can be very effective to add smaller geometry details such as brick and mortar or the gaps between timber boards. We will look at these advanced render options in *Chapter 8, Photorealistic Rendering*. For now, just keep in mind that there are options to avoid highly detailed 3D geometry and still make it look good.

Can I reduce the number of segments in an arc or circle?

If you keep these two criteria for modeling 3D details in mind, learning to model low polygon curves and circles is all the extra knowledge you need. We'll look at this now to see how easy it is to produce low polygon curved models.

All circles and curves in SketchUp are made up of straight lines. The default number of straight lines in a circle is 24. The following screenshot shows the straight lines that build a circle:

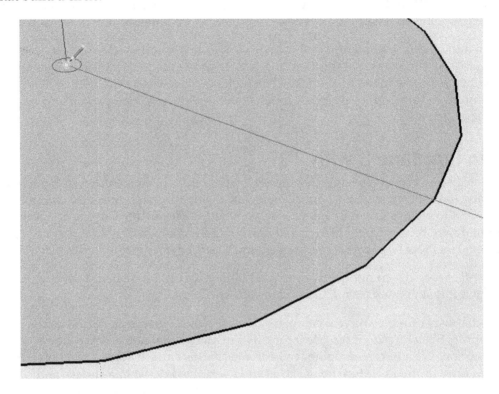

To create a cylinder with a low polygon count, perform the following steps:

1. Draw a circle and zoom in to the edge. You will see facetted edges as shown in the preceding screenshot. This is because SketchUp draws circles and arcs as a series of lines to create the curvature.

2. Now push-pull the circle to create a cylinder.

3. To find out how many polygons are being used to make up the cylinder navigate to **Model info | Statistics**.

4. The number of faces will be 26 (24 for the sides plus 2 for top and bottom). Now delete this cylinder and draw another circle. Select the edge only.

5. Right-click on the edge and select **Entity Info**.

6. Change the number of segments to 8.

7. You will be able to see easily how many segments (straight lines) make the circle.

8. Extrude the cylinder and check the number of polygons again. The number of faces now is just 10.

9. Notice that SketchUp still smoothes out the cylinder surface by hiding the edges even though it is hardly a curve any more.

This method can be used for all the circles and arcs to reduce the amount of segments wherever this will not affect the final rendering; this means most objects, and especially any small or distant objects.

Making circles easy to snap to later

Keep the number of segments to a multiple of four. This allows you to inference-snap to the quadrants of the circle or cylinder later, which can be very useful.

In a rendering program, all the SketchUp faces are converted to multiple triangles. So, there will be twice as many polygons as there are square faces in SketchUp. The following screenshot shows three cylinders with different segment counts in a typical rendering application:

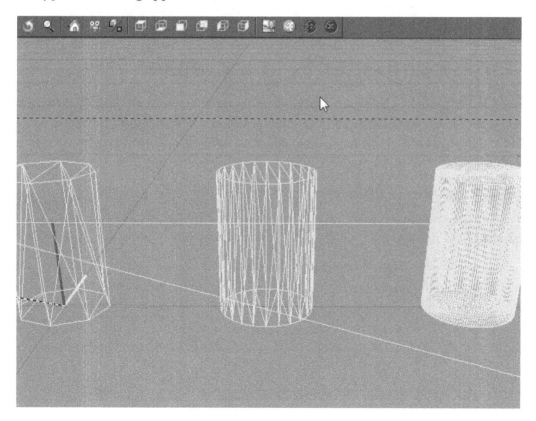

Notice in the next screenshot of the rendered cylinders that there is no visual difference between the second and third cylinders made from 24- and 128-sided circles, respectively. The first one was made from just 8 SketchUp segments and though it looks bad up this close, it would still render fine for a small or distant object:

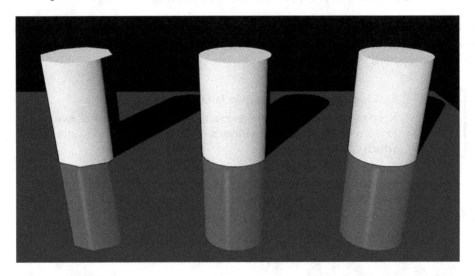

Using components to increase productivity

If you have come to SketchUp without any prior knowledge of 3D CAD, one of the features that will absolutely amaze you is **components**. When you create a component, you can copy it as many times as you like. These copies are all linked to the original component and are called **instances**. If you now change something in one of the instances, all the other copies will also change!

Imagine how much difference this single capability will make when modeling your building. The following are some of the benefits that'll allow you to ease your work:

- Identical things only need to be drawn once
- Modifying one tree, roof tile, or fence panel will update all that exist in the model

- Components can be created as crude placeholders first and fleshed out later
- You can save components to an external file and edit the details there without the rest of the scene present
- If you want to replace all the components in a scene, you just reload another component in its place

To organize your model, you can also use **groups**. Groups are more for keeping parts of geometry together in one place and to separate them from other geometry. Groups don't have the additional benefits like components have that allow all the features mentioned in the preceding list.

How to benefit most from using components

To benefit from using components, we just need to think smart. In your mind, break everything down into its smallest common parts. So, for example, ask the following questions while using components:

1. Can the item be split in two and mirrored?
2. Are there items of geometry within the component that can be drawn once and repeated (subcomponents)? For example, panes in a window.
3. Can I rotate, flip, or scale instances of a single component to create different unique items?
4. Can I modify an instance of a component to create some visual variety?

Using dummy components

What do you do if you need to modify a component that's hard to see or get to? Create an instance somewhere else in the model where you can see it better to modify it. When you're done, just delete it. You can also use this method when SketchUp is being a pain. For example, some modeling activities such as `Follow-Me` don't work so well on small geometry. So make a component, copy it somewhere where you can see it clearly, and scale it up by a factor of `10` or `100`. Now you can edit it without any problems.

Also, have you noticed that the Sandbox tools only want to work on a horizontal surface? Have a go at creating a surface, make a component of it, and then copy and rotate it as shown in the following screenshot. When you work on the horizontal copy, the vertical ones are updated instantly to create some undulating metal cladding.

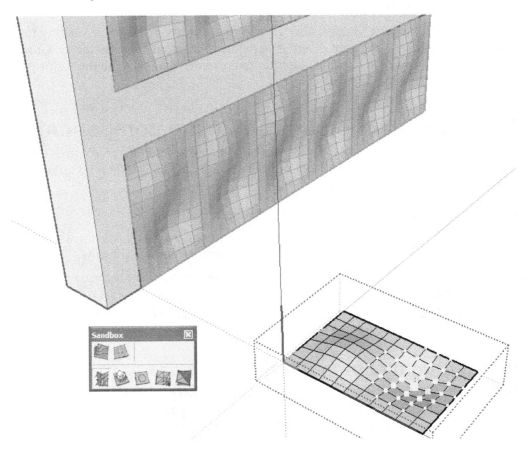

Using the Outliner for easy access

One of the most under-used features of SketchUp is the **Outliner** view. Most people don't even know it's there! Navigate to **Window | Outliner**. You should see something as shown in the following screenshot:

This is the list and hierarchy tree of groups and components in the scene. Notice that you can click-and-drag these around. Click on one now and drag it over another component. It nests itself underneath that component. In this way, you can control how components nest within others. You can also:

- Select deeply nested components to edit without having to double-click multiple times on the screen.
- Right-click an item in the list and use the context menu to edit components and groups directly.

- Reveal hidden items because you can't see them on screen when they're hidden! Hidden groups and components are still displayed in gray in the outliner.
- Save and reload components.

The **Outliner** window will become indispensable to you as you progress.

 Always close or minimize the outliner when using plugins as it can slow things down.

Why you should name components

Make use of the component naming fields as much as you can. When you create a component, give it a meaningful and distinct name to identify it among other components. Depending on what rendering software you use, this info may carry across to the renderer so that you will be able to select components by name. You can access these functions within the **Outliner** window via the context menu.

Also, think about what you will want to select once you have exported to the renderer; for example, components with different materials, foreground and background items, items you're not sure if they will make it into the final render, and so on. Selecting elements that are not part of a group or component within the renderer is always more difficult than within SketchUp.

3D Warehouse components – problems to be aware of

Using the 3D Warehouse will save you bags of time. However, it's not a panacea for all illnesses. When searching from the 3D Warehouse, be wary of the following points:

- Commercial (copyrighted) models that are passed off as someone's own work
- High polygon counts and large file sizes
- Sloppy modeling methods that won't allow a correct render
- Incorrect measurements and scale

The way to avoid problems later on is to save the component to your hard drive first rather than importing it into the model directly. Open the component up once you've saved it, and take a good look at it using the outliner (to see what's hidden) and navigate to **Model Info | Statistics** to check the number of faces. You'll get a good feel for this when you've done it a couple of times.

Purging 3D Warehouse components for your own use

Here is one way of purging components, but you will probably work out your own version of it:

1. Save the component to your hard drive as a file and open the file in SketchUp.

2. Open the **Outliner** window and inspect the structure of the model.

3. Highlight each group or component in the **Outliner** window and identify the corresponding geometry in the scene. You can rename the groups/components, if it helps you.

4. If you want to keep the structure of the groups within the component, double-click on each component to enter into the edit mode.

5. Select all faces within a group and check via the **Entity Info** window that all elements are placed on **Layer0** (the default layer).

6. Make sure that the dominant material in the component model is set to the **Default** material (the half-gray-half-blue button in the materials browser). For example, a car component can have materials assigned to the rims, the tires, and the windows, but the body should be set to default.

7. If you have back faces showing (gray instead of white), right-click on them and select **Reverse Face** to rectify this.

8. Remove or replace parts of the geometry that have too many polygons for your requirements. If you just want a car on the street, you don't need to see the steering wheel or every single bolt head.

9. Delete anything that you don't want in your component (excessive details, leftovers from the modeling, and so on).

10. Navigate to **Window | Model Info | Statistics** and click on **Purge unused**.

11. Check the scale and change the size of the geometry if required.

12. Move the geometry near to or on top of the origin. This will be the point you snap to when you insert the component into your scene.

13. Save it with an explicit filename in your component folder or library.

Default material

Leaving geometry without material (that means only with material called **Default**) is often a good way to go because the component takes on whatever material you give it once you've inserted it in your scene. So, for example, a car with the material **Default** applied to the bodywork can be inserted multiple times in your scene but each time with different body color. The rest of the materials in the component (such as tires or chrome) aren't affected.

Quick material removal

If a component has too many materials attached, one way to quickly remove them is simply to open the component separately. Open the **Materials** pallet and select the **In-Model** tab. Select and delete materials here without affecting other components or groups in your main model.

You have also aligned the orientation of the polygons to face to the outside of the component. This is important because some renderers will not show the back face of polygons properly or ignore them altogether. Moving all elements to **Layer0** will ensure that they are always visible. You can move the entire component instance to another layer to control its visibility, but you don't have to be afraid that your car is suddenly missing its wheels because you switched off the wrong layer.

People posting to the 3D Warehouse usually don't create components with photorealistic rendering or low polygon techniques in mind. You always should check the content of third-party components and test if they work well with your renderer.

Handling challenging modeling tasks

We're going to look at some of the most common modeling tasks you need to know about. There is no dark art to any of these, but just good common sense and proven methods of modeling. You will be able to use these techniques time and time again:

- Windows and doors
- Roofs, flashing, and ridge tiles
- Curtain walling
- Masonry
- Roads and pavements

Windows and doors

Don't model these! Have a search on the 3D Warehouse and see what you can get. There's a plethora of windows, so you should be able to find what you need. If not, you can use the techniques introduced in this chapter to model a door from a photograph. This also adds important texture details.

Once you are happy with the door or window component you have obtained, you need to decide how to use them in the model. This will depend on the kind of architectural visuals you want to produce (which you have already decided on in *Chapter 2, Collecting a Toolset*). If it's non-photoreal, it doesn't really matter how you place them. Just stick the components to the wall of your building. However, with photoreal, you will probably want to see reflections on the glass, and also see through it into the room behind.

In *Chapter 5, Applying Textures and Materials for Photorealistic Rendering*, we are going to set up a photo-textured room behind the window. For now, we will place the window and create a cavity behind it ready for texturing later. The cavity serves to simulate the room behind the window without having to model it. To create this cavity, perform the following steps:

1. Place your window component on the wall.
2. If the wall face is part of a group or component, double-click to edit it.
3. Draw a rectangle roughly the size of the room on the wall.
4. Push-pull to the depth of the room. Your building should now look as shown in the following screenshot:

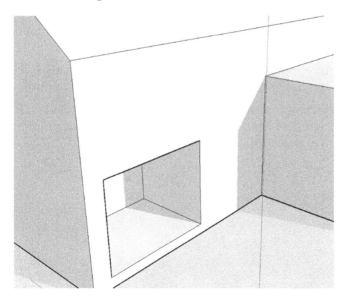

5. Select all the five inner faces of the room and create a component but leave the **Cut opening** option unchecked.

6. Give the component a useful name such as `bedroom interior`.

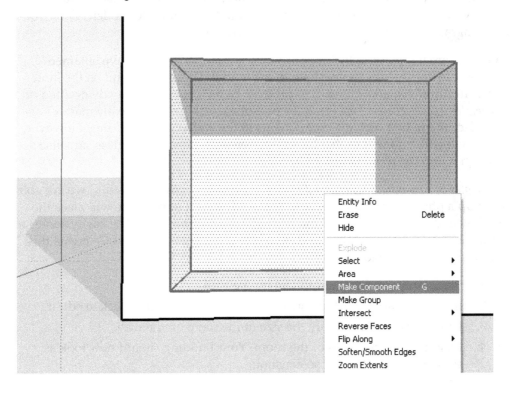

7. A face will appear that covers the entire wall, including your newly created room component.

8. Select your window component and place it on the wall. It might cut an opening if it has been modeled with the **Cut opening** option.

9. Use the **Rectangle** tool and draw over your window. If you have an arched window, you will have to use the **Pencil** tool and trace along the outline until a polygon is created that covers the opening.

10. Delete the rectangle or polygon. Your window component is now visible again as you can see in the following screenshot:

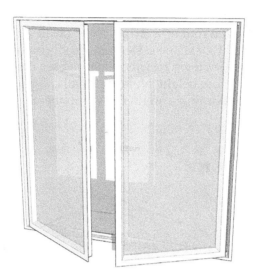

The reason we've cut a hole in the wall is that we can't be sure SketchUp's automatic hole cutting feature will work when the model is exported to a rendering program. Also, we don't know whether the windows you downloaded from the 3D Warehouse have this feature enabled correctly. Either way, retracing the outline of the window with the pencil or rectangle tool will work. Repeat this simple process for each visible window. You only need to do this if you're aiming for photoreal rendering later.

Now, check your window component and make sure the window pane has a material assigned to it that you will recognize later. If not, label it `window-glass` or similar. This is so that you can swap the material out in one go when you get to your rendering program. All the different types of windows in your scene should use the same material for the glazing.

Roof

Roofs in SketchUp are a doddle as you already know. There are one or two important tricks to bear in mind, however:

1. Make the roof a separate component.

2. First push-pull the flat roof upward a little to create a 3D box. This will make creating the pitched roof shape easier and also form the basis for fascias and so on. In the following screenshot, you can see the roof footprint being extruded to the full roof height. Note the small coordinate-axes symbol that indicates the local coordinate origin of a component:

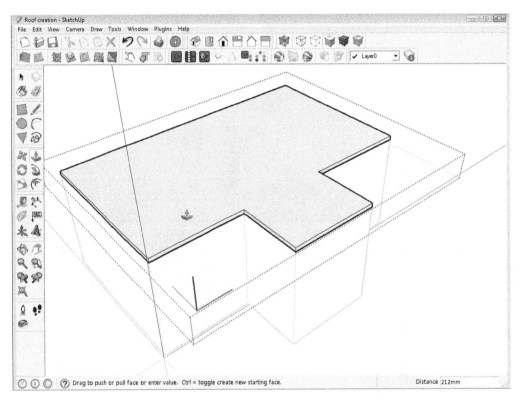

3. Model items such as gutters and drainpipes separately (and only if you need to).

Some people advocate modeling individual roof tiles for added realism. This isn't necessary unless the roof is the main focal point of your visual. Any texture you create by photographing an existing roof is already far more realistic than modeling tiles, because of the variation in color, weathering, and size that you will achieve. In *Chapter 5, Applying Textures and Materials for Photorealistic Rendering*, we will look at creating tiled textures from your own photos or pictures offered on manufacturers' websites.

You should make an attempt at valley gutter flashing and ridge tiles because this makes a big difference to the realism of a roof.

Flashing details

Lead flashing at intersections of the roof is a breeze in SketchUp. Just follow these simple steps:

1. Select the **Tape measure** tool.

2. Click on a valley line. When you move the mouse now a construction line parallel to the valley line will be attached to the cursor.

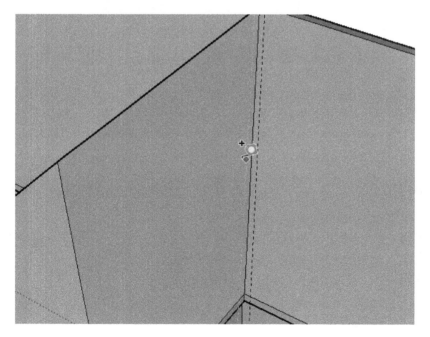

3. Move the mouse to one side of the valley line as shown in the preceding screenshot.

4. Enter a suitable distance and hit the *Enter* key. A construction line appears at the specified distance from the valley line.

5. Repeat the steps on the other side.

6. Draw over the construction lines using the **Pencil** tool as shown in the preceding screenshot.

7. Fill the new faces with a dark gray color with the **Paint bucket** tool.

Modeling ridge tiles

Ridge tiles are a little trickier because of the weird angles we get at intersections of
pitched roofs. We are going to create a very basic ridge tile component and copy it
along the ridge and hips (you can see this in the screenshot at the end of this section).
Making it into a component means that if we want to make the tile more complex
later, we only need to modify one tile, and the rest will update along with it.
To create the tile, perform the following steps:

1. Find a tile manufacturer website or brochure if necessary.

2. In a new SketchUp file, draw a basic end shape of the tile.

3. Use as few polygons as possible (see the *Low polygon modeling
   techniques* section). Click on the arc and use **Entity Info** to reduce the
   number of segments.

4. Finish the underside off flat as shown in the following screenshot:

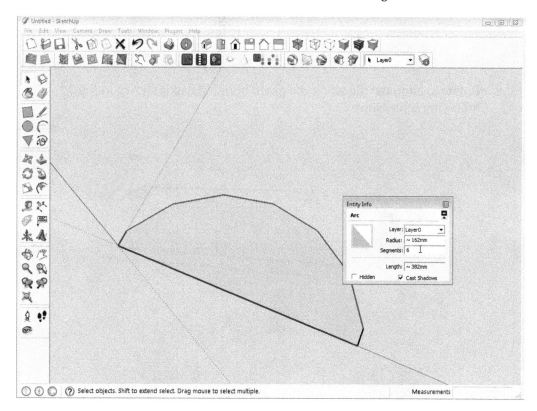

5. Scale the model if necessary.

6. Push-pull to the correct length.

7. Place the tile centered at the origin as shown in the following screenshot:

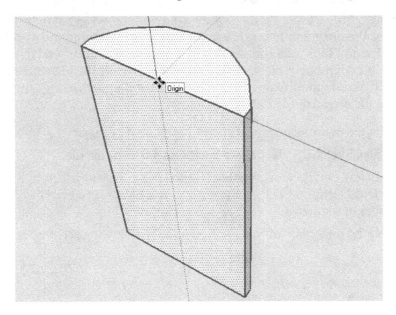

8. Rotate to align the tile along the green horizontal axis shown in the following screenshot:

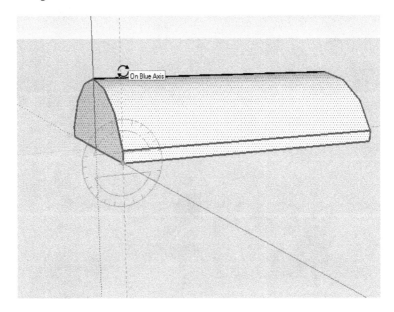

9. Save the model.

You have now created a simple ridge tile using a minimum amount of geometry. You made it a closed form so that it renders correctly even though it may not be placed snugly on the roof. We also moved the tile to the origin (where the axes cross), so that when you insert it into your scene you insert it at the center position. You're now ready to insert it into your scene to create the roof ridge.

Copying the tiles

In your building model, insert the tile component and place it at the corner of the ridge. If this is a horizontal ridge, the tile may line up quite easily. With a sloping ridge (hip), it's much more difficult. Through a process of trial and error, you will need to line up the tile along the ridge using the **Move** tool and the rotation grips shown in the following screenshot:

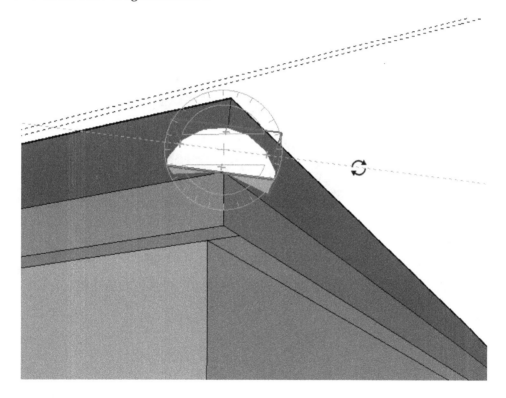

Now, perform the following steps to copy the tiles:

1. Select the tile.
2. Hit *M* to activate the **Move** tool.

3. Click on the intersection of the tile and ridge as demonstrated in the following screenshot:

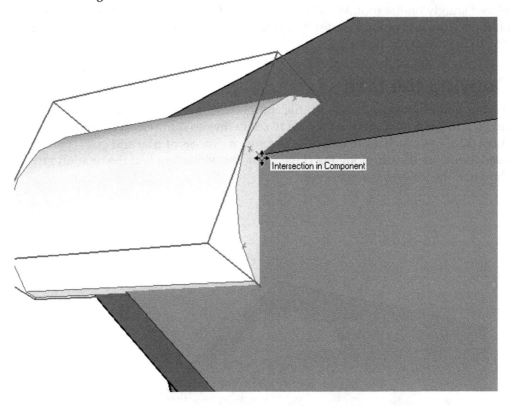

4. Hold *Ctrl* to toggle **Copy** mode.
5. Click on the far end of the ridge to create the final tile.
6. Type / followed by the approximate number of tiles (for example, /23), then hit *Enter*.

7. Change the number until you get just about the right fit as shown in the following screenshot:

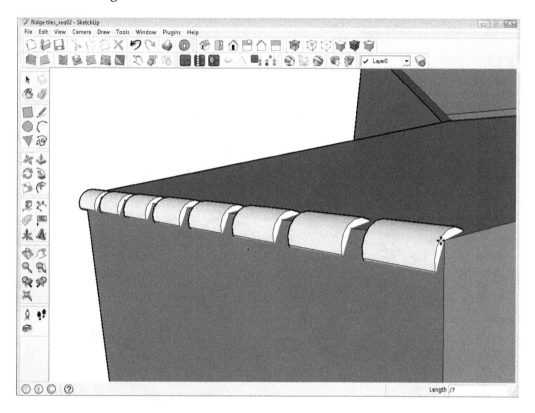

8. Double-click on the first tile.

9. Push-pull the top face to resize.

10. Slight inaccuracy over here is fine as it adds to the realism.

After you have done one hip, create a component of the group of tiles. You should be able to copy, rotate, and flip this component to create the other hips. Finally, make a unique component of any end tiles that need to be shaped, and shape the ends as shown in the following screenshot:

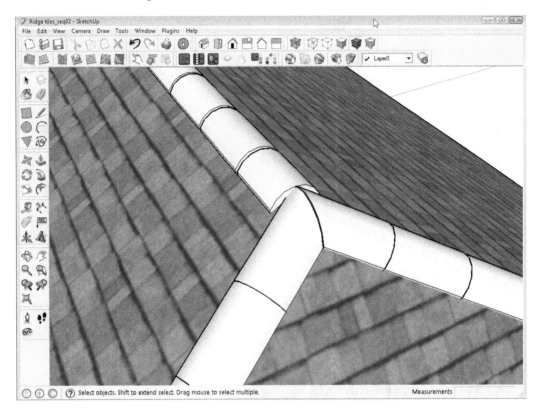

 Try copying the component where you can access it easily. Create a box or rectangle through the intersection of tiles where you want to slice them, and use **Intersect with Model** and **Erase** to cut it.

Curtain walls

Large expanses of glass may need some detail in the window mullions or other structure to look pleasing to the eye when producing photoreal visuals. When you introduce photoreal material qualities, you will pick up these small details easily. You learned how to do this in *Chapter 1, Quick Start Tutorial*, and it is also covered in more detail at the end of this chapter in the section on rounded edges.

If you are modeling for non-photoreal visuals, you probably don't need this level of detail. Just remember to use components for the upright and horizontal members of the frame so that additional detailing such as chamfers or fillets just need to be done once but are repeated over the whole facade. Give the glazed areas a consistent material name as discussed earlier. You can see an example in the following screenshot:

Masonry features

Masonry features such as stone or brick arches are best produced with photo textures. However, it will help at this stage to trace round the edges of a feature and set it in relief a little with **Push-pull**. The following screenshot shows a work in progress model entirely done with this method and you can see how effective the raised detail on the pillars is when rendered. No other texturing has been added to this scene apart from a single photo.

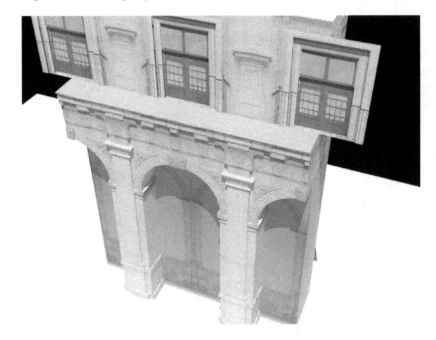

Roads

Roads are often in the foreground in visuals, but think: does anyone really want to see how great your tarmac modeling skills are? So, hopefully you'll be able to obscure most of your road and footpath areas with foliage, people, or cars later. However, when modeling, we need to take a couple of really easy steps that add a great deal of realism to our roads and paths. No one will notice when you do it but they certainly will if you leave those details out! The following are some features of roads you may not have thought about before:

- Pavements are always raised above roads
- Roads usually have curb stones
- Paved areas usually have edging stones

Realistic roads and pavements

You are now going to lower the roads in your scene and add a curb or edging feature, which can then be textured later on. Begin with the following steps:

1. Trace around the edge of the road or pavement using the **Pencil** and **Arc** tools.

2. Select the edge and use the **Offset** tool to create edging (curbstones, paths, verges, and so on).

3. Use **Push-Pull** to drop the road level down the blue axis.

4. Put a chamfer on the curb only if you are going for close-up photoreal images.

The following screenshot is an example of these elements in practice:

Landscaping with sandbox – watch your polygon count

If you have a CAD plan with proposed levels, you can easily draw around some contours and use the sandbox tools to create landscaped areas. The only thing to bear in mind when using the sandbox tools for visualization projects is that the more detail you put into the contours, the more polygons you get in the 3D mesh. So use a few straight lines to approximate the contours.

The same goes for creating a mesh from scratch using the **From Scratch** feature of the sandbox tools. Limit the amount of squares as best as you can. SketchUp and your renderer will create a smooth curved surface between the mesh edges anyway.

Modeling for realistic highlights in interior scenes

Here is one final section on a very important trick for interior and close-up scenes. If you are modeling your scene aiming at photorealistic presentation, you need to read this bit for instant added realism!

What's the problem with sharp edges?

If you model the basic shape of the box, as shown in the following screenshot, and do not add some natural imperfections to the edges, you'll obtain something flat and lifeless as the following screenshot, no matter how good your rendering skills are:

In real life, light reflects at corners and edges because they are always slightly rounded or chamfered. Even the edge of a knife has some imperfections if you look closely enough. So, if you're modeling anything for a close-up view, you need to add in this edge detail. In the following screenshot, you can see the same box with some tiny chamfers at the edges. Can you see the difference in realism? The small highlight along the edge gives you a sense of material and surface properties.

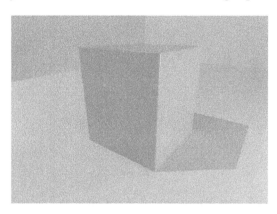

If an object is further away from the camera, you don't need to worry about it because the extra detail will be lost in the final image. The highlight would just fall *between the pixels*. It is also not necessary for non-photoreal visuals because there are no highlights at all.

The RoundCorner plugin

Of course, you can go ahead and start creating the rounded edges with the **Arc** and **Push-Pull** tools. You will quickly learn that it takes a lot of time to add these small details to all edges. However, thanks to the amazing SketchUcation Plugin Store, you can just download a Ruby extension that does it all for you: the **RoundCorner** plugin by the user Fredo.

Search for **RoundCorner Fredo6** in the Plugin Store (see *Chapter 2, Collecting a Toolset*, for an introduction to the plugin system). You first need to download a current version of **LibFredo** and then the actual plugin. The installation is fully automatic, thanks to the SketchUcation tools, but you should also download and read the PDF manual. The functions of this plugin are as follows:

- **Round corner (for fillets)**: Enter the radius and number of segments
- **Sharp corner**: This function is the same as round corner but with a sharp corner where edges intersect
- **Bevel (for chamfers)**: Enter the edge offset

Remember to click outside your geometry when you have finished selecting your corners. The following is a screenshot of the plugin in action:

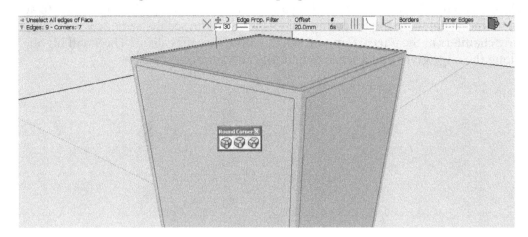

 Always save before you use any plugin just in case SketchUp decides to throw a curveball.

Preparing for photorealistic rendering

In the discussion of materials and front- and back-face orientation of polygons, we have already touched on some limitations you may encounter when using external renderers. SketchUp is designed for quick and sketchy projects and uses OpenGL for its visuals. Photorealistic renderers use a number of techniques that have other requirements for their input.

The following are some of the most common conflicts between SketchUp and third-party renderers that you should look out for when preparing scenes for export:

- **Polygon orientation**: As mentioned earlier, not all renderers can handle the display of back-facing polygons. Even if they are able to render the reverse side of a face, it will certainly cause issues when you assign an emitting material to the face to simulate light. Verify the orientation of all polygons in your model before you export.

- **Two-sided polygons**: SketchUp can assign different materials to the front and the back of a polygon. This is not common in computer graphics and most renderers will only allow you to use a single material for both sides. To avoid any issues try not to assign materials to the polygons directly. Use the default material for polygons and assign the final material to groups and component instances. This will also help you when you have to reassign materials in your render application after the export.

- **Follow-Me components**: The Follow-Me feature changes the orientation of a component based on the current camera location. If your renderer doesn't offer a similar feature on its own, you are most likely not able to reproduce this effect. For stills, this should not be a problem because the exported scene will be a snapshot with the right orientation of your components. But if you want to render an animation or create several views of the same scene, you will see some of your entourage reduced to flat billboards or lines. Replace 2D Face-Me components before the export with 3D objects to avoid this issue.

- **Automatic openings**: In the *Window and doors* section, we retraced the outline of the window to make sure there is an opening in the wall for the window component. While the automatic creation of openings is very handy in SketchUp, you can't be sure that it will translate well to your external renderer. If your exporter supports this feature out of the box, you are good without the extra manual work. Just make sure to test it first!

- **Material assignments**: One major argument for the use of external renderers is the variety of real-world materials you can use in your image. You can show surface texture and light reflections just as in reality. But how do you change these materials after you have assigned them in SketchUp? Can you just give an object a new material or do you have to replace the definition for all other elements in the scene at once?

- **Transparency**: In SketchUp, you can make any material transparent just by changing the **Opacity** value in the properties. Photorealistic renderers use different material types for opaque, translucent, and transparent materials. To achieve proper transparency, you have to assign the right type of material to your windows.

- **Clean geometry**: Using SketchUp, you can create impressive designs very quickly. You don't have to care about the proper length of elements because you can always hide a wall that is a bit too long behind something else. With physically based renderers — especially those that are radiosity-based — the paper-thin geometries used in SketchUp can cause problems for the lighting calculation. The results are artifacts such as light bleeding in your final render (light that seeps in at the corners of a room).

The only way to avoid these issues is to model the geometry precisely and sometimes even with their real physical extents; walls should be built with two polygons (one for each side) and should properly stop where they meet with another wall or building element. The following screenshot illustrates the intersections of two walls, on the left, in a hurried and messy way, and on the right, with a clean connection and physical extension to all parts:

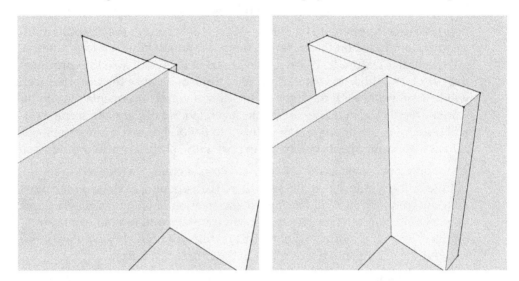

Luckily, most renderers today are fairly robust against this type of artifacts but a clean model is still something to strive for.

- **Instancing and proxies**: Thanks to components, you can quickly generate a large number of polygons in your scene and if your renderer allows you to substitute a simple _LR component on the fly with a complex 3D object, this count can go much higher during the rendering process. You also want to make your plants and people look realistic, so your renderer has to be able to handle all this complexity with reasonable speed. While you are preparing your model in SketchUp, you can cheat with some low-polygon placeholders but once you go for the final render, all that detailed geometry needs to be processed all at once. Make sure your renderer doesn't meet its limits too early.

- **Scene structure**: While this is not necessarily a cause for inconsistencies, it is good if your exporter converts the groups and components to a corresponding hierarchy in your renderer. If you are using the **Outliner** window a lot, chances are that you are so used to it that you will miss the option to navigate your scene via groups and subgroups.

Summary

Congratulations! You have now learned most of the extra skills you need to model for architectural visualization. Using these methods in various ways throughout the modeling stage will ensure that you have a scene ready for rendering. You will have saved bags of time by not modeling what you don't see, and you will have saved even more by thinking about the level of detail required.

You have learned how to use an amazing feature (components) to model things once and then utilize them many times. And you've seen how grabbing and cleaning models from the 3D Warehouse can enrich your scene through hardly any effort on your part. Furthermore, if you follow the good practices in this chapter, you will not suffer from a slow computer and you will always know just where your components are.

You are now ready to texture your model, which is the topic of our next chapter.

5
Applying Textures and Materials for Photorealistic Rendering

This chapter is mostly concerned with applying materials and textures for added realism in SketchUp or other rendering software. If you're aiming for artistic styles such as pencil or watercolor, it is often better to use an untextured model. In this case, skip this chapter for now and go to *Chapter 6*, *Entourage the SketchUp Way*.

We are now going to work through the various texturing processes together. Texturing is the process of applying color patterns (usually taken from photographic images) to 3D surfaces to add more realism or simulate more detail. You will set up great-looking textures one by one until your whole scene looks realistic.

In this chapter, you will learn the following:

- When and why to use textures
- The process overview chart
- Using SketchUp's own textures
- Extracting great textures from your own photos
- Using Match Photo to generate real-life textures
- How to create seamless tiling textures
- Applying, manipulating, scaling, and editing materials
- Creating, storing, and sharing custom material libraries
- Image formats, size, and compression
- Tweaking textured models for realism using GIMP

The methods you are going to learn are highly effective and, at the same time, they are the most robust and versatile methods possible.

Deciding to use textures

At first, you need to decide if you should be be texturing at all. As you can see from other examples, investing time in texturing does not always equal better visuals. You can go for a simple native SketchUp output, watercolor style, or other **non-photorealistic rendering (NPR)** styles, which will be less time consuming and, perhaps, provide you with a better outcome. If this is the case, you can just skip over this chapter for now and go straight to *Chapter 7, Non-photoreal Visuals with SketchUp*.

So, what are the benefits of texturing? If it is done well, texturing can:

- Reduce the amount of detail you need to model
- Allow you to use lower render settings to get the same realism
- Increase the rendering speed (this is especially important for animations)
- Create almost photoreal visuals in SketchUp without the need for rendering

These benefits are most pronounced wherever movement is involved, for example, in animations or demonstrations of real-time walk-throughs. This is because photo textures have shadows, highlights, secondary light bounce, and all the other elements of realistic lighting already built in. The real world and your camera are the rendering engines of photo textures!

The texturing process flow chart

The process that we suggest you follow is shown in the following flow chart. It shows how you can start with any of the basic modeling techniques you learned about in the previous chapter to end up with a superbly textured scene.

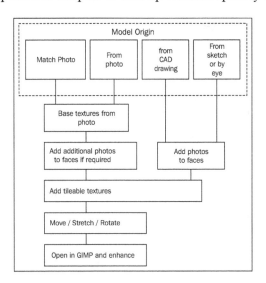

In this chart, you can see the modeling techniques (discussed in *Chapter 4, Modeling for Visualization*), **Match Photo** and **From photo**. They already provide photo images for textures. For any other surface that needs textures, you have to provide additional images (**Add additional photos to faces if required**). Smaller polygons, or surfaces where generic materials will do, can be textured with tileable textures (**Add tileable textures**). To make these fit your model, you may have to adjust the position and size of the texture (**Move/Stretch/Rotate**). Finally, you can add specific details to your generic textures to make them look more realistic (**Open in GIMP and enhance**).

The mistake that most newbies make is applying stock tileable textures and then stop there. This sometimes makes for dull and often unrealistic images. Also, the same basic textures that come bundled with SketchUp keep cropping up!

Rule of thumb

If, after texturing, your model doesn't look like a photograph in SketchUp, it won't in your renderer either. If you get texturing right in SketchUp, the renderer will merely add soft shadows and more realistic illumination and antialiasing (soft edges), turning a great model into an exceptional render.

Beginning with basic photo textures

You're going to start by applying base textures from which you will build upon later. It's like applying an undercoat when decorating, or if you're an artist, it's like laying down a watercolor wash of some basic color. You can add these base textures using your own (or others') photographs, which will add a level of unparalleled realism to your renders or SketchUp output.

There are four ways to create these initial textures:

- From Match Photo
- From the textures already present in a model created from a photo (this method is described in *Chapter 4, Modeling for Visualization*)
- Using seamless textures
- Using Google Street View

Let's look at these individually in more detail now.

Starting with Match Photo textures

If you've set up your scene using the Match Photo functionality (see *Chapter 3, Composing the Scene*), you already have a great basis for your texturing process. You can now project the photograph onto your model, like shining a projector onto the wall.

1. Click on the Match Photo scene tab.

2. Select the geometry you want to project onto.

3. In the Match Photo settings window, press the **Project textures from photo** button.

4. Orbit the model to see your textured creation!

Here is the Match Photo model you saw in *Chapter 3, Composing the Scene*. Sang has used it to create an extension to his house (he wishes he'd had a slightly larger budget).

You've now got a model that is already partly textured and ready for additional textures if necessary. Go ahead and do this in the next section.

Using textures from the photo modeling process

In *Chapter 4, Modeling for Visualization,* you learned how to model from an image. This resulted in a textured model shown in the previous screenshot. Similar to what we discovered with Match Photo, you now already have a partially textured model. The back of the model is still blank, but this might be OK if your scene is set up for viewpoints from just one side. If you require additional textures on the back, for example because you're going to animate the scene, you can add more textures using the methods presented in the next section.

Using basic seamless textures

You will learn all about seamless textures in a moment. For now, if you have started your model from scratch or from a CAD drawing, you can use SketchUp's textures to cover the model in roughly the right materials. You can also just use color fills with a similar hue to your desired material. Do this also to fill in the gaps if you've used either of these two methods.

The closest you may have come to texturing is using the materials pallet (paint bucket) and the textures that come with SketchUp. This is absolutely OK. The basic textures provided in SketchUp are very good and provide an easy starting point. A word of warning though: many people can spot these textures a mile off, because SketchUp is so popular. So, at the very least, you should modify them a little, as you'll see later in this chapter (the final box in the process diagram).

Applying SketchUp's own textures

Applying SketchUp's own textures is very simple. SketchUp comes with many repeatable textures. To apply these, perform the following steps:

1. If necessary, double-click to edit the component or group.
2. Click on the **Paint Bucket** tool icon.
3. Select a texture material from the materials pallet.
4. Click on the face to apply the texture.

The face will show the basic texture.

Scaling textures

You now need to make sure that the scale and orientation are correct:

1. Click the **In Model** button in the materials pallet.

2. Click on the texture you just applied to your face.

3. Click on the **Edit** tab.

4. Here, you can change the scale of the texture by clicking on either of the two dimension boxes shown in the following screenshot. Change the values until the texture looks correctly sized on screen.

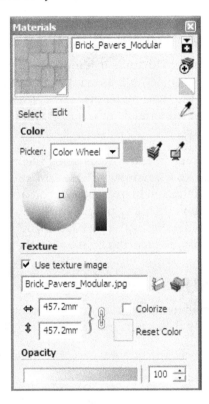

Coloring textures

On the **Edit** tab of the **Materials** pallet, you can also find several ways to change the color of your texture. On a Mac, these options are available via the icons at the top of the materials browser window. Changing these will only modify the texture within your model, not the actual texture library. So, go ahead and experiment with the settings!

Setting	Use
Color wheel	Click the mouse anywhere on the colored wheel to change the hue of the texture, and use the slider for brightness value.
Hue, Lightness, and Saturation Hue, Saturation, and Brightness Red, Green, and Blue levels	These are the three different ways to achieve more exact colors. These can be edited using the three sliders or by inputting numbers if you really need to!
Match the color of an object in SketchUp	Click on this icon and then select a basic color from an object within SketchUp.
Match the color on screen	This icon is the same as the preceding one but you can click anywhere on your computer screen. This is an excellent feature if you're copying a photo or matching a model to an existing scene.
Colorize checkbox	Use this if you have a particular hue that you wish to use on the texture. It ensures that all the colors throughout the texture are locked to the hue you have selected (such as a grayscale image using your hue instead of gray).

You have just applied SketchUp's own textures to your model. Often, it becomes necessary to scale the texture because it doesn't look quite right. Bricks and paving are more or less the same size but may vary from country to country. Timber textures can have many different sizes to simulate different wood grains. Also, coloring the same textures slightly gives us the scope for many more materials using the same basic textures.

When you type a number into either of the scale boxes, the texture resizes at the same time on screen. The x and y dimensions of a texture are linked to keep the texture in its original aspect ratio (the ratio of the image sizes). If you want to edit these values individually, just click on the chain-shaped icon next to the dimension values first.

Using Google Street View

Using photos directly from Google Street View is a new and amazing way to texture models. Use it to find buildings or building features similar to the ones you're modeling and then load the images straight into your SketchUp model. Here's an example of a roughly textured model using just Street View images. It needs a lot more work if you're going to use it in the foreground, but it could conceivably be good enough at a distance or in a quick-moving animation. It normally takes just 5 minutes to create texture models using Google Street View.

Traveling the world for real textures

For this exercise, you need an active Internet connection, because SketchUp will be accessing Google Maps.

1. Draw a rectangle, push-pull it, and click on the front face to select it.

2. Right-click and select **Add Photo Texture**.

3. A window opens and connects you to Google Maps. You can now type in an address in the textbox of the browser window. Type an address near the location of your project.

4. Use the mouse to place the little yellow man in a street. If Street View images are available, these streets will turn blue.

5. In the top window, navigate around using the arrows on the road until you find a house with a garage.

6. Double-click on the side of the house or garage to zoom in. You will have a view like the one shown in the following screenshot:

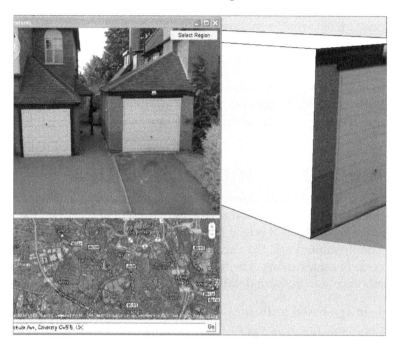

7. When you have zoomed in enough, click on the **Select Region** button.

8. Move the blue pins around to enclose the area you wish to capture. I'm grabbing the front of someone's garage.

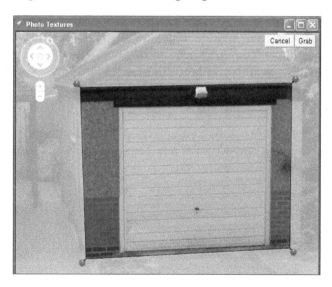

9.   When you're done, click on **Grab** (or **Cancel** to reselect a better view).

10. Your SketchUp model updates with the texture!

Google has done all 3D artists a massive favor. All the buildings in the world are available to you as long as Google sends a photo car along the road. To put it in perspective, you can browse the biggest buildings texture store in the world!

Use this method to quickly grab textures for elements of your design that are standard features on many buildings. If there's anything particularly new or complex in what you are creating, you can spend a little more time modeling it from scratch.

Advanced texturing techniques

You've now got a partly textured scene (using one or more of the discussed methods), which is ready for detailed texturing. You will already be able to see whether your scene works as it is or whether some changes need to be introduced to make the composition work. Go ahead and make any changes at this stage before you spend too long on texturing. The following two sections will explain these texturing methods in much more detail:

- Single image-based texturing
- Seamless (tileable) texturing

You will learn how to manipulate the textures you've already got, enhance them, and add new ones.

Applying whole photographs as textures

I think that, by now, you have an idea why SketchUp is so revolutionary for architectural visualization. You don't need to rely on texture creators any more, because you can just use your own photos in Match Photo, create seamless textures, or utilize Google Street View to pop the real world into your models. You can now further capitalize on this by using any photograph to texture your model.

You've already learned all the skills that you need to do this in the previous chapters. Use these same techniques now to cover any blank face with realistic textures from photographs.

Where to find texture photos

Ask yourself whether the building you are creating has any building materials, cladding, or features that are not already used in other buildings. If they have been used before in an existing building, you don't have to model them from scratch. Somewhere on the Internet or in your neighborhood, there will be a photo you can use.

Here are some examples of places to look online:

- In Flickr, you can use the **Advanced Search** option to search by geographical location and limit your search to images under the Creative Commons license with the options for commercial use and modification. You can use these images in your model without restrictions. Also, try `www.flickr.com/map` to zoom in to the location of your model.

- You can also use Google Images. Again, respect the license and copyright of any image you find.

- You can refer to the gallery sections of manufacturers' websites such as Krono for wood flooring (`http://kronooriginal.esignserver2.com/gallery.do`). Some of these might even offer you a CAD service, where you can download textures and 3D models of their products to use in your models.

- You can use "royalty-free" photos from image broker websites such as `www.Istockphoto.com`, `www.BigStockPhoto.com`, or `www.gettyimages.com` (there are plenty!). The price to pay for the rights to use the image may be justified for sites and objects that you would otherwise not be able to get.

- You can refer to the architectural websites such as `http://architizer.com` or `www.archdaily.com`. It may be a bit time consuming to track down the photographers and negotiate usage rights for these pictures, though.

However, don't limit yourself to the Web. Some of the best texture images will be your own. Even taking photos with your smartphone will often give you better textures than what you can get online. Here are some tips for your own photo hunt:

- Take the images square on. This will reduce the obstruction of details on large objects and reduce perspective distortion on small areas.

- Step as far back as possible and use a zoom lens. This too reduces obstruction by overhangs and distortion of vertical lines.

- Avoid sunlight and shadows. Try to take your pictures on an overcast day where shadows will not be prominent on the buildings. Shadows that are present on the texture image stay fixed and do not change with the sun in your model. Only in some cases, such as plaster details on a façade, the shadows are welcome to give added depth.

- If you take pictures of an existing site context, try to do all the shots at the same time. The weather, sun, and shadows should be consistent throughout all your images in the model.

- Avoid the need for a flash. The flash will illuminate your picture only in close proximity to the camera, but distant areas will be visibly darker.

Go through all your old photos to find those that feature buildings and other areas of texture. Copy them into a `textures` folder somewhere on your computer for ready access whenever you might need them. When you have some spare time, go through them and crop and straighten the texture portions with GIMP. There is more on this in the later sections.

Setting up a fake room

Here's an example of how to utilize images in your scene. When rendering a building with large windows, all we need to do is set up a billboard image of a room behind the window, such as the one shown in the following image. Someone on Flickr took the photo for me. Thank you!

However, what if you're making an animated flythrough and the camera passes by the window slowly? The image behind the window won't move in the right way. The answer is to mock up a quick Match Photo room. Have a go yourself!

1. Start with a new model.

2. Find a suitable picture of a room.

3. Start Match Photo as you did earlier and select the photo.

4. As it's a concave room rather than a convex outside of a building, select the **Inside** grid style, as shown in the following screenshot:

5. Set up Match Photo as you did in *Chapter 3, Composing the Scene*, but use the back and right-hand side or the left-hand side walls.

6. Draw a rectangle to cover the back wall of the room and push-pull it towards you until it fills the screen.

7. Delete the face filling the screen.

8. Triple-click the geometry to select all the remaining faces.

9. Right-click and select **reverse faces**.

10. Click on **Project Textures from Photo**. You should have something like the following example:

11. Scale as necessary to get a more appropriate room size if you have discrepancies in your Match Photo. As you can see in the following screenshot, my Match Photo created a super-long room:

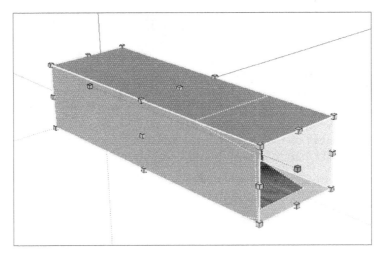

12. Add in any extra colors or textures if you need to spruce the room up a little using the **Paint Bucket** tool.

13. Now, save the scene and remember the filename.

14. In your building model, insert the room as a component behind each window and flip it if necessary, depending on where you'll be viewing it from, as shown in the following screenshot:

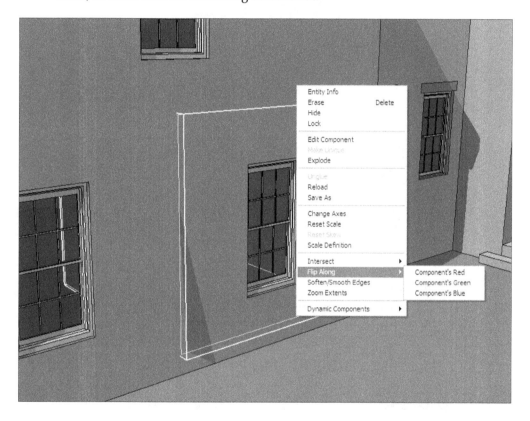

You now have a room behind each window that will behave more or less correctly on camera! The reason for all this is that when you have a moving camera in an animation, things farther away from the camera appear to move slower than the foreground. So, if you have set up a room with just a flat image behind the window, it will look all wrong.

This method allows you to quickly make a photorealistic room, which behaves right with a moving camera, without the hassle of modeling everything in there.

Night scenes

These fake rooms are great for night scenes where the room interiors are much more visible in contrast to the dark outdoors. Set up a light in the room (find out how in *Chapter 8, Photorealistic Rendering*) and see the result.

Creating balsa wood film scenery props

You're going to work out this next part of the process yourself. I have been raving for most of the book about the revolutionary way in which SketchUp allows you to handle digital images, but you'll only ever really benefit from this if you throw your existing workflow out of the window and embrace the SketchUp one.

Based on what you've learned so far, surf the Internet or explore your own image collection. What's the biggest thing you've modeled or need to model that you can get rid of and replace with a simple image?

1. Find a picture depicting an object for your model or scene.
2. Start a new SketchUp model.

3. Import the image (**File | Import**) and draw around the area you want to keep with the pencil tool.

4. Create a billboard 2D cutout or a Face-Me component with it like the following one (but maybe lose the leopard skin…).

5. Alternatively, create a quick Match Photo scene like you did with the room.

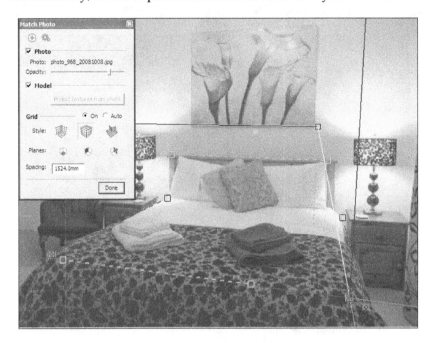

6. Draw in some rough geometry to match the object's geometry.

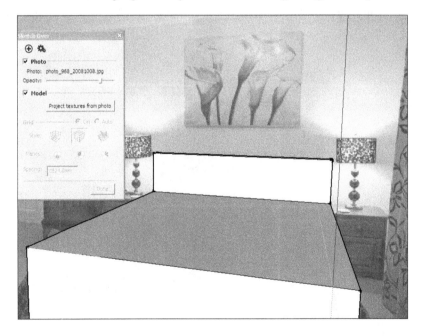

7. Project the textures.

8. Remove any unused image parts from the scene.

9. Save the scene as a component.

10. Insert the new component into your full-model scene.

The final output of the image is shown in the following screenshot:

Using, finding, and creating tileable textures

In this section, you will learn all about beautifying your scene further with tileable textures. These methods can be used in combination with all of the other methods you've learned so far. The following section applies to any texture, whether it is tileable or not.

Manipulating textures

Most of the time, you will want textures to match your geometry fairly exactly, such as when applying brick to a wall close-up. We want mortar joints to line up with the edges. Once you have sorted out the basic scale of the texture, you can now rotate, move, and scale it with the mouse.

Exact texture placement

You learned the method of manipulating the photograph of a house in *Chapter 4, Modeling for Visualization*, using pushpins. We will now look at the other ways of doing this.

1. Select a face with the texture already applied.

2. Right-click and navigate to **Texture | Position**.

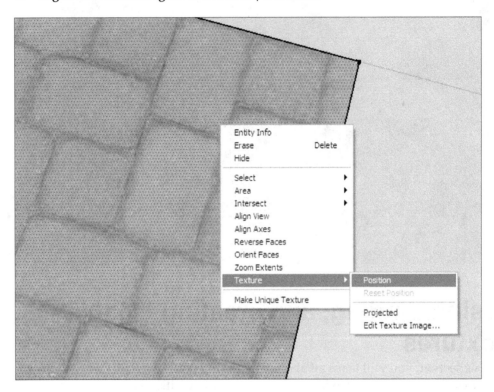

3. Click and hold one of the pins and move the mouse as follows:
    °   Use the **Red pin** to move
    °   Use the **Blue pin** to scale the texture
    °   Use the **Green pin** to scale or rotate
    °   Use the **Yellow pin** to distort the texture (for perspective correction)

You can see the four differently colored pins in the following screenshot:

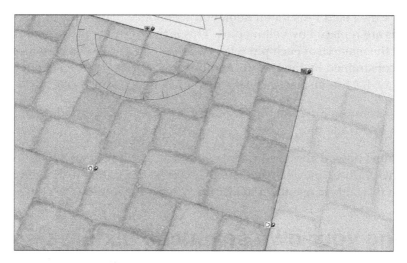

4. Play around with these. At any time, you can reset to where you started or undo what you just did by right-clicking on the texture and selecting **Reset** or **Undo**.

The different colored pins do slightly different things and can be used to manipulate the texture to fit correctly onto the geometry. You can do this with any texture, whether it came from a photo or a tileable texture. Editing a texture in this way only affects the face you're working with.

Now, notice the other features listed in the right-click menu:

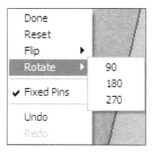

The **Flip** option enables us to flip the texture left/right or up/down. The **Rotate** option enables us to rotate the texture at 90, 180, or 270 degrees. These two are easy to understand, but what does **Fixed Pins** do?

The free pins mode

If you untick the **Fixed Pins** menu item, you will notice that all the differently colored pins are replaced by yellow pins. This is the free pins mode, and it lets you stretch the material at each pin wherever you want it. This is very useful because you're not constrained by the transformations described earlier. Each pin behaves in the same way. It's like an elastic sheet stretched between four posts.

Again, play around with this a little, because it will set you in good stead for what we're going to do later on.

Now you know how to apply, edit, and colorize the textures that you found bundled with SketchUp. Once you've created some textures yourself, as explained in the next section, you'll be able to use them in just the way you intended!

Creating your own seamless textures

Learning how to create your own texture materials for use in SketchUp is one of the most useful skills you can learn. Here, we are presenting two methods using **GIMP** (the **GNU Image Manipulation Program**) or Photoshop. First, you will learn how to prepare an image for use as a texture, and then we will look at two methods to make them tileable (in other words, seamlessly repeatable). You'll pick up the first method in minutes and use it all the time.

Correcting perspective in GIMP

Often, your source photos will not be taken square on to the object. This is not a big problem. Just perform the following steps to remove the distortion from the image. The steps are illustrated using **GIMP**, but you should find the same features in other image editing software such as Adobe Photoshop.

Keystone correction cameras

Some digital cameras have an automatic feature called "white board capture" built in (such as the Casio Exilim range). This is a fantastic way of skipping the step of correcting perspective and will save you a lot of time if you're using textures regularly. It works with any rectangular surface. Some smartphones also provide a feature like this, or at least, there is an app for it...

Perform the following steps for correcting perspective in GIMP:

1. Start with a photo taken orthogonal to the surface (with as little distortion as possible).

2. With the rectangular selection tool, select the area to be used as a texture. A square is the easiest.

3. Select **Perspective Tool**, as shown in the following screenshot:

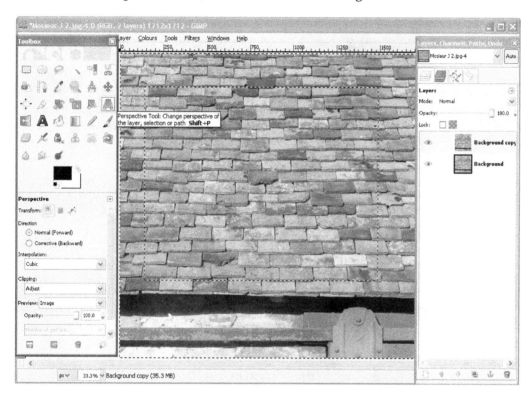

4. Drag one of the corners out until you feel the distortion has been corrected.

5. Release the left-mouse button to see what you have done. You can see the straightened version in the following screenshot:

6. Repeat as necessary. Use the dotted line of your selection as a guide.
7. When you are done, click on **Transform** in the perspective tool dialog box to apply the effect permanently.
8. You now have a perspective corrected area of texture. Use the **Crop** tool to crop the texture within the area you corrected.

You selected a square area so that you could see where the edges of the area were. Using the **Perspective Tool**, you corrected the perspective distortion in the photo to make sure that the image lined up with the edges of the selection box. This is a trial-and-error process, and during it, the image remains malleable for as long as you need. When you are happy, just press the **Transform** button to fix the changes. Even then, you can still go back to the original by selecting **Edit** | **Undo**.

You did all of this simply because textures are always applied to flat surfaces, so they have to be near-enough flat images of the material. Now that you have done this preparation, you can go ahead and turn it into a seamless texture!

Tiling via an automatic filter

This method is great for textures with little distinguishable details such as the following:

- Grass, leaves, or other ground cover
- Water and sky
- Concrete and asphalt

It is not so great for repeating regular textures such as brick, roof slates, or ceramic tiles. I'm using a dry stone wall photo in this example workflow:

1. Open your photo in GIMP.
2. Click the **Crop** tool.
3. Set the cropping options to **Fixed** and **Aspect Ratio**.
4. Type in 1:1 for the aspect ratio.

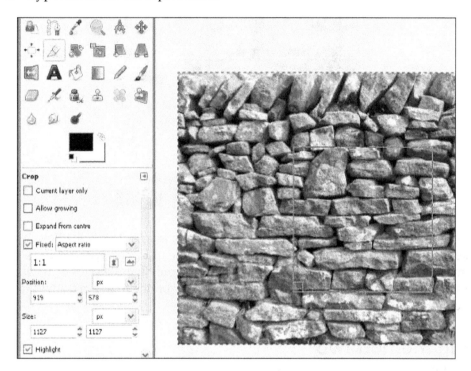

5. Drag a box over the photo. Notice that you've fixed it to be a square box, as you can see in the screenshot.
6. When you're happy, hit *Enter*.
7. Choose **Filters | Map | Make Seamless**.
8. Open **Image | Scale Image**.
9. Enter a value for the image size (1024 pixels or less) and select **Cubic**.

10. Click on **Scale**.

11. Save a copy by navigating to **File | Save a Copy**.

Here is the image with the filter applied to it:

You applied the **Make Seamless** filter to your texture image. This will allow it to tile in SketchUp without you seeing the edge between the tiles. You reduced the size of the image before you saved it because SketchUp can only handle sizes of 1024 x 1024 pixels max with the default settings. More discussion on the image sizes will follow later on in this chapter.

Tiling method two

If you still want to create a better texture from the outset, there's a second method. It takes a little longer (or a lot longer to get it perfect), but the results are cleaner.

1. Open your original straightened texture in GIMP.

2. Crop a square, as you did earlier, but make sure that the pixel size is an even number!

3. Open the **Layers** pallet by navigating to **Windows | Dockable Dialogs | Layers**.

4. Click on the **Duplicate Layer** icon (at the bottom).

5. Right-click on the new layer and select **Edit Layer Attributes**.

6. Change the layer name to Texture.

7. You now have a **Texture** layer, which you will modify, and a base layer, which you will use as a reference.

8. Click the **Texture** layer in the **Layer** pallet to select it.

9. Navigate to **Layer | Transform | Offset**.

10. Click on the **Offset by x/2, y/2** button and select **Wrap around**. Then, click on **Offset**.

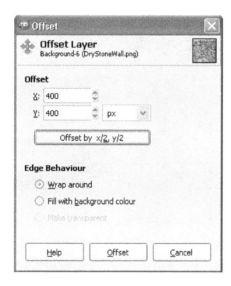

The idea now is to paint over the edges that have been wrapped into the middle.

1. Click on the **Clone** tool.

2. Turn off the visibility for the **Texture** layer (the eye icon).

3. Select the base image layer in the **Layer** pallet.

4. Hold down *Ctrl* (*Cmd* on the Mac) and click somewhere on the base image.

5. Turn on the visibility on the **Texture** layer, and select it in the **Layer** pallet.

6. Start painting. Areas of the base image will clone onto the texture image. Keep the **Texture** layer at the top to see your changes.

7. Select a fuzzy brush for this and increase the size if it makes it easier. You can see my settings in the following screenshot. The dotted circle is the brush I'm using.

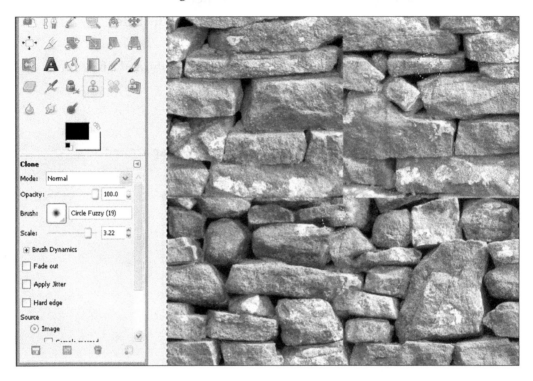

If you prefer, you can *Ctrl* + click inside the texture image instead and use parts of that to clone over the middle area.

This method has much more flexibility than the previous method and can yield more pleasing results with a little practice. However, don't get too bogged down with getting this perfect. Using a two-layer approach allows you to sample (clone) from the original image to paint over the offset image. Folding the image in on itself using an offset of x/2 and y/2 ensures that the image will tile seamlessly.

Let's now apply this texture to a scene and save it to your own texture library.

Importing a texture into SketchUp

You're now ready to use this modified image in SketchUp to create a material.
Once you've done this, you can use it like a regular SketchUp material.

1. In the **Materials** pallet, click on the **Create Material** icon (top-right corner).
   On Mac, right-click on an empty space in the pallet and select **New Texture**.

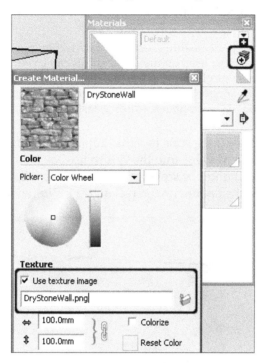

2. Type in a material name (Windows only).

3. Select the folder icon in the **Texture** section of the dialog (Windows only).

4. Navigate to your image file and click on **Open**.

5. On Mac, you can now enter a good name for the material (it defaults to the
   filename) and a rough size for your texture. This should correspond to the area
   that the picture represents in real life. On Windows, you will be returned to the
   material properties dialog, and you can set the name and size there.

6. Click on **OK** to confirm the creation of the new texture material.

7. Your new material should appear in the **In Model** list of materials.

8. To return to the edit dialog, select the new material icon and click on the **Edit** tab (Windows) or right-click and select **Edit** from the context menu (Mac).

9. Create a rectangle of 1 m x 1 m using the **Rectangle** tool.

10. Select your material and apply it to the surface.

 Don't worry if the texture doesn't look perfect or if you can see the pattern repeating itself on the surface. This can be edited when we get to the later steps of texturing (see the diagram at the beginning of the chapter). The important thing at this stage is to cover large areas of our model with realistic photo textures as fast as we can.

11. You'll be able to see if the scale is right. Adjust the texture size in the edit dialog by typing the desired value into the **Width** textbox (a horizontal double-arrow icon on Windows) until the scale looks OK (see the following screenshot). You can see that the texture on the rectangle gets updated as you type.

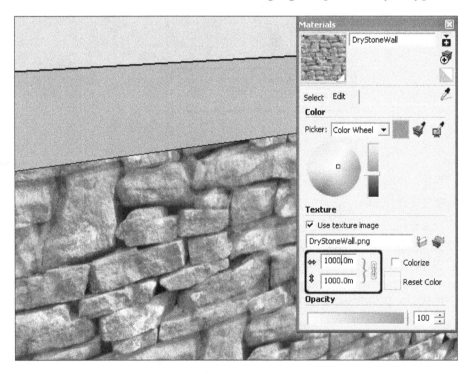

12. You can modify the *x* and *y* scales separately by clicking on the chain symbol first.

Saving a material to a library

Congratulations! You've now created a new material in SketchUp. It's an achievement that will make SketchUp texturing much easier and more versatile for you from now on. Once you've done it a few times, you will realize it's not that hard at all. Using these methods, you can create a library of real-world textures for lively architectural visuals.

Now, the last thing that we need to do is save the texture and make it easily accessible for later use. You can even share it with others. Unfortunately, you can only save individual textures on Windows. On a Mac, you have to copy the whole list of materials to save each to a new file. Here is how to save a single texture on Windows:

1. Right-click on your material icon and click on **Save As**.

2. Navigate to where your SketchUp program is stored
   (`C:\Program Files (x86)\SketchUp\SketchUp 2014\`).

3. Find the `Materials` folder.

4. Create a folder called `My Materials` or something similar (see the following screenshot).

5. Type in a name for the material and click on **Save**.

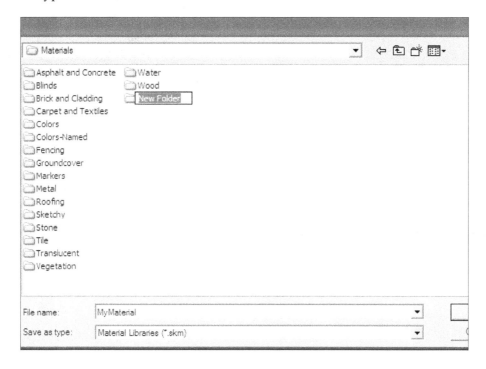

Because you created the new folder in the default `SketchUp 2014\Materials` folder, it will be listed in the materials pallet as a new collection. Just open the materials browser and navigate to **Materials | My Materials** to find the material you just saved. You can use this process to extend your standard collection of SketchUp materials.

To save your texture on a Mac, you first have to create a copy of the current material collection or start a new one:

1. From the **List** drop-down box below the materials icons, choose **New…** or **Duplicate…**.

2. Enter the name for your new collection, as shown in the following screenshot:

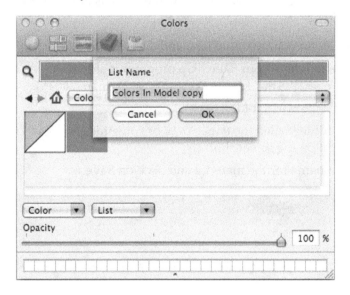

3. Make sure that you are in the new collection by selecting a different list first and then return to the newly created one. The new collection will now be empty.

4. Continue creating new materials in the same way as described earlier.

Whenever you quit SketchUp, the materials will be saved as new `*.skm` files in the folder that corresponds to the new collection. The new folders will be located in your personal SketchUp support folder, `~/Library/Application Support/SketchUp 2014/SketchUp/Materials`.

Quick recap on textures

You just created a texture from your own photo or from the images you downloaded, inserted it into SketchUp, and saved it into a new dedicated library. This is the bedrock of texturing! If you used the first method, you will notice that once you have applied the new material to your model, you may see a repeating pattern. When covering large areas, this doesn't look too great. In some cases, the repeating pattern may be obscured and not so obvious. If this is not enough, you can edit out the repetitive image elements by tweaking the textured faces in GIMP later.

You're now all set up. Everything in your model has basic textures applied to it, and what doesn't need a texture just has a color applied to it.

Advanced image considerations

So far, I haven't mentioned image file types such as JPEG or PNG, because it hasn't mattered to the fundamentals of texturing. However, there are some tricks that make a huge difference to the quality and size of your SketchUp files, and therefore, the speed at which you can model and render your scenes. We are going to quickly discuss the salient points and then come up with a method that will allow you to benefit from the various options you have.

Texture size

As you may already know, digital images are made up of pixels. Pixels are dots (picture elements) of color, and each image is made up of a grid of these dots. So, for example, a small computer screen has around 786,000 pixels in a rectangular grid measuring 1024 by 768 pixels. A digital camera might take pictures of 8 megapixels or 3264 x 2448 pixels.

In SketchUp, the maximum size for a texture image is limited to 1024 x 1024 pixels by default. If you select a larger image as texture, it is reduced in size to fit to this maximum size. This is a historic value from the time when computer and graphics card memory was more limited than today. Nevertheless, it still allows for a decent texture quality given that most surfaces will only cover a few hundred pixels or less in the final rendered image.

For large elements close to the camera, you may want to increase this value. You can find a corresponding setting by navigating to **System Preferences | OpenGL**. The **Use maximum texture size** option is not set by default. If you add a check mark here, you can use textures up to 4096 x 4096 pixels.

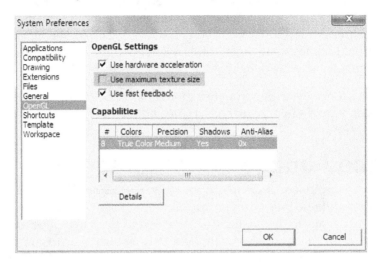

Still, don't go crazy and import all your textures in 4096 x 4096 from now on. Use sizes above 1024 x 1024 pixels only for the elements that are close up and important in your image frame. This will keep your SketchUp file size in check and enable you to work faster.

File type

Secondly, file type matters a lot. JPEG files are much smaller on your hard drive than the corresponding PNG files, because they use a lossy compression algorithm. This process removes details that are not important for the human visual perception. Unfortunately, this happens every time the file is saved, so JPEG (or JPG) is not a good format to use for images you want to edit.

PNG, on the other hand, can retain an identical copy of the image and still achieve a reasonable compression rate. It is a good choice if you want to modify your textures later but still are concerned about your overall file size in SketchUp. Regardless of the file type you choose to store your files on your hard drive, once they are loaded into the scene, they will still take up all the memory of the uncompressed image. So, make sure that you have a good graphics card with plenty of onboard memory.

Compression

When saving an image in the JPG format, you will be presented with the following box:

Moving the **Quality** slider will change the quality of the image from very compressed (poor quality but low file size) to hardly compressed (very good quality and large file size). The trick is to get a balance between low file size and image clarity. You will see a significant reduction in the file size with a quality setting of 80-85, while the image will not show any obvious degradation. I usually don't compress my images more than this, because the gain in file size is not worth the sacrifice in image details.

You have to experiment a bit and also adjust the setting based on the image content. An image with large expanses of similar colors (sand dunes, for example) will compress much better than a picture of a palm tree with many feathered leaves.

Balancing size and compression

The following image shows a stone wall texture that has been compressed too much. Can you see the blurred and jaggy artifacts the compression has introduced? The overall idea of the stone wall is still there, but individual stones and gaps are washed out and show little surface details.

This is what saving JPG at low-quality settings does to an image. This is OK for distant objects, but not for close-up ones. So, what do we do?

Here's the deal: save three versions of your texture images with the following sizes and quality settings:

Image format	Reuse/resave	Uses
PNG at large size (up to 4096 x 4096 if you want to achieve the best results)	This can be reused and resaved repeatedly without the loss of quality	This is used on all close-up surfaces where the texture will be further altered using **Edit Texture Image** in SketchUp (explained later)
JPG at large size (1024 x 1024) and adequate compression (say, 80 quality)	This cannot be resaved	This is used on all close-up surfaces that will stay as they are
JPG at low size and high compression (say, 512 x 512 at 50 quality)	This cannot be resaved	This is used on surfaces far from the camera

This way, we have all the bases covered. Here's the workflow:

1. Save the high-resolution image in PNG format and import it into SketchUp.

2. Open the image in GIMP and select **Image | Scale Image** to reduce the resolution to 1024 x 1024.

3. Click on **File | Save as Copy** in GIMP and save the image as a JPG with a quality setting of 80 or 85. Name it the same as the PNG, except add a _LR or _MED to the end of the filename.

4. In GIMP, go to **Image | Scale Image** again and set the image size to 512 x 512 or even 256 x 256.

5. Click on **Save As** and reduce the **Quality** slider to **50**. Append _ULR or _SML to the name.

Import the second and third image into SketchUp as new materials, but keep the texture size the same so that it matches the hi-res version. You should be able to replace the image texture without the need to scale the texture once it has been applied.

Now, you have a high-resolution texture for close-up details, a medium texture for general use, and a low-resolution version for distant objects with a small memory footprint. Here is the dry wall model again with our own hi-res texture applied to it. Much better!

By the way, there is no point in using the medium- and low-resolution texture in the same model. Once the material/texture is used in the scene, it will not be loaded again and again each time it is used. So, a good way to start with texturing is to use your low-resolution texture for all the surfaces and only load the medium-quality texture if you see that the quality is not enough. Use the high-quality texture for all the surfaces that you are going to edit further with the steps mentioned in the following section.

Modifying textures for added realism

Once a surface has a texture applied to it using any of the methods we've looked at, it can be edited with an image-editing software. This is handled from within SketchUp, so you don't need to mess around exporting and importing images.

Telling SketchUp to link to an image editor

Before you try to modify textures using an image-editing software, you need to tell SketchUp which program to use.

1. Open the Preferences window (**SketchUp | Preferences** or **Window | Preferences**).

2. Select **Applications**.

3. Click on the **Choose** button.

4. On Windows, navigate to the directory where GIMP is installed; this is usually C:\Program Files\GIMP 2\bin. On a Mac, choose Gimp.app from the Applications folder.

5. Click on **Open** to apply the selection.

The GIMP default installation location on Windows is shown in the following screenshot:

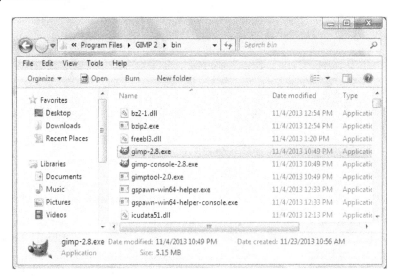

You have now set up SketchUp to open GIMP each time you need to edit a texture image. You can pick any image editing software you are comfortable with, such as Photoshop or Picasa.

Making unique textures for surfaces

Before you can open an entire surface texture in GIMP, turn it into a texture that is unique to the face of the texture, or you will end up modifying the texture on all surfaces in the model:

1. Right-click on a surface and select **Make Unique Texture**.

2. Right-click again and navigate to **Texture | Edit Texture Image**.
3. GIMP opens up with the texture that is ready for editing!

You just created a separate texture image for one particular surface in the model. This creates an image that will cover the entire surface and detects any cropping and holes such as window openings. If you don't create a unique texture first, GIMP will open the tiled texture image for editing. This means that any changes you make will be seen on all the instances of this texture throughout the model.

Editing textures in GIMP

Now, the textured image of the entire face that you selected is open in GIMP. You can modify whatever you wish. When you save the changes to the image and go back into SketchUp, the texture will be updated. You may have to use the **Export** or **Overwrite** menu option to create an image in the original file format if you add new layers or channels to the image while you are editing.

As you can see from the following texture I opened, the image here is only 178 x 337 pixels. This is a little too small to do high-quality editing with it. Although the picture already shows features specific to this wall (such as the frames around the windows), you can see the poor quality of the texture. So, instead, I'm going to go back to SketchUp, apply a standard brick pattern, and create a new unique texture from the standard brick image.

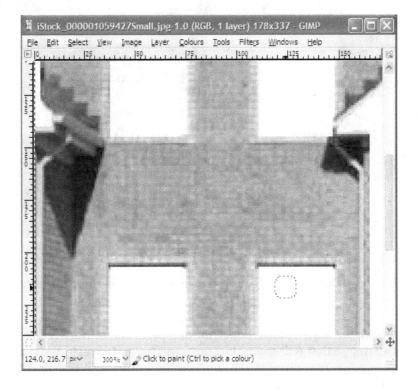

As you can see in the following screenshot, I now have a larger image of 1071 x 2048 pixels to play with. This is much better! This is because each SketchUp brick texture tile is 250 x 250 pixels, which covers about 1 square meter of wall. When we create a unique texture specific to a surface, SketchUp repeats this tile until it fills the whole wall area.

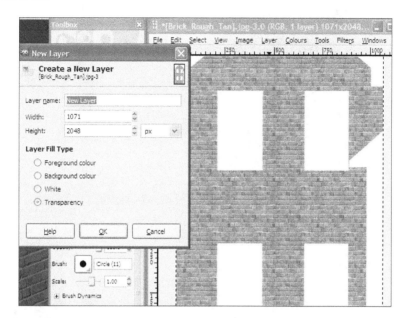

Adding some muck and variation

Hats off to the SketchUp folks for creating such a clean texture, but in real life, we wouldn't expect it to be so uniform. You're going to apply some variation with GIMP now.

1. Create a new layer by selecting **Layer** | **New Layer**.

2. This will create a transparent layer over the top of the original one. You can now modify this without being afraid of spoiling the original texture layer.

3. If you can't see the **Layer** pallet, press *Ctrl + L* (*Cmd + L* on the Mac).

4. Click on the new layer to select it.

5. Select **Fill Bucket** and select a texture or gradient fill.

6. Click in the image window to fill the entire layer with the gradient color.

7. Now, navigate to **Filters | Render | Clouds**. Experiment with the options. You should see a pattern like the one shown in the following screenshot:

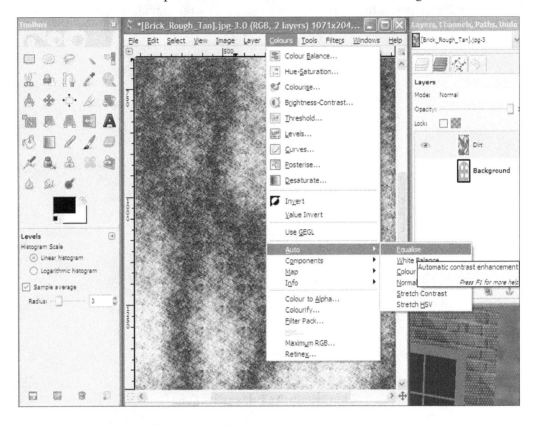

8. Navigate to **Colors | Auto | Equalize** to stretch the range of contrast (see the preceding screenshot).

9. Now, take the **Opacity** slider of the layer down to **10** (in the **Layers** pallet).

By adding a light translucent layer with a random cloud pattern, you have now added some simple variation to the texture. You can do this for all your textured surfaces one by one or just the ones closer to the camera. At this point, you can also add more detail, such as hanging flowers, to the texture.

Adding extra elements to a texture

Perform the following steps to add extra elements to a texture:

1. Open an image that contains extra elements.

2. Draw a selection around the area, as shown in the following screenshot:

3. Select **Edit | Copy**.

4. Go to your original texture image and select **Edit | Paste**.

5. In the **Layers** pallet, right-click on **Floating Selection** and then select **To New Layer**.

6. Use the **Move** tool and the **Scale** tool to get the pasted image element in position as demonstrated in the following screenshot:

7. Select the new layer in the **Layers** pallet.

8. Right-click and select **Add Layer Mask**.

9. Click on the mask to select it.

10. Select the paintbrush and paint out all the background bits you don't need, as you can see in the following screenshot:

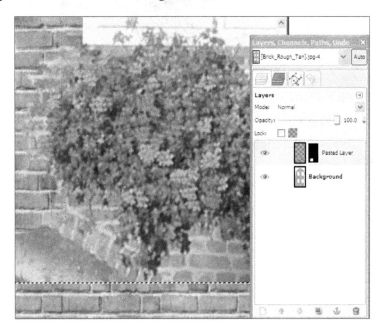

There is more about layer masks in *Chapter 9, Postproduction in GIMP,* where you will get to grips with GIMP in much more detail.

11. Click on **File | Save a Copy** to save a master copy somewhere as a GIMP *.xcf file. The XCF file format is GIMP's native format that preserves all layer information for future editing.

12. Choose the menu **Image | Flatten Image**.

13. Finally select **File | Export** or **File | Overwrite** to update the texture image in SketchUp.

14. Your textured face will update with the changes you made. You can see the result in the following screenshot:

You have used layers a lot to create your image composition, but all this will be lost when you save and go back to SketchUp because the image is saved as a JPG or PNG, which can't save layers. Saving a copy of the file in the native application format before you flatten the image can be a real time saver. Saving it as a GIMP (*.xcf) or Photoshop (*.psd) file will retain all the layer info, and it won't lose any detail either, so you can come back to it and make edits as many times as you like.

Adding extra detail

Now, it's your turn. See how much difference you can make by adding little details where it matters. Try adding lintels to your windows by taking the texture from an existing photo, like the one shown in the following screenshot:

In the preceding image, you can see the brick pattern of a lintel that is used in the following image in a different scenario. Would you have noticed that the lintel is from another building?

Knowing when to call it quits

I've been known to spend days texturing and then, finally deciding that I didn't like what I'd done anyway. I replaced the hand-crafted image with a tiled texture, and it was adequate. So, don't get drawn into games such as adding cats behind a window. Refer to your original scene setup drawings to identify areas that can benefit from more details and ignore parts of the scene that are peripheral in your camera shots or too far away to show any details.

Summary

I think you are now fully clued up in the art of SketchUp texturing. As you've seen, SketchUp has some amazing tools to help you along the way. Now that you've made the best use of textures, you can rest assured that your model will render beautifully.

In this chapter on texturing, we discussed when it is appropriate to use textures. Sometimes, it's best just to leave this stage out completely and go for an NPR look (see *Chapter 7, Non-photoreal Visuals with SketchUp*). We also discussed tileable textures and a couple of ways to make your own textures. Don't forget to keep taking photos and keep a library for future use.

We used Match Photo to greatly speed up the texturing process and make use of digital photos wherever you want. Finally, we looked at ways to tweak texture images in GIMP to add realism. This is all accessible easily with SketchUp linked to GIMP.

We also discussed lots of other stuff, all of which combines to give you the wherewithal to create quick, great-looking textured models ready to render or print straight from SketchUp. You can now go to the next chapter on entourage, which is a weird name for people, cars, and trees…, or you can go straight to *Chapter 8, Photorealistic Rendering*.

6
Entourage the SketchUp Way

When pitching a great design to a client, your pitch will stand or fall, based on the presentation of architectural visuals. However, your visuals will stand or fall with the quality of the entourage, that is, additional elements such as furniture, plants, and people that add lifelike variation to the image. In fact, a promising design can be marred by bad entourage. As entourage is not specific to a project, you can build up a library of entourage components in SketchUp and choose suitable elements to add to your scene.

Entourage of professional quality is hard to create. Obtaining in-focus photos of trees, with the right light and background, and then clipping around them to remove all the background elements can take forever. That's why, quality entourage has its price.

In this chapter, you will find out ways to find or create entourage that you will be happy with. If you don't have the money to spend, you'll learn how to create your own entourage. We will look at some of the best resources you can use to do so quickly and easily. You'll also learn how to use this entourage within your SketchUp workflow.

In this chapter, you will learn the following:

- Where to find high-quality, free photoreal furniture models
- How to overcome problems with foliage
- How to create 2D people to use repeatedly
- Where to find good plant entourage and how to generate it
- Where to use entourage in your workflow to obtain the best results

The notice hierarchy

The notice hierarchy is a term I think I've made up on the spot. But, wherever it comes from, it's not a bad way to describe something you've probably experienced: If you walk into a room, there are certain things you'll notice first. If these things are missing, you'll notice something else first, and so on. Here's my take on the order of the "notice hierarchy":

- People
- Animals
- Furniture
- Lights
- Carpet
- Pictures

This might not be entirely accurate, and the order may vary from person to person. What's interesting though is that you can choose exactly where the viewer (the client) looks for his first impression. We all know that first impressions count, right?

So, what would you like your multibillionaire client to see first when showing them their new apartment development?

- A smiling, relaxed young couple
- A toaster

It's all about transporting the viewer into the image you've created. So, when you show people inhabiting the space in the same way in which the client would wish to, you've put the client into the scene. Neither men nor women, rich or poor think nostalgically about the great bread toasting they did this morning.

Supporting the scene

Actually, there's an even more important consideration. No matter how good your rendering is or how good an impression your entourage makes, if there's a single piece of really bad entourage in the scene, it gets noticed first. So, the very first goal of using entourage is to not ruin your scene!

Entourage elements have their own style and quality. Therefore, sometimes, the best advice is to leave it out. Some of the best visuals show a building on an open background, like the one by the SketchUp user, REVI21ON, shown in the following image. The rich texturing provides variety and a sense of scale all on its own. Any entourage you'd want to place in this scene would have to match up with the superb detailing of the building itself. Would you want to spoil it with entourage?

If you make sure that you always use entourage sparingly, you are more likely to spend some time on finding good quality entourage to fill the spot.

Be the marketing exec

You are a salesperson, and the most effective architectural visuals are sales documents. If you treat them as such, you will never go wrong. Think about this for a minute and internalize what it means. You need to pull out all the stops to create the vision of your client's dream space. The easiest way you do this is not by getting every minute detail of the building right, but with well-selected and well-placed entourage. Entourage brings life to your scene.

In the rest of this chapter, we will go through how to use entourage to help you make this impact.

Choosing entourage

Let's evaluate your choices at this stage. I suppose there's little difference between all these options in the final visual, but obviously, some types of entourage will suit you more than others. However, be warned; it's easy to drift aimlessly on the Internet trying one thing after another. To help you, I've included a quick reference table so that you can compare the relative merits of each option side by side.

At which stage do I introduce entourage?

There are three options here, as illustrated in the first column of the following table:

Design stage	Difficulty to use	Quantity available	Formats
SketchUp	Easy	High	SKP, 3DS, DWG/DXF
Renderer	Medium	Medium	3DS, OBJ
Postproduction	Difficult	High	Images

Broadly speaking, the level of difficulty of introducing entourage will increase further along the production process you are in. So, as already discussed in *Chapter 3, Composing the Scene*, it is best to set up at least entourage place markers in SketchUp right at the start. The disadvantage of introducing detailed entourage (high polygon and detailed textures) into SketchUp is that it tends to slow the program down to a snail's pace. The way to get around this is discussed in this chapter when we look at swapping high/low detail entourage.

Many visualization artists leave entourage to the last moment, even introducing it in the postprocessing stage in Photoshop or GIMP. Traditionally, it used to be difficult to set up a 2D billboard-styled entourage in modeling or CAD software. This is not the case with SketchUp. So, there is really no need to learn all the skills required to do this successfully in GIMP or Photoshop. If you already have the skills and a library of images, you might still like to do it this way. Postproduction, however, is the last stage in the digital production pipeline, and so, it is your last chance to fix anything that might have gone wrong with a rendering. You can save your entire image with a well-placed car or tree.

What I suggest is that you introduce entourage at the SketchUp and rendering software stages. The two work so seamlessly together that you will be able to keep both programs open, using the best features of each to populate your scene. While most entourage can be introduced in SketchUp and taken directly to your renderer, you will achieve the best results with objects that are in the renderer's native file format and are introduced into the SketchUp scene on the fly during the export. We will introduce this workflow for Thea Render in *Chapter 8*, *Photorealistic Rendering*, and set up a library of replacement components.

What's my acquisition strategy?

An acquisition strategy is the posh way of saying "be consistent". Unlike me, who has a bit of everything on my computer, in lots of different file formats and visual styles, software for creating this or that is spread over several hard drives so that I can never find it. It pays to decide the best way of acquiring entourage for you and then sticking to it. The broad choices are to buy it, find it on the Internet, or make it yourself.

	Quality	Suits your workflow	Money	Time
Buy	Medium/High	Not always	High	Low
Find	Low/High	Not always	Low	Medium
Make	Medium/Low	Yes	Medium	High

So, how much time or money do you have to spend? What quality do you expect? It might always seem wise to buy entourage, and this is true to the extent that you will have more time to work on a design. This will be quite significant the next time a deadline approaches. However, even entourage that is bought doesn't provide everything, and you might have to adapt it to your workflow. On the other hand, you can get exactly what you want by searching a little and spending some time on making it yourself.

For example, trees are usually sold as either 2D images for postproduction or high-polygon 3D objects. You might prefer 2D face-me cutouts. Making entourage, as you will see from the tutorial on 2D people further on, is not so difficult for some types of entourage. You can also use software such as tree generators or character creation software to make it easier for you. Other objects, such as vehicles are best left to the experts.

2D or not 2D, that is the question

The following is a table showing what type of entourage is available for each category: people, trees, vehicles, furniture, backgrounds (such as city scenes), and skies. For each of these, there are pros and cons for 2D or 3D based on the availability, quality of the outcome, and ease of use. In addition, there are the types of output to consider. When aiming for stills, then 2D will usually be sufficient. 2D isn't resource hungry (unlike high-polygon 3D trees), and actually, it is more photorealistic than 3D when the entourage is made from photos. You'll learn how to make photo-based 2D entourage in this chapter. For animation, the decision is more difficult. Sometimes, a 2D entourage will look, well, just like a cardboard cutout:

	Availability		Suitable for animation		Cost		Software to help	
	2D	3D	2D	3D	2D	3D	2D	3D
People	Yes	Yes	Yes	Yes	Med	High	GIMP, Photoshop	Poser, Daz Studio, Makehuman
Plants and trees	Yes	Yes	No	Yes	Med	Med	RPtreemaker	Vue, NGPlant
Vehicles	No	Yes	N/A	Yes	N/A	Low	N/A	N/A
Furniture	No	Yes	N/A	Yes	N/A	Low	N/A	N/A
Backgrounds	Yes	Yes	Yes	Yes	Low	High	Vue Easel/ Esprit	Vue, Bryce
Skies	Yes	No	Yes	N/A	Med	N/A	Photosphere	N/A

We will show you how to use a sky image as a background in *Chapter 8, Photorealistic rendering*, and use a (free) city model for our tutorial in *Chapter 10, Animations*. The other groups of entourage are discussed in the following sections.

Furniture

When creating interior views, the furniture you choose is of paramount importance in establishing the look and feel of the image. While people are not used to discerning the build quality of architecture, they are very well equipped to judge good or bad furnishings. This is because everyone buys furniture, and everyone spends most of their lives inside. So, when you look at an interior visual, most of the impact will be created by the furniture, not the room itself, as you can see in the following image:

This fact gives rise to the continuing need for good 3D models of furniture, much of it branded. Since design houses want their designs to show up in interior visuals, they often find a way to provide free models to us. It's just a matter of finding them.

Before SketchUp came along, most visualizers used 3D Studio (later 3D Max) to create architectural visuals. So, there are years worth of content around the world in the old 3D Studio format, *.3DS. Guess what? Lots of it is good stuff; it is free, and you can insert it directly into your renderer.

[Go easy. Some of the best interior renders I've seen show an empty room with just one visually interesting chair in it and great lighting.]

Manufacturers' websites

Some manufacturers of designer furniture understand that they need to offer high-quality 3D models of their products to motivate architects to add them to their visuals and hopefully, add them later to their finished buildings. With the increasing popularity of SketchUp, some companies also started offering SketchUp files. Generally, these files are converted from a high-quality source and are very detailed (read very high poly) and can slow down your workflow significantly. These files are very good to produce photorealistic renderings but may need to be simplified for an acceptable performance in SketchUp.

A few manufacturers with a downloadable collection are:

- `www.hermanmiller.com`
- `www.fritzhansen.com`
- `www.sanitec-kolo.com`

The 3D Warehouse

There are bags of SketchUp furniture to choose from in the 3D Warehouse, and the amount of good quality gear is going up all the time. However, not all of the stuff there is suitable for high-quality SketchUp-based output and photorealistic output. If you're going to export your scene to a renderer, make sure that you check out the section on cleaning up 3D Warehouse components in *Chapter 4, Modeling for Visualization*.

List of websites

Once you've done your own search, try these great free sites, too. Remember to save, catalogue, and organize your downloads; otherwise, you will find it impossible to locate it later when you need it, with file names such as `1234asdf4qwe.zip` being commonplace; don't say I didn't warn you!

Try the following websites for furniture models:

- `Archive3D.net`
- `Turbosquid.com`
- `Flyingarchitecture.com`
- `3Delicious.net`
- `Resources.blogscopia.com`

To further explore what is there on the Internet, free or paid, you can go to the list of links at www.3Dlinks.com and navigate to **3D OBJECTS | Commercial 3D Objects** or **3D OBJECTS | Free 3D Objects**.

People cutouts

We're going to learn how to make 2D face-me people that can be used both in photorealist and non-photorealistic rendering. With this method, you can build up a stock of people that you can use, no matter what the required output is. The following are the applications for this type of entourage:

- Black and white with sketchy edges
- Colored with sketchy edges
- Textured within SketchUp
- Photoreal rendered

The following pictures of the same man correspond to these four output types. At first, here is a black-and-white sketch. The lines are not too crisp and have a bit of hand-drawn quality:

The next image shows the same jogger in a cartoon-style rendering. The lines in this picture are a bit sharper, but the first impression is created by the colored cloth and body shape:

One further step is shown in the next image where the jogger's cloth and body parts are created with a photographic texture. Note the realism that this further detailing adds to the person:

Finally, you can see a photorealistic rendering of the street. It looks like the jogger is really running along the street, thanks to the quality of the textures and the shadows that a tree casts on his legs:

So, you can see that this entourage works with every type of output. There are many ways of creating entourage, but this is possibly the most versatile way and offers the following benefits:

- Works with any rendering software
- No transparency to mess up the renderer
- Correct scale, no resizing needed
- Casts shadows
- Inserted within SketchUp, not within the renderer or as a postprocess
- Easy to make with any skill level

Creating 2D people components

To create a high-quality 2D component of a person, follow these steps:

1. Search for a high-quality, high-resolution picture of a person with a good contrast to the background.
2. Open the image in GIMP.

3. Navigate to **Filters | Enhance | Unsharp Mask...** if it is necessary to enhance the sharpness of the image.

4. Crop the image near the person using the **Crop** tool to take away any excess area of the image. Do this by dragging a box around the person; then, press *Enter* when you are done.

5. Save it as a PNG image. This is a non-lossy format that is suitable for repeated editing (see *Chapter 5, Applying Textures and Materials for Photorealistic Rendering*).

6. In SketchUp, navigate to **File | Import** and choose **All Supported Image Types** in the drop-down box.

7. Select the image (make sure that the **Use as image** checkbox is selected).

8. Click on **Open** and place the image into SketchUp.

Scaling the person

The image you just imported needs to be set to the correct size for a person. This can be easily done with the **Tape Measure** tool:

1. Select the **Tape Measure** tool and measure the distance between the bottom of the feet and the top of the head.

2. Now, type the approximate height of the person. Just take a guess.

3. Click on **Yes** in the following pop-up dialog to confirm that you want to resize the model.

Tracing the outline

In the next step, we will create the outline of the person as a SketchUp polygon:

1. Switch the view mode by navigating to **Camera | Parallel Projection** and then click on the **Top View** button (or navigate to **Camera | Standard Views | Top**). You should see the image flat on your screen.

2. Zoom in using the scroll wheel of the mouse.

3. Select the **Pencil** tool.

4. Click on the edge of the person and trace around the silhouette.

5. Make sure that **on face in image** shows each time before you click (see in the preceding image).

6. You will find it best to get the lines well within the edge of the person, so no background shows on the cutout.

When you are done, you will now have a completed outline, like the one shown in the following image:

Applying the photo texture

Finally, we add the image texture to the polygon and remove the background:

1. Select the cutout, and right-click and select **Reverse face** to get the white face to the top if necessary.

2. Select the image, right-click on it, and select **Explode**. The photo is now projected onto the cutout person.

3. Erase the background.

Checking for halos

A halo is the glow that you see around some entourage, making it look fake. It appears when there is some light background left in the cutout and the component is placed in front of a dark object.

1. Turn off the edges by navigating to **View | Edge Styles**. Uncheck both **Profiles** and **Edges**.

2. Export a 2D image, open it, and check for a black line around the edge of the person.

3. Change the background to black by navigating to **Window | Styles | Edit | Background Settings**. Click on **Background** and change the color to black, as shown in the following screenshot:

4. Export the image again and now check around the edges for bright lines.

5. If any edges need adjusting, turn the edges back on and redraw those lines to cut away the bright or dark pixels.

You've just created a 2D person cutout, which you can use as a face-me component in SketchUp. The photo you used has been projected onto the cutout so that it's good enough for photorealistic rendering.

Now, click on the **Hidden Line** view button, and you'll notice that there's no detail apart from the outline. There's still a little work to do if you want to use this entourage for non-photorealistic visuals.

Drawing the innards

You can now add some detail on the inside of the person, such as the edges of clothing, hands, neck, and hair. Once you have done this, your entourage can be used for any of the SketchUp styles. The following is the basic plan to get you started:

1. Using the same method that you used earlier, trace in some internal details.

2. Create a copy of the cutout person.

3. On the copy, fill in blocks of color using the **Paint bucket** tool.

You'll now have two versions of the same person. The one on the left-hand side can be used for photoreal visuals, and the one on the right-hand side can be used for artistic or sketchy styles, including the methods in *Chapter 7, Non-photoreal Visuals with SketchUp*.

Creating the face-me component

With the coloring and texturing complete, you now have to convert the polygon into a SketchUp component:

1. Triple-click on the first copy you made.

2. Create a component and label it `Man running_PR`.

3. Select **Always Face Camera**.

4. Select **Set Origin** and place the origin where the feet touch the ground, as shown in the following screenshot:

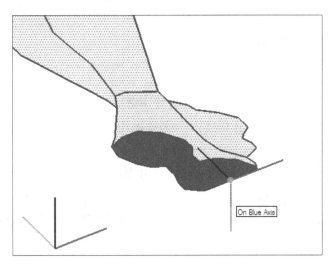

5. Place the **red axis** along the lower horizontal edge of the cutout and click.

6. Place the **green axis** perpendicular to the cutout plane, so that the blue axis lines up with the center of the person (see the preceding image).

7. Click on the **Create** button to create the component.

8. Right-click on the new component and select **Save As**.

9. Browse to your component library and save the new component as `Man running_PR.skp`.

10. Repeat the preceding steps with your second copy, but call it `Man running_NPR.skp`.

To switch between the versions, just right-click and select **Reload**, then select the _PR or _NPR version, and click on **Open**.

You made a component from the 2D cutout and told SketchUp where the axis should go to place the person upright into a scene. This means that when inserting the component in future, it will always appear with the middle of the feet placed at the cursor. Even more importantly, as a Face-Me component rotates to follow the camera, you've told SketchUp where the center of rotation in the component is. You have labeled your components with a suffix so that you can easily swap between them, depending on what output you plan to produce.

3D people and the uncanny valley

In human aesthetics, the "uncanny valley" refers to the negative emotional response that almost-human features can cause. It means that we sympathize more with an anthropomorphic, but a clearly mechanic "face", like that of the Pixar character Wall-E, than we do with an artificial face that tries too hard to imitate human features but is slightly off in details such as the hair or skin tone. Our brain is programmed to spot minute details in facial expressions and body language, and when our perception registers that something is off, it triggers an emotional warning.

In the field of computer graphics, this effect can be found quite frequently. A character in a video game may move "a bit stiff" or the hair on a 3D person model may look too compact to be real. Even in big movie productions, directors will more likely scan the face of an actor with a 3D scanner and motion tracking to get the expressions right, rather than relying on a completely computer-generated character.

For architectural visualization, this means that we have to be extra careful when using 3D entourage for people. Using 2D cutouts from photographs, you can create convincingly realistic people that look real, because they are real in the picture. You only need to choose photos that match the lighting conditions in the 3D scene, and it will be hard to see the difference. If you use 3D character models, you don't need to worry about the lighting, but everything else should be perfect or the only non-photoreal element in your rendering will be your people entourage.

A (cheap) alternative to super-realistic 3D models is an abstract representation of human figures in the image. A translucent silhouette can convey the sense of scale and proportions just as well as a 3D model, without the need for top-quality skin texture and clothing. Try this option to see if it fits your presentation style and your client's taste. If it doesn't work for your project, you can always replace the simple cutout with a whiz-bang 3D component.

Vegetation

We have already looked briefly at vegetation in *Chapter 3, Composing the Scene*, and talked about how important it is for the effectiveness of a visual. Hopefully, you have already included some great vegetation in your scene by cutting 2D billboards from photos. However, for some applications, especially when aiming for an animated output, you might need some other vegetation.

Non-photoreal sketchy trees

In non-photoreal scenes, cartoon-style trees look great. You can create these easily yourself by starting with a tree photo and tracing around it as you've just done with the person.

The following image is an example of a sketchy tree. Have a go at making one now from a photo. Then, follow the earlier steps to create a face-me component:

Want an automatic veggie maker?

RPTree Maker from Render Plus allows you to generate 2D trees from within SketchUp and place them into the model. It saves a PNG with alpha mask on a 2D face-me component. The alpha mask is a black–and–white image of the tree showing SketchUp, and other software, where to clip the image. You can download a free 30-day trial version of RPTree Maker from the Render Plus website (www.renderplus.com).

Vue from e-on software (www.e-onsoftware.com) has to be the top choice for computer-generated vegetation. The foliage engine within Vue creates an infinite variety of different random trees and shrubs at the click of a button. Depending on how much you spend, you can gain greater control over this, and even create your own species. For any outdoor scene with a large amount of foliage, it is well worth looking at Vue, as its render engine is built specifically for handling the massive polygon count created by lots of 3D vegetation. Vue is regularly used in movies to simulate forests and even entire ecosystems.

For Vue Version 10 and younger, there is also a SketchUp exporter plugin available. This simplifies the export of SketchUp scenes for rendering in Vue.

Vehicles

Many people are fascinated by cars, boats, and planes. So, there is always a large amount of hobbyists who have taken it upon themselves to model their favorite vehicle in SketchUp. These models end up in the 3D Warehouse, where even more enthusiasts modify them and upload them again. So, you should be OK finding any vehicles you may need. If you need a specific brand and model, you can use one of the commercial collections. As always, a quick Google search will get you started.

One problem with the 3D Warehouse models is that each author has his own style of modeling. If you need 30 different cars for a road scene and each of these has different materials and textures assigned to them, you're going to have a nightmare when you want to change and modify them. To avoid this, build yourself a library of good-quality models with a matching style. Sometimes, these are given away for free by some of the commercial model libraries. Alternatively, spend some time in SketchUp, reducing the unnecessary materials or polygons from the downloaded components.

Summary

In this chapter, you looked at the challenges and solutions for using entourage that will enhance and not detract from the visual appeal in your scenes.

Specifically, we covered where to find entourage and what to look for in high-quality entourage. We discussed when to choose 2D or 3D entourage for best effect and how to create your own high-quality 2D entourage, which will work for all types of image output. Finally, you learned to decide when to buy entourage, when to make your own, and when to scrounge around on the Internet for free stuff!

We also discussed at what stage in the workflow you should use entourage, and we came to the conclusion that in most cases, inserting stuff either in SketchUp or the rendering application is preferable to the postprocessing stage.

Now that you've learned enough to get your scene populated with entourage, you can get on to the real fun of creating the visualization images. This is the topic of the next chapter.

7
Non-photoreal Visuals with SketchUp

In architectural visualizations, non-photoreal images are images that maintain the characteristics of the processes that created them. A simple form is a 2D or 3D line drawn straight out of a CAD application. More advanced images use 2D graphic techniques to increase the realism of the scene, just like architects used to do in the past with their hand-drawn perspectives.

As the name suggests, SketchUp does sketchy styles extremely well. You can get pleasing visuals straight out of the box by hitting a few buttons, and you can take things further by exporting an image to an image processor such as GIMP. In this chapter, you will learn how to do both of these. In particular, you will learn:

- How to produce images in SketchUp's own sketchy styles
- How to create a watercolor style output (the *Dennis Technique*)
- How to simulate the effect of black-and-white pencil drawings

In the process, you will also learn about the tools that will help you experiment with your own styles. The Dennis Technique is illustrated in the following image by Dennis Nikolaev, to give you an idea of what is possible with the tools presented in this chapter.

SketchUp's native output

Let's get started immediately with some sketchy output. SketchUp has some fabulous built-in sketchy styles that you can always fall back on when you don't have the time or inclination to do anything more adventurous. Just because they're quick and easy to use doesn't mean they're not great. Other CAD software developers would kill to get automatic output this good.

Keep a settings diary

Often when you discover a great look in SketchUp, the perfect combination of styles, shadow, face, and background settings, you never remember how to recreate it the next time. So, why not keep a list at the back of your desk diary or even start a SketchUp notebook especially for this purpose?

All you need to know to get a great-looking sketchy output from SketchUp is how to access, and maybe modify, the built-in styles. These styles completely control how you view every aspect of what you see on screen:

- Background color or image
- Overlay or watermark

- Sky and ground
- Line thickness and texture
- Line jitter, extensions, and endpoints
- Face style and opacity

All these settings are covered in detail in the online help of SketchUp. You can access it by navigating to **Help | Knowledge Center**.

Editing SketchUp's built-in styles

For the purpose of this book on visualization, you're going to look at what you specifically need to know to create architectural presentation drawings. You can then experiment to find out the rest if you want to.

1. Make a start by opening any SketchUp model.
2. Go to **Window | Styles**. This opens the **Styles** pallet.
3. In the **Styles** pallet, go to **Assorted Styles | Brush Strokes on Canvas**.
4. The view of your model changes to reflect the style you selected.
5. To modify this style, for example, click on the **Wireframe Face Style** button, as shown in the following screenshot, or choose from the menu **View | Face Style | Wireframe**:

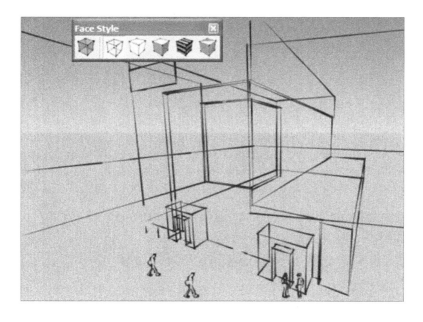

6. This only changes the view temporarily. Now, click on the **In Model** icon in the **Styles** pallet.

7. The style thumbnail in the top-left corner of the window is shown with a circular arrow to indicate that you changed the settings of the style. On Windows, you can also hover the cursor over the thumbnail to see a pop-up notice.

8. While you're watching it, click on the thumbnail to update the in-model style with the current style settings.

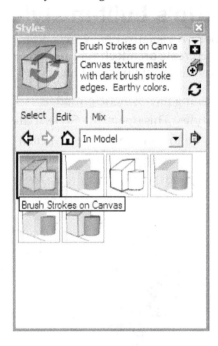

When you clicked on the thumbnail icon, your update to the style was saved in the model. However, don't worry; this won't affect the original style in the system style pallet that will be available in every new SketchUp file you create. If you do wish to save your new modified style for use in other models, you can do so as follows:

1. Right-click on the style icon in the **In Model** collection.

2. Select **Save As** from the context menu.

3. Pick a location and save the style as a *.style file.

Why is this important? Well, every scene has a style associated with it by default. So, when you change the drawing style in SketchUp and then create a new scene, it will always display your modified style. You can even use scenes to switch between drawing styles. You can also disable the option to save the style with the scene in the **Scenes** pallet.

However, all that is saved with the scene is the name of the style, not the actual settings. You have to update the style, as shown in the preceding steps, to apply any temporary changes to the style itself so that they can be recalled when you return to the scene.

Get some style!

So, why don't you experiment a bit with styles now? Start with a simple model you drew, or download one from the 3D Warehouse. Now, set up five scenes with different views and styles. Experiment with the settings in each of the scenes you've set up. Then, save your changes to a new style if you like the result. Feel free and experiment, because when you reload SketchUp, you will not have ruined any of the default styles.

Saving 2D images in SketchUp

Whenever you save a 2D image, I'd recommend that you create a scene tab. If you have one set up already, but you changed the shadows or view in any way and want to keep the changes for your output, right-click on the tab now and select **Update**. This means that if you need to save the image for this view again, you can use the scene to return to the exact same setup. The camera angle and other view settings will be restored whenever you click on the scene tab.

1. Maximize the SketchUp window (top-right corner of the window).

2. Set up your scene with styles, shadow settings, camera angle, and field of view (you learned about these in *Chapter 3*, *Composing the Scene*).

3. Go to **View** | **Animation** | **Add Scene**.

4. Go to the **Styles** pallet, click on **In Model**, and then click on **Update Style with Changes**.

5. Select the menu entry **File** | **Export** | **2D Graphic**.

If you have the Pro version of SketchUp, you will be able to export images in the following scalable CAD and Vector 2D file formats: AutoCAD (DXF, DWG); Portable Document Format (PDF) and; Encapsulated PostScript (EPS). Some of these are a must when working with CAD or illustration software.

6. Select **PNG** if you plan to work further on the image or don't want to lose detail; select **JPEG** if you need a low file size and don't plan to modify the image further.

7. Click on **Options** and set the **Width** to 3000 pixels. The vertical dimension will change automatically to match the aspect ratio of your main SketchUp window. On Mac, you have the option to set the image's **Height** independently, but not on Windows.

8. Click on **Anti-Alias** if you'd like softened edges. Usually, you will want this box ticked.

 Screen limitations to be aware of

As SketchUp exports what you see on screen, the size of the exported image depends on the shape of your SketchUp window. So, if your window is roughly a square, the image will come out roughly like a square when you export it. When you maximize your screen, it will come out roughly like the shape of your monitor. However, even then, it is affected by how many toolbars you have at the sides and top. In short, if you want an output with repeatable size, you need to keep your workspace setup consistent.

This is a basic overview of how to generate sketchy styled output from within SketchUp. However, as a pro architectural visualizer, you will need something more polished. In the rest of this chapter, you will find out how to combine several of SketchUp's styles within GIMP to give even better results. This process is known as a non-photoreal (NPR) visualization technique.

The Dennis Technique

The Dennis Technique is the quickest and most fun of all NPR techniques developed so far for SketchUp. The skills you'll learn here will allow you to experiment and develop your own particular preferred style or technique.

The method gained a huge following after the architect, Dennis Nikolaev, posted the following image for review in the gallery section of the SketchUp Pro user forum. To great clamor, he agreed to provide us with a run-through of his method, and having done this, he proceeded to mentor and encourage those of us who were trying to copy it. The Dennis Technique was born in a 400+ post thread!

It turns out that the big trick, or secret if you like, behind the Dennis Technique is speed. You need to be quick in everything you do: quick, rough mouse movements, quick decisions on whether you like what you see or want to erase it. The whole process should take no more than half an hour once you're used to it, and this lack of time investment will make you willing to be bold and use flourishes you wouldn't usually consider. "Getting it right" is not the idea here. In fact, it spoils it. You can see why by looking at this close-up of Dennis' original:

This close-up shows the roughness, which actually provides the desirability of the image. It is as if watercolor has been applied to a hand-drawn pen and ink drawing. Follow the steps here exactly so that you gain an idea of why each step is required. When you've done it like this once, you can add your own embellishments.

Setting up the Dennis Technique in SketchUp

The following picture shows a dwelling in SketchUp. I've taken this one from the 3D Warehouse. It might be easier for you to do the same rather than using your pride and joy project, simply because you'll be defacing it beyond recognition, and this can be quite upsetting! Choose a really simple model like this one.

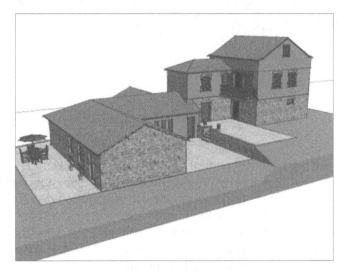

First, you will set up three scenes, which you will export to GIMP later. Each scene has its own style setting that describes the visual appearance. They are:

- Color Wash
- Lines and shadows
- Lines only

Before we start, maximize the window so that you keep the window size consistent between the image exports. Also, make sure not to move the camera between the scenes. Compose your scene if you have not done so already.

Creating the Color Wash image

The first scene and style to create is the Color Wash:

1. If you have selected any style other than the default one, go to the **Styles** pallet now and select the **Default Styles** collection.

2. Select the **Shaded with Textures** style.

3. In the **Styles** pallet, press the **Create new Style** button (the one with **+** in it) and call it `Color Wash`.

4. Go to the **Edge** section on the **Edit** tab and turn off the display of **Edges** and **Profiles**.

5. Still on the **Edit** tab, click on the **Background Settings** button.

6. Turn the **Sky** option off. Set the **Background** option to blue, and turn the **Ground** option on.

7. Click on the thumbnail image at the top-left corner of the style manager to update the style (Pro version only).

8. Turn shadows on and experiment with time and date settings until you like the result.

9. Go to **View | Animation | Add Scene**. This fixes the camera, style, and shadow settings of the new scene.

10. You may get a message like the following one. Click on **Save as new style** and hit **Update Scene**. SketchUp recognizes that you modified the style settings and makes you aware of the possible consequences. Saving a new style is a quick way to avoid any issues.

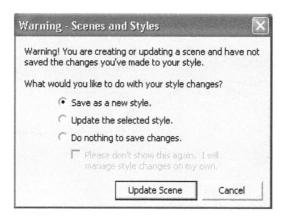

You should have something like the following screenshot: just colors and textures, but no lines. We'll call this the Color Wash scene.

Lines only

The next style we need is the opposite: no colors or shadows, only lines:

1. In the **Styles manager**, select a sketchy style with a white background. I've used the **Sketchy Charcoal** style here.

2. Make sure shadows are turned off.

3. Now, create a new scene tab. Call this `Lines Only`.

Lines and shadows

The final style that we need combines lines with a shaded view:

1. Turn shadows back on and create the final scene.

2. Call the scene `Lines and Shadows`.

3. You can mess around with some of the edge settings here if you like.

Optional selection layer

Optionally, you can now also create a flat colored image, which you will just use for masking and selecting areas of color in GIMP. Use the **Shadow Settings** dialog box with the settings shown here.

Uncheck the **Antialiasing** box in the image Save options when you export this image. This is useful when you get more advanced with GIMP, as you can select areas of color to work on. You might want to do this to simulate real watercolor, where you would apply one color at a time.

Exporting the scene tabs

You have just set up three scenes to save different style settings. It's now time to export these scenes to 2D images.

1. First, save your SketchUp model. This means you can come back to it and re-export the images if you need to.

2. Go to **File** | **Export** | **2D Graphic**.

3. Select **PNG** as the file format from the drop-down list.

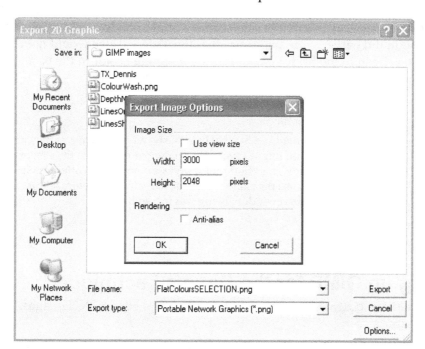

4. Click on the **Options** button.
5. Type 3000 into the **Width** field (see the preceding screenshot); the height will adjust automatically.
6. Click on **OK** to close the options window.
7. Type in a filename and click on **Save**.
8. Repeat the preceding steps for each of the three views you just set up. I suggest you use the filenames ColorWash, LinesShadows, and LinesOnly. Do not change the size of your SketchUp window to create images of equal size!

You now have the three views set up. They will be opened in the GIMP image editor. You should have this downloaded and installed already from *Chapter 2, Collecting a Toolset*. If you prefer, you can use Photoshop, but you have to translate the instructions to match the Photoshop tools. The fourth optional view is there just to help you select areas of color easily.

Setting up scenes (page tabs) first rather than just manually exporting views is important. This will allow you to come back and make changes to your model and re-export the images at exactly the same camera angle, shadow setting, and style setting as you did earlier. You made sure that the style settings would not change by clicking on **refresh** in the **Styles** pallet. Putting a flat blue color in the background allows you to select and replace the sky with an image in GIMP.

Keep the screen the same

Annoyingly, sometimes SketchUp exports images exactly as they are on screen. So, you might save a file, change or maximize the size of the SketchUp window, and find that it saves a completely different view. To combat this, use the same computer and always maximize the SketchUp program window before saving an image.

Now, on with Dennis' magic formula!

Setting up GIMP for the Dennis Technique

You should have ColorWash, LinesShadows, and LinesOnly PNG images, all of the same size.

1. Once you have opened GIMP, go to **File | Open**. Select the ColorWash image and click on **Open**.

2. If the **Layers** pallet is not visible already, open it now by navigating to **Window | Layers, Channels, Paths, Undo**.

3. The image now appears as the **Background** layer in GIMP.

4. Now, select **File | Open as Layers**.

5. Hold down *Ctrl*, select the other two images, and click on **Open**.

All three images will now be open in GIMP as layers. Your screen should look roughly like mine. If you need to rearrange your layers, you can click-and-drag them with the mouse.

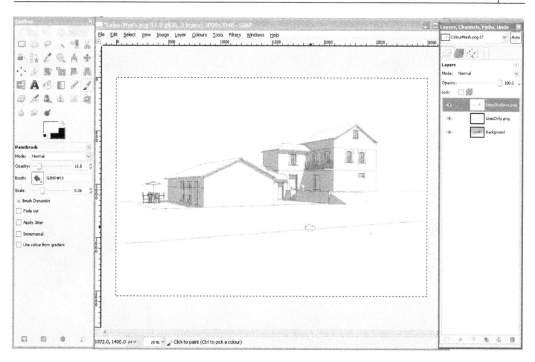

At first we will remove the blue colored background from the ColorWash image to make space for sky image:

1. Click on the **ColorWash** layer in the **Layers** pallet; then, click on the **Duplicate Layer** button at the bottom. This will create a copy of the **Background** layer.

2. Click on the eye icons for the other layers to hide them so that you can see the new layer.

3. Select this new layer by clicking on it in the **Layers** pallet.

4. Let's call this layer `ColorWash1.png`.

5. Right-click on the new layer and select **Add Alpha Channel**.

6. Select the **Fuzzy Select** tool (aka *Magic Wand*) from the main tools pallet and change the **Threshold** value to 1. Click anywhere inside the blue sky area to select it.

7. Hit *Delete*.

8. The sky is now transparent (checker board pattern) and ready for you to insert a sky image behind it. Go to **Select | None** to reset the selection area.

Now, you need to simulate the inaccurate random characteristics of paint and pen.

1. Go to **Filters | Distorts | Ripple**.

2. Alter the settings as shown in the following screenshot:

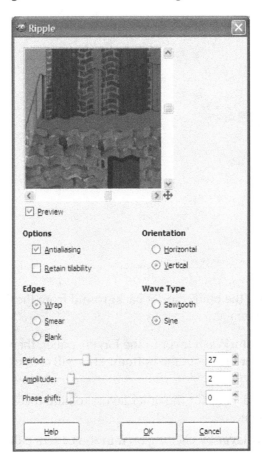

 If your image has repeating textures, these won't look too good. So, try using the **Oilify** filter instead of or in addition to the **Ripple** filter. All we are trying to do here is introduce some variation. You can experiment with many of the filters to achieve your own version of this effect.

3. Click on the LinesOnly layer and make it visible again.

4. Change the **Layer Mode** value of the LinesOnly layer to **Multiply**. You should now have something like this:

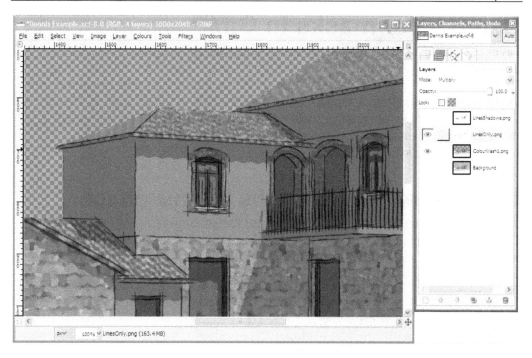

If you're new to GIMP, then please give yourself plenty of time to get used to it. You'll find it worth it in the end. So far, you have opened your images as layers in GIMP. Layers work like see-through sheets on an overhead projector or tracing paper if you prefer this analogy. We stack them on top of each other and mask bits out from each, so that the final image we get is a composite of all three. The layer stack you've got so far is shown here. The LinesOnly layer has been set to **Multiply**, which will project only the lines (dark pixels) onto the ColorWash layer below.

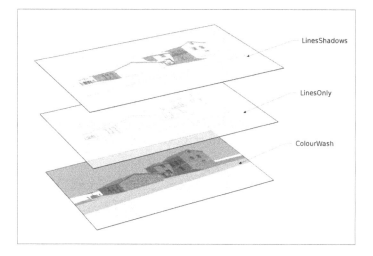

Using layer masks in GIMP

Layer masks are a key feature of pro image software and the main reason we're using GIMP. A layer mask is a black-and-white image associated with an image layer. Wherever you paint black on the layer mask, you will be able to see through the layer. Wherever there is white, you will not be able to see through it. This is a nondestructive way of creating "holes" in a layer, where the layer below will show through. There's some more information on using layer masks in *Chapter 9, Postproduction in GIMP.*

Using layer masks for the Dennis effect

You're going to use layer masks now to create "holes" in the LinesShadows layer. This will allow the painted area to show through from the layers below. You'll be able to see how it all works by performing the following steps. Don't worry! There is not much to it and you will get to grips with it really quickly.

1. Click on the eye icon on the LinesShadows layer to switch it back on.

2. Right-click on this layer and select **Add Layer Mask**.

3. Select **White: Full Opacity** and click on **Add**.

4. Select the mask (the white rectangle that has appeared beside the layer).

5. Click on the **Paintbrush** icon.

6. Select a large rough brush. Don't select anything too round or smooth. I like the **Galaxy, Big** brush that comes with GIMP.

7. Hold down *Ctrl* and use the scroll wheel of your mouse to zoom in a little on the center of the drawing.

8. Quickly and roughly, paint over the most important areas with full opacity. Wherever you paint (in black) on the mask layer, the color of the layers below it will show through the LinesShadows layer, because the black areas on the mask layer are converted to transparent areas of the image layer.

9. In the **Paintbrush** pallet, change the **Opacity** to around 50 percent.

10. Paint in some more areas.

11. Reduce it further to 20 percent and paint over any larger areas of color to simulate a watercolor wash effect. Go over some areas more than once to build up color.

Here's the image so far. It doesn't look great, but then it doesn't have to! You don't need a lot of skill for the Dennis Technique. That's why it's so popular.

In the following screenshot, you can see the rough brush strokes I've made to produce it. The black areas are the focal point where I used 100-percent opacity. In the various shades of gray you can see where I have used the 50-percent or 20-percent opacity brushes.

Now, I'm feeling the pain with you here. I'm just following the method as I write, so you're not getting a dressed-up version. I'm no artist either, just a CAD guy, maybe like you are. If I can do it, then you can do it, too.

You've been punching holes in the sketchy black-and-white top layer to allow the paint through from the layers below. Doing this quickly tends to give the best watercolor sketch effect that we're after. It also saves loads of time. Bear in mind that you're not actually deleting anything here. You can simply go back with a white brush on the mask layer and reinstate whatever you like, or neaten it up if that's what you want. We've also left lots of uncolored areas in there to give the pencil sketch feel. If in doubt, look at Dennis' originals earlier in the chapter.

Dennis Nikolaev's tutorial page

True to the generosity he showed back in 2005/2006 when he first showed us his "little graphic trick", Dennis has also set up a tutorial on sketchucation.com. You can find it at http://sketchucation.com/resources/tutorials/48-advanced/200-dennis-technique or search for Dennis Technique in the forum's search box.

Using a sky image in GIMP

The Web is full of stunning sky photos, and you have, no doubt, your own amazing holiday shots. Just grab the one you like, and follow these steps to insert it into your composition. Or why not just point your camera upwards on a sunny day?

1. In GIMP, go to **File** | **Open** and select the sky image.

2. This will open a new GIMP image window. Working in this has no effect on any other image you may be working on, although they share the same pallets and option windows.

3. Use **Image** | **Scale Image** to resize the sky to match your scene's images. It doesn't matter if you have to distort the sky a bit; it won't be visible in the end.

4. Go to **Filters | Artistic | Oilify** and increase **Mask size** and **Exponent** until you get an oil-paint effect similar to this:

5. Now go to **Select | Select All**.
6. Use **Edit | Copy** to copy the whole image into your clipboard.
7. Switch back to your Dennis window.
8. Just in case you're still editing a layer mask, click on any layer icon in the layer pallet to deselect the mask.
9. Now, select the menu **Edit | Paste**. The sky image will be copied into your composite image as a **Floating Selection (Pasted Layer)**.
10. Right-click on this floating selection and select **To New Layer** from the options to convert the floating selection to a proper image layer.
11. Change the name from **Pasted Layer** to Sky Image or similar.
12. Move the new layer just below the ColorWash1.png layer in the **Layer** pallet.
13. Select the bottom layer (**Background** or **ColorWash.png**), and use the **Fuzzy Select** tool to select the sky area again.

14. Go back to the top layer, click on the mask, and roughly paint in some sky as you did earlier. The selection you just made will limit all the brush strokes to the sky area so you won't be changing your existing building mask.

You inserted a sky image into the main scene and turned it into a layer. This was put just below the color wash layer, which had the sky deleted earlier. So, only the sky area shows through this layer. You then used the magic wand on the original sky area to create a selection to protect other areas of the image from changes.

Creating a vignette layer

The idea of the vignette layer goes back to the early days of photography when the artists would blur the edges of the image during the process of developing the print. As a composition tool, it helps you focus the eye into the image and take away edge distractions. The idea here is to start with a completely white mask and gradually reveal only the areas you really need to see. It's very minimalist, but that's what sketchy visuals are!

1. Create a new layer at the top of the stack and select **White** as the **Layer Fill Type**.

2. Create a layer mask as you did earlier.

3. With a large brush and opacity at 20 percent, just reveal the largest extent of what you need to see. Leave a good white border around the edges.

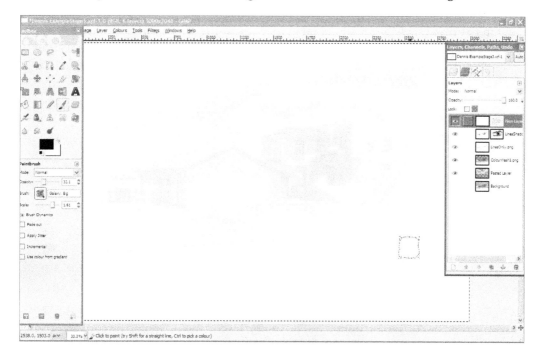

4. Go over the inner areas you want to highlight again.

5. With a 40-percent opacity brush, half the size of the first one, uncover some of the focal areas bit by bit—but be sparing.

6. Change your brush to a white one with full opacity, and paint out all the areas that are irrelevant or distracting.

Modifying the final composition with new SketchUp output

My final image is shown here. It's not great, mostly because the textures weren't great in the first place, but it is much better than before. Repeating mechanical textures, like the ones shown in the following image, look really fake in the Dennis Technique. I also don't feel the lines are sketchy enough, and I may have been too heavy-handed with the main colored area. So, what can I do about it? Lots!

Using layer masks has allowed you to apply lots of effects to the final image while not damaging the underlying layers. So, you can just go in and swap them with some better ones! You can also go back to any of the layer masks and reveal more or less of each layer, neatening things up as you feel the need. Nothing is ever lost.

Modifying the Dennis Technique

This can be challenging because it's open ended. However, you're up to it.
So experiment!

1. Go back to your SketchUp model and try out another sketchy-lines style. Choose a really scruffy one if you can find it, and modify some settings yourself, too.

2. Re-export this image as a **PNG** file to use as a new `LinesOnly` layer.

3. In GIMP, insert the layer as you did earlier, and move it next to the original one in the **Layer** pallet, but turn off the old layer using the eye icon. How does it look?

4. Now, change some colors and textures in SketchUp and export a new `ColorWash` image.

5. Replace the `ColorWash` layer with the new one and reapply the **Oilify** filter or **Ripple** filter if you want to.

6. Modify some of the layer masks, too, and see what you get.

7. Save the results of each change as an image and print them next to each other. Write notes next to each image so that you can get the effect again next time.

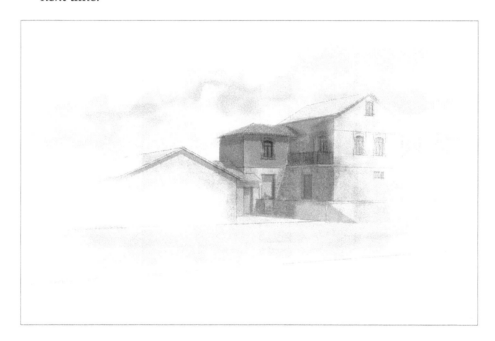

Here's my final image, and you can see the layer stack I ended up with in the following screenshot. Remember, only the layers with an eye next to them contributed to the final image. You can see the original LinesOnly and ColorWash layers, which I have switched off. Also, I went for a combination of two pencil styles in the end.

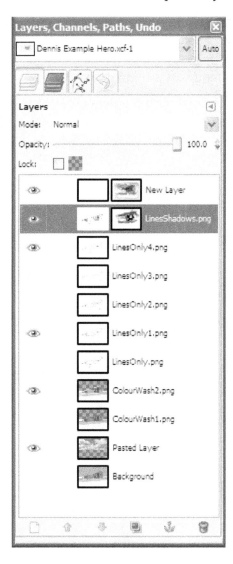

Richard's sketchy pencil technique

By now, you have probably learned all you need to know about creating non-photoreal artistic compositions using SketchUp and GIMP. All the skills are contained in the Dennis Technique you've just mastered. However, let's look at a pencil-only method that takes these techniques still a little further. This method relies just as little on artistic judgment and skill, because most of the pencil look is created automatically. It's developed from a technique that we named the *Richard Method* because of Richard Jeffrey who first proposed it on the original SketchUp forum during the Dennis thread. Here is Richard's wonderful pencil image:

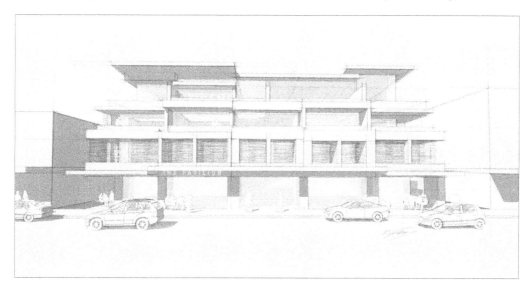

Setting up the Pencil Sketch Technique in SketchUp

To prepare for the Pencil Sketch Technique, you have to create scenes and styles in SketchUp corresponding to the following images. They can be based on any black-and-white sketchy line style from the **Styles** pallet.

All the settings listed below can be modified via the **Edit** tab on the **Styles** pallet:

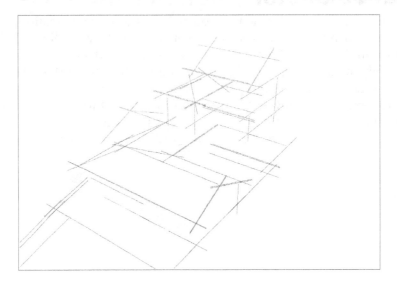

The **Heavy Construction Lines** style consists of the following:

- Large line extensions
- Low detail slider
- No shadows

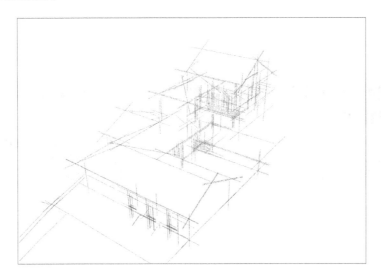

The **Light Construction Lines** style, similar to **Heavy Construction Lines** but with some exceptions:

- Higher detail slider
- No shadows

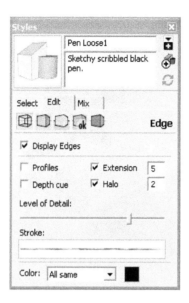

These first two styles are created using the **Level of Detail** slider with high values for the **Extension** option, as you can see in the preceding screenshot.

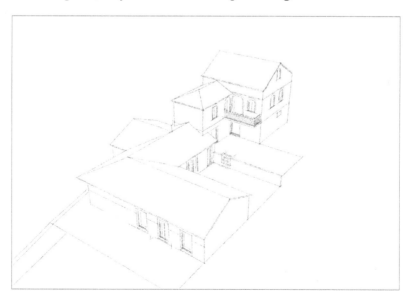

The **Outline** style:

- Use an unmodified sketchy-lines style
- No shadows

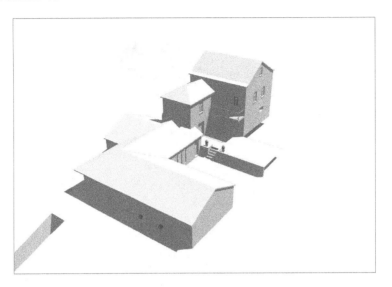

The **Pencil Shading** style:

- Select the monochrome face style
- Shadows on
- Turn edges off

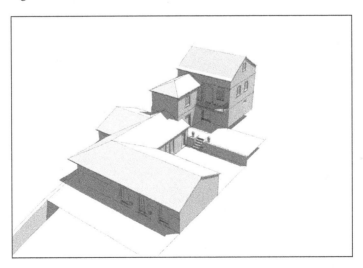

Finally, the **Dirty Hands** style:

- Same as the previous style
- Except with sketchy edges switched on

Setting up the Pencil Sketch Technique in GIMP

Now that you have set up all the styles, it's time to export the images as you did earlier. Then, switch to GIMP and continue with the following steps:

1. Open all images as layers in GIMP as you did with the Dennis Technique.
2. Select the layer with light construction lines.
3. Go to **Layer | Transform | Offset**.
4. Move the layer slightly by a few pixels (see the following screenshot) to give the lines a construction-line feel.

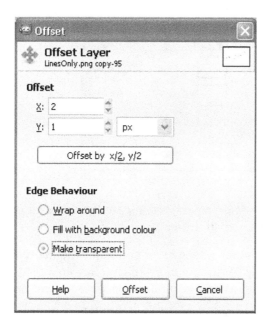

5. Alternatively, you can use **Filters | Distorts | Lense Distortion** on this layer.

6. Arrange the layers, and change the mode and opacity as shown in the following screenshot:

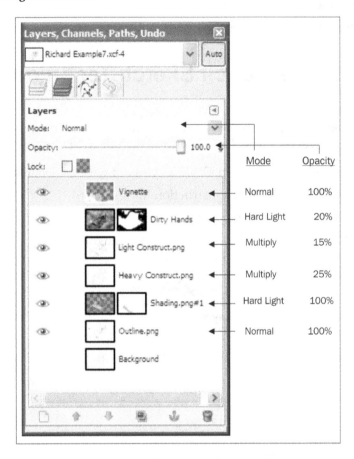

In this layer stack, you set up layers to simulate the different pencil marks you would expect to see in a pencil drawing:

- The Light Construct.png layer simulates the many faint construction lines done at the beginning of a sketch. They are offset or distorted slightly to give the idea that they were drawn over a second time

- The Heavy Construct.png layer is the same, but has fewer lines and a heavier line weight (opacity)

Creating pencil shading in GIMP

We will now be working on the **outline**, **pencil shading**, and **Dirty Hands** layers to create the final image. So, let's get started on these.

1. Select the **pencil shading** layer (`shading.png`).

2. Select the **Select by Color** tool from the main tools pallet.

3. Set the **Threshold** option to 1.

4. Go to **Filters | Blur | Motion blur**.

5. Set the **Length** to 10-20 and **Angle** to however you like it to simulate the direction of your pencil strokes.

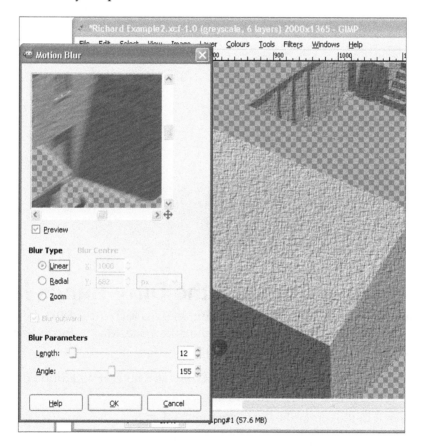

The content of the layer is blurred in the direction you specified.

6. Select the layer in the **Layers** pallet. Select the **move** tool and move it back approximately within the sketchy lines (use the arrow keys for small steps).

7. Select **Colors | Brightness-Contrast**; then, increase the brightness and contrast a little until it looks like pencil shading.

8. Set the **Layer Mode** to **Hard light** or **Grain extract** as preferred.

9. Now, mask out any areas where you don't want this shading to be, like you did in the Dennis method. You can see me doing this here to take away the shading from the windows:

Adding some grunge – the Dirty Hands layer

Just as the Dennis technique had a magic step, so does Richard's. The following might not seem like much, but it makes all the difference. Master this, and no one will be able to tell that it's not genuinely hand drawn.

1. Import your **Dirty Hands** image in GIMP as a layer if you didn't do it with the other images.

2. Move it to the top of the layer stack and select it.

3. Go to **Filters | Render | Clouds | Difference Clouds**.

4. Use the default settings and click on **OK**.

5. Go to **Filters | Noise | RGB noise**.

6. Leave the settings at the default values and click on **OK**.

7. Roughly, mask and erase anywhere you don't want any smudging. You can see this in the following screenshot (all the hatched areas are masked/erased).

8. Set the layer opacity to 15-20.

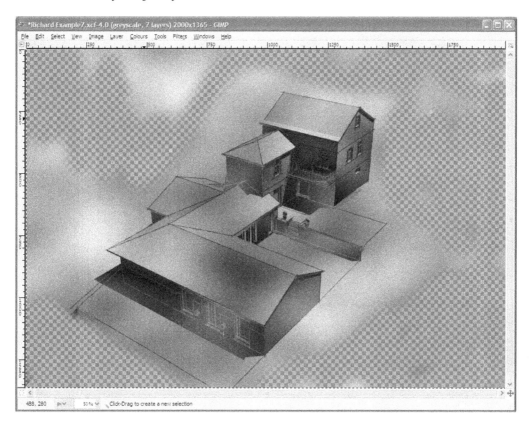

Finishing touches

Your image is almost complete. The following final steps will add some filtering to enhance the appearance of the paper-drawn sketch:

1. As with the Dennis Technique, add a vignette layer to finish the composition.

2. Save a copy in GIMP's xcf format to allow you to edit it further some other time if desired. This format retains all the layers and masks.

3. Choose **Image | Flatten Image**. This will remove the layers and masks, and you are left with an image with a single layer.

4. Use **Filters | Artistic | Apply Canvas** to create a paper-grain effect.

5. Choose a depth setting to suit your taste. You can see here how the paper-grain effect shows the smudged graphite just like when you do it by hand.

6. Save this final image as a PNG file. Here's the completed image:

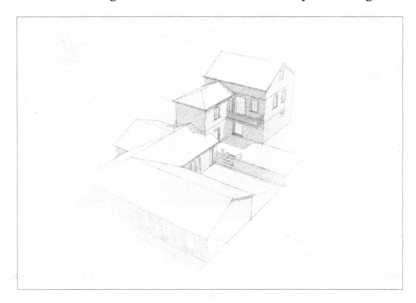

Summary

In this chapter, you have learned all the basics you need to create artistic visual styles using GIMP. You have learned how to use layers to build up a composite image from SketchUp output and how to use filters to modify SketchUp's native styles. You created and edited layer masks to avoid erasing original image data. You finally used the Dennis Technique to produce fast sketchy watercolor art and the Richard Technique to create eerily realistic pencil art.

These methods will become the staple of your visual output, simply because they're quick and easy to achieve, yet the client can be seriously impressed with it. These styles are sketchy and loose, ideally suited for presenting early design concepts. In the next chapter, you can take your designs further and produce photorealistic visuals.

8
Photorealistic Rendering

In this chapter, you will learn how to render photorealistic architectural visuals with SketchUp and Thea Render. You will already be familiar with the basic process from *Chapter 1, Quick Start Tutorial*. This chapter goes into a little more detail, giving you the why, as well as the how. This is what we are going to cover in the chapter:

- Why you should learn and use an external renderer
- What to expect from photorealistic renderings
- How to use the Thea for SketchUp plugin
- How to insert high-quality 3D entourage into your SketchUp model
- How to assign photorealistic materials and advanced lighting
- How to create renderings with multiple channels for postprocessing

Why use an external renderer?

If you have followed the chapters in this book so far and also did some exercises on your own, you should by now be fairly comfortable with producing artistic and convincing presentations. So, you may ask yourself why you should spend time and money on learning another rendering program that just shows the same thing that SketchUp does.

There are several features that an external renderer (also called a render engine) can add to SketchUp. Here is a short overview of computer graphic technologies and terms to help you understand the workflows you are about to learn. Perhaps, you already know about the points discussed in the following sections and just cannot put a name to the various features. In this case, this Computer Graphics Primer is a small aid to help you talk the talk.

Geometry

One simple improvement is that pure render engines do offer a much higher limit for polygons in a scene than an interactive editor such as SketchUp can handle. Therefore, your final image can contain geometry with a much higher level of detail than the SketchUp scene you are editing. At the end of this chapter, we will introduce proxy components, a way to use simplified components as a placeholder for detailed library objects.

Materials

In SketchUp, a material is a combination of color, texture, and transparency. The simplest materials only use the color information, and this is often enough for illustrations or conceptual drawings. If you want to make objects look realistic, you need to add a few more properties that physical materials have. Photorealistic renderers, therefore, have more options to define materials and even special material types such as opaque and transparent materials.

Most common are the specularity and roughness settings. **Specularity** defines the amount to which highlights from light sources are reflected off a surface. A highly specular material will show strong highlights along the edges and where a light source is mirrored on a flat surface. **Roughness** characterizes the shape of these highlights: Little or no roughness will give the highlights a sharp edge. With increasing roughness, the boundaries of the highlights will become more and more blurred.

You have already seen how much the appearance of an object in SketchUp can improve by applying an image texture. With Thea, you can reuse the textures you have applied in SketchUp and have them transferred identically into the Thea rendering. In fact, you need to apply a texture in SketchUp to define the texture coordinates that Thea relies on for the mapping. With these coordinates in place, you can use other texture-based effects to improve the appearance of the object.

We already mentioned the term **bump mapping**. This is a method to give a 3D surface additional depth and detail by modifying the surface characteristics based on an image. It is frequently used to simulate small surface irregularities on a smooth surface such as the bumps of an orange skin or in a close-up of a plastered wall. For more complex patterns, often the same image as the one used in the image map is used for the bump map. The end effect is that a brick wall will look as if there were real grooves between the bricks. In the following screenshot, you can see a flat texture without bump mapping (in the left-hand side) and the same material rendered with a strong bump mapping enabled (in the middle):

Bump mapping is only the illusion of structure on a flat surface. To create real geometric details based on images, a technique called **Displacement Mapping (DM)** is used. With DM, the renderer will subdivide a surface into tiny elements and then move these up and down a bit based on the image texture. This creates real 3D details without the need to model them in SketchUp. You can see an example of displacement mapping on the right-hand side in the preceding image. Note the displacement at the edge of the surface. Also note that even the surface of the bricks is a bit displaced, which causes ragged shadow lines.

Unfortunately, displacement mapping is also very resource intensive to render. Use it selectively in your scene and only for surfaces that are close-up, where you will be able to see the additional level of detail.

The options mentioned earlier are standard in advanced render engines these days and can be applied to opaque materials. A more recent addition is **subsurface scattering (SSS)**, which simulates the light scatter close to the surface of translucent objects. It is important for a realistic impression of marble or wax, for example. Another physical effect of transparent objects is light refraction or **caustics**. A rippled water surface or a ball made of solid glass will cause light passing through it to refract and create lighting patterns on the floor.

To account for these phenomena, a sophisticated render engine will provide dedicated types of material for transparent and translucent objects. These will have more options than the basic opaque type and allow you to control the optical effects in the image. To learn more about these properties, consult the manual for your render application and visit the material-specific online forums.

Lighting

SketchUp is also very limited in the lighting settings. You can set the time of day for shadow calculations, but this does not influence the brightness of the scene or produce realistic penumbras. To overcome these limits, advanced renderers use a number of algorithms, which are collectively known as **global illumination (GI)**. To calculate the lighting, these algorithms consider not only the light directly received from light sources, but also the quantity that is reflected off other objects.

Daylight

Natural lighting is especially important for architectural visualization, because most of the objects will be displayed under daylight. A good **physical sky model** is necessary to create the right impression of morning or evening light. Renderers that have SketchUp plugins typically use the information about the daylight setup that you define in the shadow settings. So, you will get the same sun position and shadows in your final rendering as in your SketchUp preview.

An alternative method to create a naturally lit environment is **image-based lighting (IBL)**. This technique is used in the movie industry to capture the lighting environment of a scene to match it later in computer-generated images. The lighting is saved in a panoramic **high dynamic range (HDR)** image. When this image is used as a texture for a sky dome, it recreates the lighting environment that was present when the image was captured.

 To learn more about HDR images (including how to take your own), visit http://hdrlabs.com/news/index.php. In their **Galleries** section, you can also find a nice selection of HDR images for testing.

Artificial lighting

An option to create artificial light sources for architectural lighting is also not available in SketchUp. Commonly used are point lights with an omnidirectional distribution and spotlights that limit their output to an opening angle. Both types are usually only logical points in space and are not represented by any geometry. To work with them in SketchUp, some kind of placeholder geometry is necessary.

Large luminous surfaces, such as a fluorescent tube, can be created with an area light type or a special emitter material property that can be applied to a surface. For light fittings with complex light distribution, some renderers have the option to apply an **IES file** to a light source. IES is short for IESNA LM-63, a file format defined by the Illumination Engineering Society to represent the distribution of physical light fittings in lighting analysis and rendering applications. In exterior scenes, a few well-placed point lights and spotlights can achieve a big effect. The appearance of interiors can benefit from the added accuracy provided by IES distribution files.

[More information on IES files is available at
www.helios32.com/resources.htm#Formats.]

Advanced features

In addition to the ones mentioned earlier, professional rendering applications will provide a number of other features that are useful for a productive workflow and data interchange with other applications. An important aspect is the preservation of additional image information from the rendering process. Commonly used in postprocessing are **depth** and **transparency** information. Both can be saved and exported as a grayscale image and hence, transferred into an image-editing application.

You can see that there is much to be gained from using an external rendering engine, and the results are well worth the effort to follow the rest of this chapter.

Setting up for photoreal rendering

After this overview of computer graphic technologies, it is now time to look at the Thea user interface before we start exploring the features in a test scene. For this chapter, you need *Thea Render* and the *Thea for SketchUp* plugin installed (the free demo version will do for testing). As a licensed user you can also download sample materials from the **Resources** section of the website (http://www.thearender.com/) and have access to the **Materials & Texture** forum where other users exchange and discuss their own materials. Check the download and installation instructions in *Chapter 2, Collecting a Toolset*, if you don't have it already on your system.

Rendering process

The following are the steps of the SketchUp and Thea rendering process.
This process will work for other renderers, too, and is a good way of structuring your workflow, because you achieve great results in little time. For example, why find out a material hasn't mapped at the right scale only after an hour-long render? With the following process, you will find that out in a few minutes with a quick test render.

- Step 1: Preparing the SketchUp model
- Step 2: Performing an initial test render
- Step 3: Assigning materials
- Step 4: Defining lighting
- Step 5: Inserting extra entourage
- Step 6: Production rendering
- Step 7: Postproduction rendering

We are going to look at each of these steps in detail using a small test room and an atrium scene. The test room is a variation of the famous *Cornell Box*, a well-established test setup to evaluate rendering algorithms. You can also use any scene that you have set up yourself in SketchUp.

Thea for SketchUp interface

The main interface for working with Thea in SketchUp is the Thea for SketchUp plugin. The plugin gives you access to all features that are necessary to set up and render a scene out of SketchUp. This is beneficial for a quick workflow, because you don't have to switch between SketchUp and the Thea Studio application during the setup of your scene.

The Thea plugin is accessible by navigating to **Plugins | Thea Render**. It is split into two main windows: the **Thea Tool** window and the **Thea Rendering Window**. There is also a toolbar with two buttons to enable each of these windows.

The Thea Tool window

We will use the buttons and controls of the tool window to set up the camera options and add materials and other elements that will be specially treated during the export (such as lights). The window is structured in four panels (or tabs) that you can see in the following image:

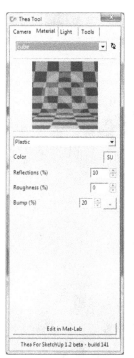

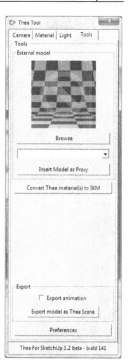

When the **Thea Tool** is active, you will also see a red frame displayed in the SketchUp 3D window that shows the field of view for the current Thea camera. This either frames the area that will be rendered or indicates that the camera view is wider than the SketchUp window via arrows to the left and right.

You will also notice that the SketchUp cursor changes when you have the **Thea Tool** window open. Depending on the current tool in use, there are a number of different cursor shapes. The default is a small cross and is used to select SketchUp materials for the material assignment.

The Thea Rendering Window

The main window is the place where you can set up, control, and view the rendering process itself. The window has a large area at the top where the rendered image is displayed. Below is a row of buttons to save and refresh rendered images and to start, pause, and stop the current render.

You can see a screenshot of the rendering window with an open scene in the following image:

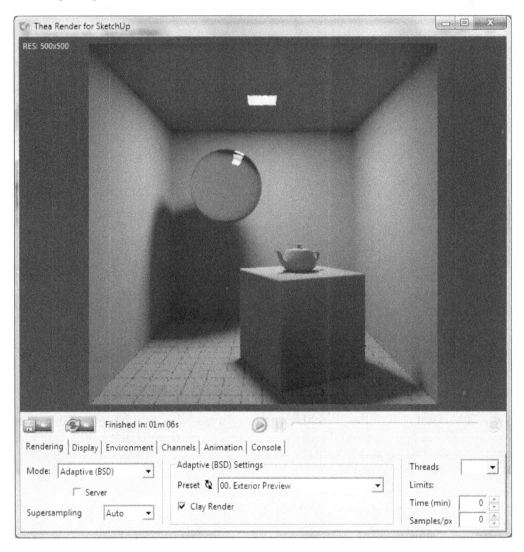

At the bottom of the window, you will find the control elements for the rendering and display of images and the advanced scene options. This section is organized in tabs, and we will discuss the contents of the relevant tabs in the following sections.

Step 1 – Preparing the SketchUp model

To follow the steps in the book, you can download the `Cornell Box` SketchUp file from `www.packtpub.com/support`. In this demo scene, the model is already prepared for 3D rendering, and there are scenes set up to follow the steps below. If you imported our test box from the 3D Warehouse (search for *Cornell Box*) or used your own SketchUp model, you should do some preparations before you can start rendering:

1. Create a copy of your SketchUp file just for rendering. You will create new scenes and content dedicated to the rendering process, and you can save all this in a dedicated SketchUp file.

2. Remove unused content. Check the model for hidden geometry, unused and obsolete scene tabs and layers, and especially materials. Purge the material list.

3. Identify the important materials in the scene, especially those that are used for windows and nearby large objects.

4. Double-check the orientation of surfaces that you want to convert to emitting surfaces or to which you want to apply a displacement map.

5. Create and save important camera viewpoints in scene tabs.

Step 2 – Performing an initial test render

You are now going to do a test render to see how the model looks like when rendered in another renderer. You can use this first test to identify areas that need more modeling or parts where you should add textures to make them more interesting.

1. In SketchUp, select the view you want to render. If you use the Cornell scene from the Packt Publishing website, select the **Step 2** scene . If you imported the Cornell box from the 3D Warehouse, select one side of the box and hide it so that you can see the objects inside.

2. Open the **Thea Tool** window by navigating to **Plugins | Thea Render | Thea Tool**.

3. Check that the **resolution** on the camera tab is set to **800 x 600** pixels, and the **aspect ratio** is set to **4:3**. These are the defaults.

4. Open the Thea render window by navigating to **Plugins | Thea Render | Thea Rendering Window**.

5. In the settings area of the Thea window, select **Adaptive (BSD)** as the render mode. Then, check that the **Preset** selection is set to **00. Exterior Preview**.

6. Click on the Start button.

Your scene will render, and you should see the progress in the image area of the window. The rendering should complete in less than a minute (depending on your computer performance, of course). The final image will look something like the following image:

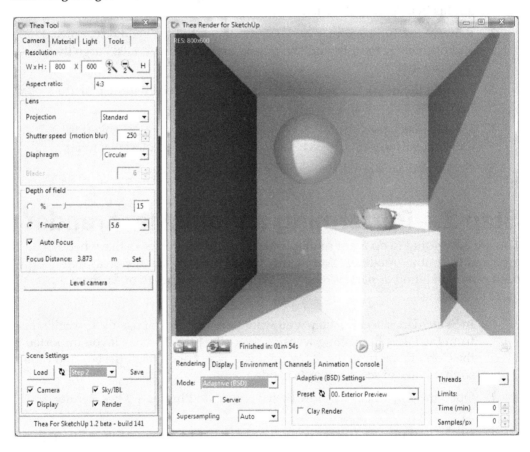

Review the rendered image, and pay attention to the following aspects:

- Check that all the textures are in place correctly. Make a note of where the textures are missing or distorted. (Note that there are no textures in our scene yet.)

- Look out for the quality of the geometry details, especially on rounded corners and smooth surfaces such as the teapot and sphere in our scene.

- Search for areas in the image that look unnaturally "empty". You should consider adding further geometry or a surface texture to make these areas more visually interesting.

- Also, look at the distribution of the objects in your scene. Remember that this is a 2D representation of your room that should look well balanced without the knowledge of the 3D model behind it.

If you have found any issues with your scene, you should now go back into SketchUp and make some corrections. This is the *export-check* loop, which you may have to repeat a few times. The more you get used to SketchUp and your rendering application, the less you will need to do this. However, for now, there is a lot to learn by performing this exercise, so the time is well spent.

Common import bugs and how to rectify them

The most common import bugs will be seen here at this first stage. Textures do not always scale or map correctly. This is the case with many rendering apps. The following table shows some common problems, likely causes of the problem, and how to deal with them:

Problem	Usually happens when...	Solution
Textures appear skewed or incorrectly scaled in a few isolated places.	You've stretched photos over a surface using the texture features in SketchUp.	In SketchUp, select the face, then right-click on the face and select **Make Unique Texture**.
The image is completely dark.	You may not have exported the sun from SketchUp, and there are no other lights in the scene.	In SketchUp, ensure that the **Shadows** setting is on. In the **Environment** tab in the Thea main window, verify that **Use Sun** and **Use Sky** are both checked.
The scene renders completely blank.	There may be a face in the way of the camera that didn't show up in the SketchUp view.	In SketchUp, remove or hide the face that could be in the way, or change the view just for the test render.

Clay rendering

Our small test scene does not offer much variety and detail that you need to look out for. Check out the following image for a test rendering of a fully modeled building. This scene was the winning entry for the *SketchUp Design Your Dwelling* competition in 2012 by Drew Wilgus. It has been downloaded from the 3D Warehouse, and no further modifications have been done for the render. You can get it by searching for Crissy Airfield House in the 3D Warehouse.

The image is a composite of a normal rendering (on the left-hand side) and a clay render (on the right-hand side). This is a special render setting where all material colors are ignored, and you can see only the 3D geometry. This helps you check your lighting setup, identify the detailing of the model and to decide if you need to add more of it or can do the rest with textures.

You just exported your 3D scene from SketchUp, imported it into Thea, and created an image from the scene—all with one click. It came in with the light set up exactly as it was in SketchUp. You performed a test render with basic settings and small image size to show up the errors in texture import and the overall appearance of the scene. These settings ensured fast render times for a quick evaluation of what we need to see.

You will have noticed that the lighting in our Cornell box scene is not great, and most of the scene is in shadow. This is because we used a daylight environment to render our scene, which is essentially an interior room. We will correct this in the next step when we assign Thea materials to the surfaces.

Step 3 – Assigning materials

You have seen earlier that Thea will use and import SketchUp colors and texture images in the test renders. Luckily, most outdoor materials have a matte appearance that can be well represented with the default material properties. So, all you need to do to achieve a realistic rendering is to tweak the materials that are already set up from SketchUp.

For indoor scenes, you will want to replace most of the materials with special optical characteristics that are not available in SketchUp. These are:

- **Transparent Materials**: These include windows, solid glass objects, and clear liquids. Windows and water surfaces are the most common in architectural renderings.

- **Translucent Materials**: These include frosted glass and some natural stone such as marble. They also include thin fabrics and liquids such as milk. You will find these materials mostly in interior scenes.

- **Polished Metals**: These include chrome, gold, silver, stainless steel, copper and so on. Metals do reflect light in a different way due to their surface structure, so we need a special material class for them.

- **Specular materials**: These include many types of shiny or glossy plastic, materials with coatings, and lacquered and varnished surfaces.

- **Light emitting objects**: These special type is used to represent bright and illuminated objects like a pendent light or a TV screen.

Thea has presets for the above material types, so assigning a suitable advanced material is straightforward in most cases.

Applying predefined materials

You have already set up your scene with some lighting, SketchUp colors, and texturing. It is now time to make the best of Thea's material libraries in your scene. Let's have a go at this using a metallic material for the teapot.

1. Make sure the **Thea Tool** window is open. You should see the frame indicating the camera window in your SketchUp window.

2. Click on the **Material** tab in the **Thea Tool** window.

3. Note that the cursor has changed to a crosshair with the Thea logo attached to it (unfortunately, this has not been shown in our screenshots).

4. Click on the teapot (just a single click!).

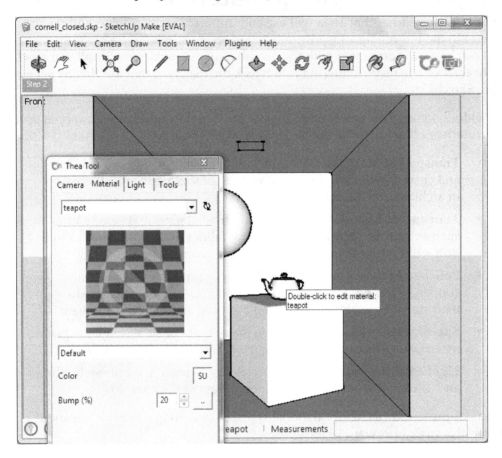

5. See how the drop-down menu in the **Material** tab has changed to display the **teapot** material. At the moment, the preview window is empty, and the material type selector below is set to **Default**.

6. Change the material type to **Colored Metal**.

7. At the bottom of the panel, click on the **Edit in Mat-Lab** button. The **Thea Material Lab** window opens. You can see the appearance of the material in the **Preview** panel. This is a combination of the basic colored metal and the color you gave the object in SketchUp.

8. If you want to change the material and use a predefined material from the Thea library, use the browser on the left-hand side to locate a suitable material. We will use the standard material **Metals | Copper Deco**.

9. Just drag the material icon of your choice from the browser into the preview window. The preview will update to show a view of the selected material.

10. Finally, click on the icon called **Accept** on the left-hand side of the window to apply the Thea material to the SketchUp material. This change will apply to all objects that use the same material in the scene.

11. The **Material Lab** window closes, and you can see the preview image in the **Thea Tool** window now.

You can go through the other materials like this. Keep in mind that complex materials with displacement mapping and so on will increase the render time. To check how your scene is getting along, do a quick test render as explained in step 2. We assume that the walls of our box are standard rough materials, so there is no need to refine these. To complete our settings, we just assign the **Thick Glass** type to the material **sphere** and the **Plastic type** to the material **cube**. Feel free to adjust the **Reflectivity** of the plastic material to give it a bit more sparkle.

When exporting plain colored materials from SketchUp, texturing coordinates (also called UV-coordinates) are not exported. So, when you come to map a new material onto this color, the texture scale will be wrong. To solve this, apply a texture-based material in SketchUp (any will do, as long as it uses a texture image rather than a simple color) before you apply the textured material in Thea.

Light-emitting materials

So far, we are still using the sun to illuminate your scene through a missing wall. What we need is a light source, and Thea's Emitter material can provide just that.

1. Select the **area light** material (either via the drop-down or by clicking on the small square at the ceiling in the SketchUp scene).

2. Select the **Emitter** material type.

3. The options for the **Emitter** material type will show in the lower half of the window.

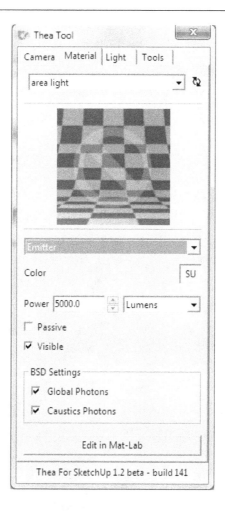

4. Set the **Power** setting to **5000.0** and **Lumens**. This is a very crude approximation for the light output you can get from a ceiling light like ours.

5. The other options can keep their default value. Just make sure that the **Passive** option remains unchecked or the emitter will not illuminate our scene. Also, keep the **Visible** option checked for this scene.

We have now placed a light source in our scene to illuminate the objects from the ceiling. Let's adjust our render settings to make use of this new light.

1. In the Thea Main window, select the **Environment** tab.

2. In the **Environment** section, disable **Use Sun** and **Use Sky**.

3. Switch to the **Rendering** tab, and set the render **presets** to **10. Interior Preview**.

4. Start the render again. When the render is finished, you will see a dark image with only the ceiling light clearly visible.

5. Switch to the **Display** tab.

6. Adjust the settings to the following values:

    ° **ISO**: 1600

    ° **Shutter**: 60

    ° **f-number**: 2.8

The objects should now be clearly visible again. If you used a different scene, you may have to adjust the values until your image is bright enough to see.

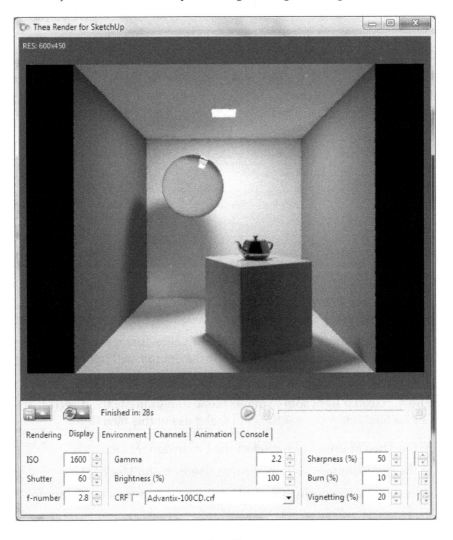

One-sided materials

If you look closely at the image and the reflection in the teapot, you will find that there is still a black hole where the front wall of the box should be. Remember that we hid the wall to be able to look into the cube. To solve this issue, you can make materials invisible from one side to look through a wall while it is still present in the scene.

1. Select the **Step 3** scene in the SketchUp example file for this chapter (only if you downloaded it from www.packtpub.com/support). This will unhide the missing wall and set up a section plane so that you can look into the scene.

2. Select the **front** material in the **Thea Tool** window. This is applied to the inside of the camera-facing wall of the box. We can use the **Default** material like we did for the other walls, so there is no need to select another type.

3. Click on the **Edit in Mat-Lab** button.

4. In the **Material Lab** window, select the **General** icon in the panel below the **Preview** panel. In the panel at the bottom of the stack, you will now see the **General** options of the material, as shown in the following screenshot:

5. Uncheck the **Two-Sided** option.

6. Click on **Accept** to accept the changes to the material and return to SketchUp.

Importing Thea materials to SketchUp

You may have noticed during your tests that Thea materials that rely on textures do not apply with the right scale to surfaces that do not have a texture on them in SketchUp. This is because the necessary UV-texture coordinates are missing on the surface. UV coordinates are used to map a bitmap image onto a 3D surface. To create these, you need to apply a textured material in SketchUp. You could choose any material and just replace it with the Thea material, but this would not give you a correct preview of the scale and rotation of the texture in SketchUp.

To generate a suitable textured material in SketchUp, you can import materials from Thea.

1. In the **Thea Tool** window, select the **Tools** tab.

2. Press the **Convert Thea material(s) to SKM** button.

3. A file browser will open in the Thea **Materials** data folder. Browse to the material you want to convert. We will use the `Materials/Floors and Tiles/Ceramic Tiles Lime.mat.thea` file.

4. Click on the **Open** button, and a new file browser will open up, asking you for the directory to save the converted material as a SketchUp `*.skm` file. You only need to give the directory path, as the filename will be taken from the `*.mat.thea` file.

5. Choose the folder and confirm with the **Select Folder** button.
    A new SketchUp material will be created.

6. Apply the new material to a surface.

7. Adjust the scale and orientation of the material by right-clicking and selecting **Texture | Position**.

SketchUp textures have a default size. High-resolution texture images, such as those available at `www.thearender.com`, will need to be scaled in SketchUp to have the correct size. On the other side, you don't have to manually assign a Thea material, because the correct material will be selected based on the material's name.

With a translated material applied to the floor, your rendering should now look like the following image:

Summary on materials

For most outdoor scenes, the only materials you will need to change are the windows, water, and metals. The rest of the time, the colors and textures you set up in SketchUp will render fine just as they are. This is because most outdoor materials are matt, not shiny or reflective.

This is just about all you need to know to get great-looking architectural visualizations using SketchUp with Thea. You will use Thea (or any external renderer) simply to create more realistic light, shadows, and reflections, where SketchUp can't do this. If you have started from the beginning of the book and worked through, you have now learned 90 percent of what you need to create great photoreal renders.

Step 4 – Defining lighting

In this step, we will introduce light sources into the scene to create a pleasing and balanced lighting environment for the space.

Preparing the test scene

To have a larger space to play with, we will use an atrium scene for this setup. Again, you can download the SketchUp file from the book's website or search for *ACME Gold* in the 3D Warehouse.

1. Start SketchUp with an empty scene and delete the default 2D person.

2. Import the *ACME Gold* atrium building from the 3D Warehouse and place it at the origin.

3. Rotate the building by 90 degrees counterclockwise to align it with the *y* axis and have the glazed atrium point towards North. This will give us better shadows for daytime studies.

4. Place the camera inside on the second floor level. Use the western corridor because the eastern side is more detailed.

5. Remove the blue tint from the SketchUp material for the atrium windows and set the Thea material to **Thin Glass** in the **Thea Tool** window.

6. Feel free to apply Thea materials to the materials used in this scene. You should also create a new material to separate the material for the glass balustrades from the window material.

7. You should set the geolocation on your scene to somewhere on the northern hemisphere, where you can get low sun angles during winter and high sun angles during summer. (We will use the location Halle in Germany to prepare for our IBL section, later in this chapter. You can see the setup so far in the following screenshot.)

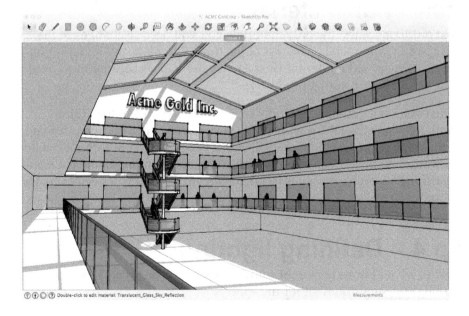

Using daylight

The easy-to-use light sources in Thea are the physical sun and sky that are created from the shadow settings in SketchUp. We will start our lighting studies with these daylight settings.

Testing the sun and sky with clay render

We will use the clay render setting introduced in step 2 to do our lighting tests. With a clay render, we can focus on the light alone without being distracted by other issues. As the model will have a light-grey, matt surface, you will be able to see exactly where and how strongly, the light is falling. It will also speed up the render significantly by having only simple materials ("clay") to render.

1. Enable **Shadows** in SketchUp and adjust the daytime settings to create an interesting shadow on the wall.

2. In the **Thea Tools** window, set the camera **resolution** to something like 800 px and the **aspect ratio** to match your scene. We will use **16 x 9** to get a nice wide view.

3. Open the Thea Rendering Window and choose the **Rendering** tab.

4. Set the render mode to **Adaptive (BSD)**. Now, you will see the detailed **Adaptive (BSD) Settings** in the central panel.

5. Use a preview **preset** for this render. Although we are inside, we choose **00. Exterior Preview**, because we have a large atrium that is almost like an outside space.

6. Check the **Clay Render** option below the presets.

7.   Start the rendering process.

Your image should be finished in a few moments. This clay render allows you to see how the light and shadows are distributed in the space.

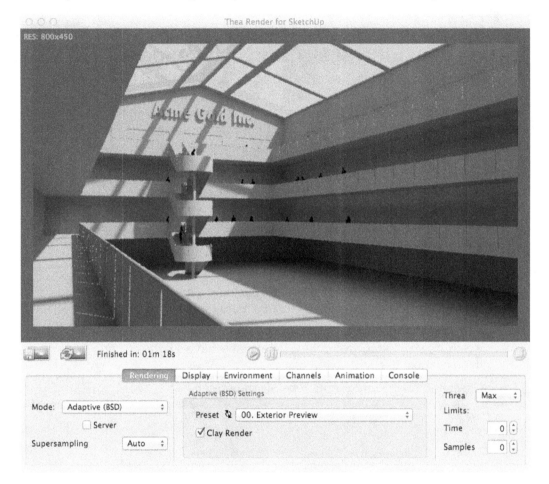

For the preceding image, you chose the **Clay Render** preset, which converted all the basic materials to a matt grey. This is very render-efficient, because the render engine does not have to calculate reflection or highlights. Thea keeps the transparency of glass during clay rendering, so you assigned a glass material to the atrium windows before the render. Other renderers might convert even glass to an opaque gray. In this case, you have to temporarily hide the windows for a clay render.

You can now make changes to the time of day and date back in the SketchUp shadow settings. This will alter the sun angle and shadows in the scene. Use the SketchUp shadows as a preview for what you will get from a Thea rendering. If you feel that the amount of light needs adjusting, you can also alter the exposure in the image by going to **Thea Rendering Window** and selecting the **Display** tab.

Adjusting the daylight settings in Thea

When you change the time of day or season for your shadow settings, you will notice that not only the position of the shadows changes but also the total amount of light in the scene. Thea has a sophisticated method to calculate the intensity of the sky and sun based on the sun's position in the sky and your scene's location on the globe. This will give you a very natural daylight environment for your scene.

Sometimes, you may wish for a more emotional setting, though. For these special requirements, you can manually set the properties of the sun and sky in the **Thea Rendering** window.

1. Open the Thea Rendering window and select the **Environment** tab.

2. In the **Environment** panel to the left, select to edit settings for the sun.

3. The central panel will now show the **Manual Sun** option. The values in the text boxes are linked to the SketchUp shadow settings. When you change the time of day in SketchUp, you can see the values for the sun angle and power update in the Thea window.

4. Check the box next to **Enable** to allow manual overrides of the calculated values.

5. Change the **Emmitance** from **Default** to **Color**. A color selector will appear next to it.

6. Click on the selector button and pick a light-orange color in the SketchUp color selector.

7. Enable the **Soft shadow** setting and set the radius to a value between 50-150 meters. The lower the value, the more blurry the shadow edges will be.

With these settings, you should get a dramatic sunset image like the following image, although the shadows are still correct for the middle of the day. Note that any coloring you introduce through the use of colored light sources can't be undone by postprocessing.

If you want to keep your options open, you should only use white light sources during the rendering and use postprocessing to add color tints.

You can also manually adjust the sky settings in a similar way, but the values used to configure the appearance of the sky are much more technical and require a good amount of knowledge to be used effectively. Luckily, there is a better way to add an impressive sky to our scene, as we will see in the next section.

Image-based lighting

We already introduced **Image-based lighting** (IBL) in our technology overview. It is now time to put this technique to practice. In particular, we will use a process called **Smart IBL**, which uses optimized images to reduce render times.

To learn more about **Smart IBL (sIBL)**, you can visit www.hdrlabs.com/sibl/index.html.

For our tests, you need to download one or more HDR images from
`http://www.hdrlabs.com/sibl/archive.html`. We will use the **Stadium Center** image by Christian Bloch in our example, because it does match the size of our building.

1. Download the zip archive for your image and extract it on your hard drive. You should find several files in the archive, among which are the following:

    ° `Stadium_Center_3k.hdr` (large file, high-resolution HDR)

    ° `Stadium_Center_8k.jpg` (large file, very high-resolution JPEG)

    ° `Stadium_Center_Env.hdr` (small file, low-resolution HDR)

2. Open the Thea Rendering window with the **Environment** tab.

3. Select **IBL** from the **Edit settings** drop-down menu in the **Environment** panel. The center panel will show a list with four checkbox options and a file browser.

4. Select the first option in the list called **Illumination**. Note that the **Use Sky** option on the left-hand side is disabled when you use this option.

5. Use the file browser to select the low-resolution `Stadium_Center_Env.hdr` file.

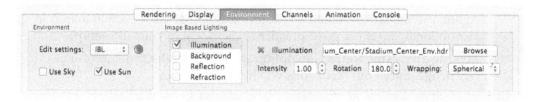

6. Click on the round **Environment Preview** button next to the **Edit settings** menu in the **Environment** panel on the left-hand side. A pop-up window will come up that shows the HDR image mapped to the sky dome.

7. You will see your current sun's location overlaid as a yellow dot on top of the image. In the HDR, the brightest area indicates the sun. Use the **Rotation** setting to roughly align the image with the sun in our scene. We have to rotate our image by 180 degrees to align it with the real sun.

8. You can do finer adjustments by tuning the time of day and date in the SketchUp shadow settings.

9. Enable the **Background** option and select the `Stadium_Center_8k.jpg` image. Apply the same rotation to this image as you did earlier.

10. Enable the **Reflection** option and select the `Stadium_Center_3k.hdr` image. Again, use the same rotation angle. (For this scene, the reflection map is in fact optional, but it is a good practice to include it in your IBL setup).

11. You can enable the **Refraction** option as well using the `Stadium_Center_3k.hdr` image, but in our scene, this will have little effect.

12. With all the images in place, you can now start a new test render. You can also disable the **clay render** option to see how your material will look like in the new light.

How Smart IBL works

The images you selected for your various options have a dedicated purpose. The lighting in the scene is provided by the low-resolution HDR image. As it provides ambient lighting, it does not have to be very accurate. However, this low-resolution image would not look good as the background for our scene, so we use a very high-resolution JPEG image instead. You can see the clouds through the atrium windows. In scenes where you can see the surroundings, the added details of the large image are important.

Finally, we also set up a reflection (and refraction) map using another HDR file. It is more important for reflections to be precise, so we use a medium resolution image for this.

On top of all this, we still keep the sun from our daylight settings to produce clearly defined shadows. The low-resolution environment image would not be suitable for this. To match the orientation of the image with our sun settings, we had to adjust the rotation of all our IBL images.

Saving the sky settings

You have spent quite some time on setting up your lighting. It would be a shame to have to do it all over again the next time you want to render an image. In the **Thea Tool** window, you can find an option to save all your scene settings that are not stored with any SketchUp objects.

1. Open the **Thea Tool** window and select the **Camera** tab.

2. At the bottom of the window, you can see the **Scene Settings** panel.

3. When you want to save your settings, just hit the **Save** button, and the options you used to render your image will be stored with the SketchUp scene.

4. To load the settings, first select the scene in the drop-down menu and then click on the **Load** button. The settings are not updated automatically when you change the scene.

Create new scenes for your render settings in SketchUp; then save and reopen the SketchUp file. The **Thea Tool** window does not update the list of available scenes automatically when you add a new scene in SketchUp.

Artificial lighting

As you have seen, you can get a really nice render using SketchUp's sun and sky settings without changing much in Thea. SketchUp passes all the necessary environment info on to Thea. However, what about the indoor scenes with artificial lighting? We are going to take the same scene and add some components in SketchUp that are exported as light sources to Thea.

Creating Spotlights in SketchUp

You will be using SketchUp to set up and edit the lights. Thea lights are treated in SketchUp like any other component. They do have a bit of extra information, but this is only important for the exporter plugin. You can use all the usual tools such as the **Move** tool to move a copy to set up the lights in your scene. You can also hide all unnecessary geometry to help you place the lights more easily.

1. Open your scene in SketchUp. You can use a new file just for the artificial lighting setup.

2. Open the **Thea Tool** menu and select the **Light** tab.

3. At the bottom of the window, there are three buttons to create a **point light**, **spotlight** or an **IES light**. Click on the **Spotlight** button to create a new light in the scene.

4. Pick the point in the scene where the light should go. The actual light will be a bit offset from the point, so you can click directly on a surface.

5. Move the cursor down along the blue axis. This defines the direction of the spot light and its initial intensity. If you move further down, the light will be brighter.

6. You can insert more than one light using the spotlight tool. Every time you place a new spotlight, a new *component definition* will be created.

7. Alternatively, use the SketchUp copy and paste function to make a copy of the existing spotlight. Copies made in SketchUp will share the same definition, so any change made to one copy will apply to all instances.

In the following image, you can see two spotlights placed under a stair landing. Note the small lines used to mark the middle of the beams. These were used to place the component in the scene.

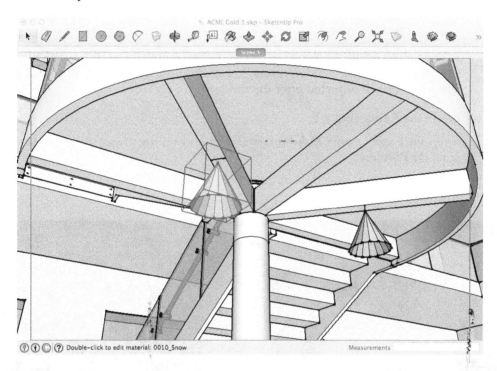

You set up a spotlight in SketchUp with default settings. You then moved the cursor down along the blue axis to show the spotlight where to point. The further you move the cursor before you click, the greater the light power.

Rendering artificial light

Notice that the sun and sky still are present in the scene, and these still need to be "switched off" for the rendering. Do this now as follows:

1. Open the Thea Rendering window and select the **Environment** tab.

2. In the **Environment** panel, uncheck both **Use Sky** and **Use Sun**.

3. If you have any IBL settings left from previous experiments, uncheck these options, too.

4. Select the **Display** tab.

5. Set the values in the left column to the following:
    ◦ **ISO**: **1600** or **3200**
    ◦ **Shutter**: **125** or **60**
    ◦ **f-number**: **2.8**

    These values set the characteristics of a virtual camera and film to calculate the brightness of the rendered image, based on the available light sources. They can also be adjusted after the rendering.

6. Select the **Rendering** tab.

7. Keep the render mode at **Adaptive (BSD)** and set the preset option to **10. Interior Preview**.

8. If you have many materials in the scene, you should also set the option to create a **clay render**.

You should get an image like the one shown above. There are two lights present in this scene, and no light is coming from the sun or the sky. That's why we changed the rendering preset from exterior to interior, because all the light in the scene will come from within. The clay render will again help you focus on a balanced light distribution while you are positioning lights in your scene.

Changing the light parameters

If you notice that your lights are too dark or too bright, you can change their settings in SketchUp using the **Thea tool**.

1. Back in SketchUp, open the **Thea Tool** window on the **Light** tab.

2. Hover over one of the spotlight components in the scene and check the status bar and tooltip.

3. Click on the spotlight. The **Thea Tool** window will change to show the settings specific to this spotlight's definition. Remember that the settings may be shared by other instances in your scene.

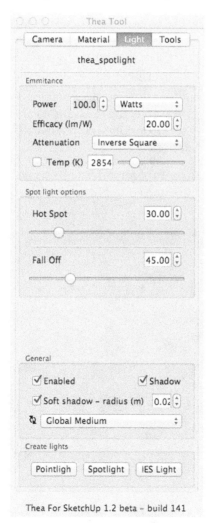

4. Under **Emmitance**, you will find the **Power** option. Increase or decrease this value according to your needs.

5. You can change the **Attenuation** option, but a physically correct light will obey the **Inverse Square** law. You should have no need to change this.

6. The spotlight type also has specific options available in the **Spot light options** panel. They are as follows:

   ° **Hot Spot** is the area under the spotlight where the core of the light beam is going to be. This value should always be smaller than the **Fall Off** value.

   ° **Fall Off** indicates the angle to which the light will gradually diminish. A larger value for the **Fall Off** will produce a wider fade from the core beam.

7. You now have a basic idea of the light power you need. Use the preceding options to set up a spotlight suitable for your needs.

8. Copy this light throughout your scene wherever you need lights with identical settings (for example, the downlights along the wall). The copies will share a common set of options and change all at once whenever you modify one of the instances.

When you are done with your setup, rerender your scene. In the following image, you can see the scene with the same spotlight copied multiple times and adjusted as necessary:

Creating a virtual light switch

Create new layers in SketchUp and assign the individual groups of spotlights to these layers. Using the layer visibility, you can now switch the groups of lights on and off.

Point lights

Point lights can be set up in the same way as spotlights, except that they don't have direction, hotspot and falloff settings. They are useful where you need a bit of diffuse lighting that illuminates the whole room. Try adding some more lights in SketchUp, both spotlights and point lights, and altering the settings in SketchUp. Do a test render to see what effect these settings have. This is the best way to learn, remember, and get a feel of the light settings that are required in a particular scene.

Adding light-emitting materials

To finish off the lighting in this scene, we need some larger ceiling lights. In order to simulate this, you're going to create some simple rectangles in SketchUp and set up a light-emitting material in Thea. We have already discussed light emitting materials in step 3.

1. In SketchUp, draw a rectangle where you want a ceiling light. Make it approximately 1200 mm long and 200-300 mm wide to keep it within the industry's standard dimensions.

2. Make sure that the bright (front) face is facing down.

3. Create a new SketchUp material and apply it to the rectangle.

4. Make a component of the rectangle and copy it to several locations near the ceiling.

5. Using the **Materials** tab from the **Thea Tool** window, assign the **Emitter** type to this material and set its output to 10000-20000 lumens (you have to experiment a bit to find the correct value for your scene).

6. Hide all the other lights. This is best done with a layer dedicated to lighting.

7. Now, create a **Clay Render** like the following one. It should show only the ceiling lights.

You have disabled all the spotlights so that you could check the level of lighting from the rectangular overhead lights. You changed the material so that the rectangles act as light-emitting materials. Notice how uniformly the light is spread from a large rectangular light source, just as you would have from normal strip lights.

You can now enable all the other lights you disabled earlier and do a final clay render again with all the lights on.

The final indoor render

You are now ready to render a preview image and the final image of your artificially lit indoor scene. As the scene is complex with many light sources and reflective materials, we are going to use the **Unbiased (TR1)** render mode. There are no options for this render mode, so all you need to do is select your image resolution via the **Thea Tool** window and hit the **Start** button.

The following image is the final image that we get after about 50 passes. It's now ready to go on to postprocessing in GIMP. This is the subject of the next chapter.

Step 5 – Inserting extra entourage

More and more 3D content is now being produced or converted into the .skp format. So, you might already have downloaded and inserted everything you need for your scene directly in SketchUp. However, sometimes, you want to insert your 3D entourage models only into the rendering application and not into SketchUp, especially if you are dealing with high-poly models.

The **Thea Browser** provides a feature that allows you to add high-poly 3D content from your Thea library into a SketchUp scene without using up resources. To follow these steps, you need some 3D objects installed in your Thea library. You can get some free sample content from http://www.thearender.com/cms/index.php/resources/free-samples.html.

1. Open the **Thea Browser** by navigating to **Thea Render | Thea Browser**.

2. A file browser will open in the Thea data folder. Navigate to **Thea folders |
   Models | Free Samples | Sample Xfrog Library** (or another location
   with your 3D library files). You can see the open browser window in the
   following image:

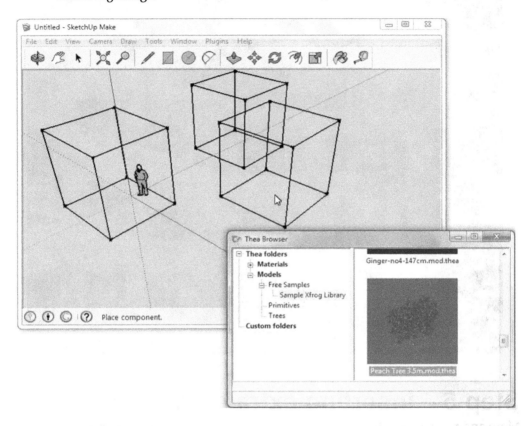

3. To select a model from your Thea library, double-click on its image on the
   right-hand side of the browser. In our example, we use a tree model with
   the name, `Peach Tree 3.5m.mod.thea`.

4. You can now place a component instance in our model. This instance will
   represent the tree in the SketchUp scene. The components are only displayed
   as wireframe boxes, so they don't take many resources to draw.

This is a good way to insert high-quality 3D entourage such as plants into a scene. You can easily create dozens of tree instances without slowing down the SketchUp interaction. When the SketchUp scene is exported to Thea, each instance will be replaced with the library model, which can have a few million polygons each. You can even scale the components in your scene, and the 3D model in Thea will be resized accordingly.

> To create a more detailed representation of your Thea model in the scene, you can save a SketchUp file with the same name as the Thea library file in the same folder (in our example, this would be Peach Tree 3.5m.mod.skp). Now, when you select the Thea file in the browser, the .skp file will be loaded as a component instance into the scene. You can add as much detail to the .skp file as you need to get a good representation of the 3D model.

In older versions of the plugin (before v1.3), you will find this feature in the **Thea Tool** window on the **Tools** tab under **External model**. You don't have a visual browser, though.

Step 6 – Production rendering

Before you start your long running final rendering process, you should do a test render to see what you will get from hours of rendering. You should do a test rendering for each new scene that shows a new part of your model or contains proxy components that are not well represented in the SketchUp 3D scene window.

Test production render

You are ready to do a "dress rehearsal" of your final render just to smooth out any other issues and make final changes. This will be a version of your final render, but at a lower resolution and with lower quality settings.

If you have created a dedicated file for your daylighting scene, open this now:

1. Open the **Thea Tool** window and check that the camera **resolution** is still set to **800px**.
2. Select the correct **aspect ratio** for your scene.
3. Open the **Thea Rendering Window** and select the **Rendering** tab.

4. Use the **Adaptive (BSD)** render mode and set the preset to **02. Exterior Medium**. This will use the biased rendering engine with enhanced quality setting.

5. Start the render process and allow it to render out to the end.

This will produce a test render with better indirect lighting and material appearances. It will take noticeably longer than the standard preview rendering, but it should still finish within a reasonable time to give you a quick feedback before the final render. You can go and get yourself a cup of tea while your computer is doing the work.

Reducing the render time

When you get back from making tea and the render process is still less than half way through (the progress bar shows you how much of the image is complete), you might want to press the red stop button and simplify some materials in order to reduce the render time.

If you have used many displacement maps or lots of translucent surfaces, ask yourself if you really need them. You could change these materials to basic materials or use a bump map instead. Bear in mind that however long the test render took, the production render will take much longer than this. So, the primary focus of your test production render is to check that your full render won't take days to complete.

Also, you can now make other small changes if you need to. When you are happy with the test image and it is rendering quickly enough, go to the next step to give it the full works with a high resolution production rendering!

The final render

For the lighting setup for most of this chapter, you have been using only sun and sky or IBL. This would apply for the majority of outdoor scenes. For this kind of scene, **Adaptive (BSD)** with exterior presets or **Unbiased (TR1)** is a good render setting. You only need to use **Unbiased (TR2)** when you have caustic refractions in your scene, for example, from a swimming pool.

On a practical level, **Adaptive (BSD)** will finish sooner, while the unbiased modes usually do not come to an end within a realistic time. You have to stop the process when your rendering has achieved sufficient quality. There are also some advanced features, which are only available for one or the other mode.

It is time for our final render:

1. Use the **Thea Tool** window to increase the camera **resolution** to **1600** or **3200px**.

2. Choose **Adaptive (BSD)** as the render mode.

3. Use the **03. Exterior High** preset.

4. In **Threads** at the far right, select **MAX**. This means your computer will be entirely busy with rendering. If you want to use your computer for something else during the rendering, reduce the value by one or two threads.

5. Switch to the **Channels** tab and enable **Depth** and **Alpha** under **Common channels**. We will discuss these in the next section.

6. Click on the Start button and wait for the rendering to finish.

You will notice that the image starts out in 1:1 scale in the preview window. Depending on your window size, you will only see the center part of the image. During the first passes, the image looks pretty crude. Once the ray tracing starts, you will see the center completed first, so you can see the quality of the final image before it is complete.

Saving the final image

1. If you used an unbiased render mode, click on the stop render button when your image has achieved a good enough quality.

2. In the **Display** tab of the **Thea Rendering** window, you can now apply some adjustments, for example, to make the image brighter.

3. Click on the **Save Image** button. You will see a file browser where you can specify the image path and filename:

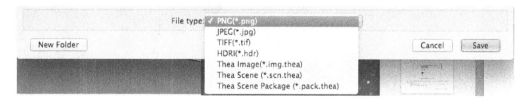

4. At the bottom of the window, you will find the option for the file type. Next to PNG, there are also options to save the image as **HDRI (*.hdr)** or **Thea Image (*.img.thea)** file.

5. Save one copy of the image as a PNG image.

6. Then, save it again as **Thea Image (*.img.thea)**.

You saved your final image as a PNG file to use it in GIMP and other 2D-graphic applications. The PNG file format is lossless, but it is still only a low dynamic range format. This means that it cannot hold all the information that Thea has produced while rendering the image. A high dynamic range format such as HDRI and the native Thea Image format can store all this and make it available for later adjustments. After a long render, you should always save the image in the Thea Image format. You never know if you will need it later.

The following is the final daylight render:

Step 7 – Postproduction rendering

You are almost done. Remember that you enabled two additional channels—depth and alpha—for the final rendering. These special render channels will allow you to do all sorts of postprocessing wizardry in GIMP, which is the subject of the next chapter.

Depth render

The first image that we will save is a depth render. It represents the z-information of the image, that is, the distance of a point to the camera.

1. Switch back to the **Channels** tab.

2. Under **Currently visible**, set the **Channel** option to **Depth**, as shown in the following screenshot:

3. Adjust the **Max Z (m)** option until you can just about see the farthest corner of the atrium. For my viewpoint, this is at 65 meters.

4. Save the image as a PNG file.

Alpha (mask) render

A mask render is a black-and-white representation of all the outlines of objects in the scene. The render will show whatever is present in the scene as white and the rest as black. This is especially useful when you need to replace the background of a scene or the outdoor view through windows. You will do this in *Chapter 9, Postproduction in GIMP*. To create the mask render, we have enabled the alpha channel in Thea. This works just the same way. The only difference is that the alpha channel shows the transparency of objects.

1. Under **Currently visible**, set the **Channel** option to **Alpha**.
2. There are no options to adjust for the alpha channel, so just save the image as a PNG file.

As you can see in the following image, the alpha channel is not very spectacular for this scene. You just see the skylights of the atrium, because these are the only areas where the background HDR image is visible. You can also see that the windows are not fully transparent, because they are shown in a shade of gray and are not completely black.

Summary

In this chapter, you learned how to take the scene you have set up in SketchUp and give it photorealistic lighting. For daylight scenes, this is as easy as hitting the Start Render button in the Thea plugin, because SketchUp has information on both the sky and sun for lighting. You also learned how to tweak SketchUp materials in Thea to add realistic highlights and surface properties.

You learned a few more advanced techniques that you can build on, in particular, how to edit materials in the Thea Materials Lab and how to fix incorrect texture mapping. You also used artificial lights and image-based lighting for your scene and verified the light levels with clay rendering. Finally, you used a test render to test all your settings before the final rendering for which you also created and saved depth and alpha channel images.

Now, it is time to go and experiment with your own scenes to put these techniques into practice. Why not make some great renderings of your previous SketchUp projects so that you can show them off and put them in a portfolio? Keep this book handy and dip into it as and when you need it; don't forget the great help forums at www.thearender.com and www.sketchucation.com, where you will be given advice.

If you want to look into other rendering software, I've listed the ones most commonly used with SketchUp in *Appendix, Choosing Rendering Software*, along with their main features based on this book's suggested workflow.

In the next chapter, you will learn how to further enhance your renderings by using postprocessing techniques in GIMP.

9
Postproduction in GIMP

In the last chapter, you created a photoreal rendering of your interior and exterior architectural models. That's a big achievement! However, whatever you do, don't stop there! There are some important things you need to do to your image before it's worthy of your portfolio.

In this chapter, you're going to learn some tricks in GIMP, which pro 3D visualizers use. You can follow these steps even if you have Photoshop, but you will have to translate the instructions per the Photoshop tools. In this chapter, you'll find out how GIMP can help you:

- Modify levels to give ultra realistic lighting
- Produce a vignette that draws the eye to your scene
- Add bloom to add a glow to the highlights
- Blur foreground or background to simulate the camera depth of field
- Add lighting effects in GIMP
- Composite several images to insert your model into real life scenes

It's a lot to cover, so let's get going. You can use some of the scenes you've already created in the earlier chapters. Create a new copy of your rendered image for each of the techniques you want to try out, so you can apply the modifications to a fresh copy each time without mixing the effects. In *Part 1 – tweaks and lighting levels* of this chapter, we will look at ways to improve a single image. In *Part 2 – compositing multiple images* of this chapter, we will combine our rendering with other image material to create a complete scene. To follow our examples, you will obviously need to install GIMP. Refer to *Chapter 2, Collecting a Toolset*, for download and install instructions.

Part 1 – tweaks and lighting levels

The rendered output from unbiased render engines is superb! When you click on **Start**, it fires rays at the scene and recaptures them in the (virtual) camera. So, it's really just a digital camera with simulated digital light. What does this mean to you and me? Well, apart from the great results, the light levels (saturation and white balance, among others) aren't always right straight out of the box. This is where GIMP comes in.

Here's the piano scene. Note the imperfections that detract from realism:

- Light shades are dull and washed out
- No clear contrast between light and dark areas
- Daylight quality is somewhat unrealistic

Often when you've done a render, you will not be entirely pleased with the result, but you just don't know why. This is usually related to something called color levels. To be accurate, color levels is just the name of the tool used to adjust the color distribution of an image. We will use it to change how the red, green, and blue values (levels) encoded in the original image are mapped to the output values of the modified image. Let's have a go at adjusting levels in GIMP, so that you can see how the RGB levels can be used to improve your image.

Adjusting levels automatically

There are several ways to fix the levels in a rendered image. Some of these are easy, and you should try these first. After that, you can look at the more involved ways of doing it, which can yield even better results.

1. Open your rendered PNG image in GIMP.

2. For a quick level fix, go to **Colors | Auto | Equalize**.

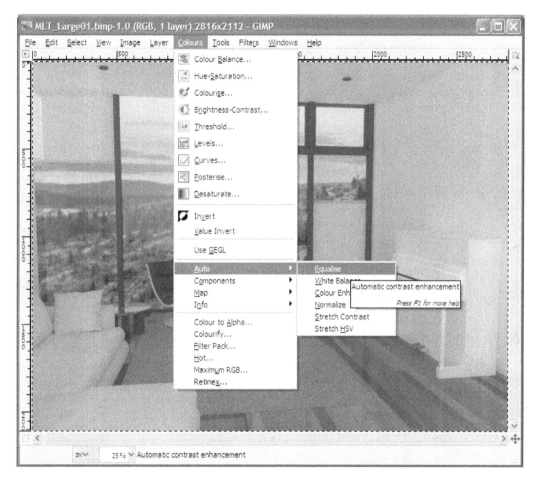

3. You will see five other automatic-level operations on the menu. If **Equalize** doesn't do it for your image, click on **Undo** under **Edit**, and try some of the others on the menu:

    °   **White Balance**: This corrects photos that have impure white or black colors

      °   **Color Enhance**: This makes colors appear more vivid without changing the brightness

      °   **Normalize**: This scans the image and stretches the brightness values across the full spectrum to make the darkest part black and the lightest part white

      °   **Stretch Contrast**: This is the same as **Normalize**, but does this for each color channel independently, so you may find that the colors have changed

      °   **Stretch HSV**: This is not frequently used, as the resulting effect can be a bit random

4. Alternatively, if you have access to other image editing software designed for quick digital photo correction, try some of the autofix settings on those (for example, Photoshop Elements or Picasa). They tend to be very effective and hassle free.

5. The last, and possibly the best, way of tweaking levels is to open the **Levels** dialog and click on the **Auto** button. Do this by going to **Color | Levels...**.

You just discovered color operations in GIMP and tried out a few automatic color-level tools to see what they did to your image. A lot of these settings may not actually create a better image, but they are available on the color menu for you to try out and see if they can improve the appearance of the render. Often they won't work because the image has more than one problem. Remember to make use of the **Undo History** option as you experiment. You will find it on the **Layers, Channels, Paths, Undo** pallet in the **Windows** menu.

Adjusting levels manually

You're now going to learn one of the most powerful and versatile image editing techniques available. Once you begin using this method, you will not need any one-click preset and will be able to tweak the lighting exactly how you want it. This is worth learning as it will give your images that extra edge.

Using the Levels dialog

At first, you are going to adjust all the color channels at once:

1. Once you have your image open in GIMP, go to **Colors | Levels**

2. The **Levels** dialog box will open and you will see something like this:

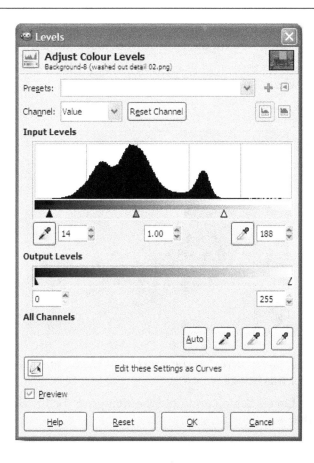

3. The graph, called a **Histogram**, shows the color values in the image (or layer) from black (left) to white (right). As you can see from this histogram, all the detail in the image is seen in the middle of the graph. The very light and dark areas of the graph aren't being used at all. This makes for a very washed out, low-contrast image. You can see part of the image here:

4. Click on the black triangle at the bottom-left corner of the histogram and drag it to the right until you hit the base of what looks like a mountain range.

5. Do the same with the white triangle to the right. The previous screenshot shows you where I've placed mine in the histogram.

6. Click on **OK**.

7. You will now have corrected the contrast in the image. Can you see how much clearer this image is?

8. Reopen the **Levels** dialog and note the change in the histogram. It will look a bit like this one:

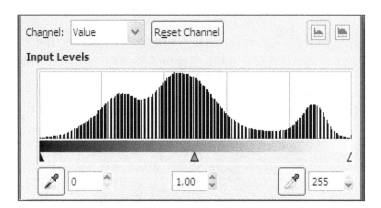

You just took the color-level information contained in the image and stretched the most used part to fit the entire value range. Note how the mountain range now fits the entire area. The brightness range of your image now spans between 0 and 255, whereas before, the image was confined to something between 14 and 188 (see the first histogram). By dragging the white and black arrows, you told GIMP to stretch the existing values over the available range, enhancing the contrast.

Adjusting the brightness balance

With the **Levels** dialog, you can also adjust the brightness of the image, as follows:

1. While you're still in the **Levels** dialog, click on the middle arrow and drag it to the left. The image preview becomes lighter.

2. Now drag it to the right. The preview image becomes darker.

3. Move it to where you're happiest and click on **OK**.

The middle arrow controls the gamma value. This tells GIMP whether to favor the light or dark values of the histogram. This is the correct way to brighten the image because none of the actual image information is lost. If you close and reopen the **Levels** dialog, you will see that the histogram has not changed in any way.

Correcting individual color channels

Now comes the really good bit. You will know that digital images are split up into red, green, and blue channels (RGB for short). Using the **Levels** dialog, you can edit each of these channels separately in exactly the same way as before. This will allow you to balance out the light levels perfectly and get rid of unrealistic color tints, or even introduce some for your own purposes:

- **Red**: This gives interiors warmer color temperature.
- **Green**: Increase this for leafy outdoor scenes. However, this makes interiors look unnatural!
- **Blue**: Increase this for realistic natural-looking light.

Note the drop-down menu above the histogram that says **Channel: Value**. This means the histogram is taking the combined value of all three channels. If you click on the drop-down menu, you can select any of the three color channels to edit separately. Do this now and use the three arrows for each color separately. Once you have used all three colors, go over them again until you are happy with the result. Then, before you finish, go back to **Value** and give the whole ensemble a final tweak.

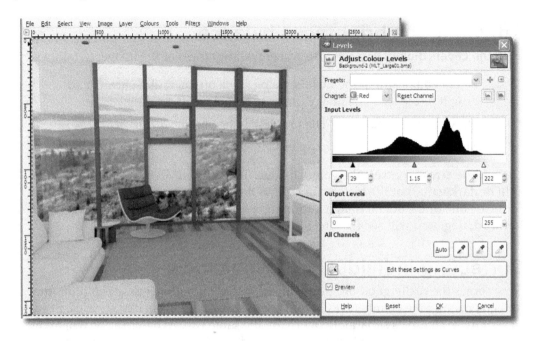

Removing unwanted image noise

Now, let's look at the final render from *Chapter 8, Photorealistic Rendering*, made with the unbiased render engine (TR1 or TR2). If you look carefully, or zoom in to a small area of the image, you will see a speckled effect.

Grainy images like the preceding one are characteristic of progressive render systems, such as the unbiased engine in Thea and other renderers. It can add an appealing film grain effect, a bit like the crackle on an old vinyl record. However, too much crackle won't allow you to enjoy the performance. If you master the noise-removal technique shown here, you will save bags of render time because you don't need to wait for so many render passes.

1. Take a render from the unbiased engine and open it in GIMP.

2. Duplicate the layer by clicking on the button at the bottom of the **Layers** pallet.

3. Select the new copy of the layer.

4. Use **Filters | Blur | Gaussian Blur**. Try a small radius of say 2-4 pixels.

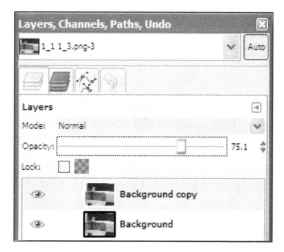

5. Use the layer's **Opacity** slider (see the preceding screenshot) to adjust the effect of this layer on the original image (shown as follows). It's a trade-off between less noise and more detail. Here is the same area again with the Gaussian Blur radius set to 3, and the layer opacity set to 75 percent.

6. Create a layer mask if you want to block out areas you don't wish to apply the effect to (go back and check *Chapter 7, Non-photoreal Visuals with SketchUp,* if you can't remember how to do this).

7. When you're done, select the upper layer and go to **Layers | Merge Down**.

8. This makes the change permanent and puts everything back to one layer, ready for you to carry out other image edits.

You created a slightly blurred copy of the image and overlaid the original with it. You then adjusted the opacity of the blurred layer, so that the effect of the layer on the final image would be reduced. This way you can fine-tune the effect.

Getting rid of noise is never perfect. Either you will lose detail or have an image with sharp details but also a lot of noise. Of course, the alternative is to use an unbiased render engine in Thea or render for a longer time. Finally, you can also try the **Depth of Field** effect, which we'll cover later, to introduce some intentional blurriness to the image. An additional benefit of this is the reduction of image noise.

Keep sharp lines with Selective Gaussian Blur

A downside of the Gaussian Blur filter is that it also blurs the edges of objects in the picture. If this is a problem for your image, try **Selective Gaussian Blur** instead by going to **Filters | Blur**. This filter has an additional setting for color differences (**Max. delta**), that is, it blurs only similar colors together but keeps the contrast at edges as is.

Using the G'MIC plugin

A more involved alternative to the quick fix you've just learned is to try downloading and installing the **G'MIC** plugin for GIMP. You can find it at `http://gmic.sourceforge.net/gimp.shtml` (It is also part of the *gimp-extensions* packages mentioned in *Chapter 2, Collecting a Toolset.*). The dialog box for the tool within GIMP is shown here:

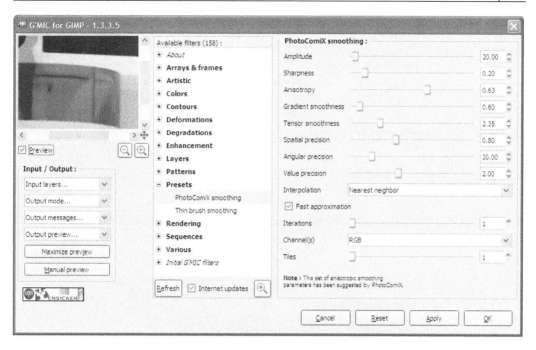

Here's the G'MIC version of our image after applying the **PhotoComiX** smoothing filter with the settings shown in the preceding screenshot. Note that on Mac, you will find this filter under the filter group **Testing**.

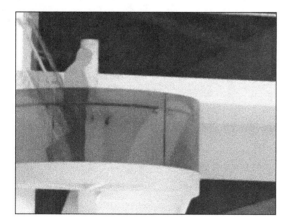

If you're up for it, download and install the plugin now using the instructions on the website. Open your image in GIMP and try some of the filters and settings until you get a great result.

If you have some money to spend on image correction software, *Neat Image* by ABSoft is hard to beat, with exceptional quality output, speed, and ease of use. You can get a free trial of this software at `http://www.neatimage.com`.

Adding light bloom

On bright days, the sun puts a halo of light around bright objects in direct sunlight. You can achieve this effect easily in GIMP. This is a good way to soften an image, making it more dreamlike.

To add a soft glow to the edge of lights, take your final render from *Chapter 8, Photorealistic Rendering*, and follow these steps. Let's start with this small area of the final render:

1. Open the image and create a copy of the image layer in GIMP.
2. Use **Gaussian Blur** on the copy with a radius of 5-10 pixels. This depends on the size of your rendering.

3. Now, increase the brightness and contrast of the layer using **Colors | Brightness-Contrast**, so you have something like this image:

4. Set the layer to **Hard light** or **Lighten only** and adjust the **Layer Opacity** to get the effect you want.

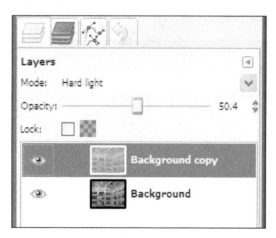

5. Go to **Layer | Merge Down** to fix the effect and allow further work on the image.

Here is the enhanced image. You can see how the light *blooms* out, rather than having a sharp edge like before.

To see the effect more pronounced, take a look at the following image rendered in Modo (a 3D modeling and rendering tool). Rendering and texturing was done by Ahmed Alireza and modeling by Branko Jovanovic.

You created a copy of the image over the top of the original one. You blurred and increased the brightness of the copy to get a halo effect. Setting the upper layer to **Hard light** changed the contrast of the layer below. Merging the two layers allows us to create some of the other effects more easily.

Now that you have learned how to create a glow manually, you can go back to your original image and try **Filters | Artistic | Softglow** and compare the two results. The **Softglow** filter can apply these changes automatically, but now you have two methods to achieve this effect: a quick fix for the whole image and a manual one, so that you can control the effect in different parts of the image using masks.

Simulating depth of field

Depth of field is an effect created by the aperture settings in a camera. It basically means that the center or focus of your image is sharp, while the near foreground and far background are blurred. Photographers use this effect to focus your attention on the foreground of an image. Applied as a post process to rendered images, it adds photographic realism.

Renderers, strictly speaking, do not have an aperture and so all the depth of field effects are artificially generated. In Thea, you can use the **Darkroom** tools to apply and modify a depth of field effect after the render. Other renderers may not have this feature or you may want to apply it selectively to an area of the image. So, here is how you can create a depth of field effect using GIMP.

For this exercise, you need to install the GIMP plugin, *Focus Blur*. Check if your GIMP installer already came with this plugin. You will find it under the GIMP menu entry **Filters | Blur | Focus Blur**. If you cannot find it there, the best way to install it on Windows is the GIMP extensions project at `https://code.google.com/p/gimp-extensions/`. This is a Windows program that installs a number of plugins for GIMP on your system, including Focus Blur. On Mac, there is no easy way to install only the plugin, so your best option is to use a GIMP installer that already includes it. The installer at `http://gimp.lisanet.de/Website/Download.html` contains this plugin.

The following are three images that illustrate this concept:

1. First is the rendered image itself. Notice all of it is in focus; you can clearly see the brick pattern on each box.

2. Here is the depth rendered image. You learned how to produce this in *Chapter 8, Photorealistic Rendering*.

3. This is the final image after the effect was applied in GIMP. You can tell the focus is on the box in the center because the other two boxes are blurred.

Creating depth of field using a depth render

At the end of *Chapter 8, Photorealistic Rendering,* we created a depth render image. It should look something like the following one. Bright areas are closer to the camera, and darker shades are further away, although for our process it does not matter which shade is used to indicate distance.

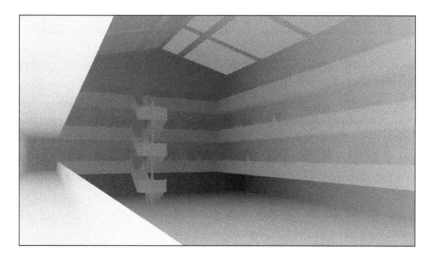

In the following steps, we will use the grayscale information of the depth render image to blur the areas of the main render image selectively, which will create a simulated depth of field effect.

1. Open the main (color) rendering from *Chapter 8, Photorealistic Rendering,* in GIMP.

2. Go to **File | Open as Layer**.

3. Select the depth render image and click on **OK**. You should now have your color rendering as the background layer and the depth map on top.

4. Click on the rectangle for the foreground color in the main tool pallet. This will take you to the **Change Foreground Color** dialog box.

5. Click on the **Eye Dropper** tool (circled in the following screenshot).

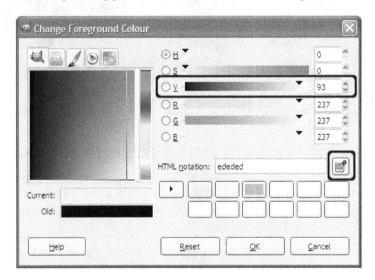

6. Make sure the depth render layer is selected, and now move the **Eye Dropper** tool over the image.

7. Hold down the left mouse button and watch the **V** value change (circled in the preceding screenshot). It moves between **0** and **100** as you move it around over the depth map, depending on the gray value under the cursor.

8. The values you are reading are a percentage of how far away something is from the camera. Write down the value you get when you pass over the area that you want to focus on.

9. That's all you need from this dialog. We don't need to set anything here, so just click on **Cancel** to close the window.

10. Turn off the depth render layer (use the eye icon), so that you can see the main image.

11. Select the main image layer so that the filter works on that layer.

12. Access the plugin by going to **Focus Blur** under **Filters | Blur**.

13. Select **Gaussian** to change the radius setting to control the amount of blur required (depending on your preference and image size).

14. You can see the effect in the preview image. Move around using the sliders to see more of the image.

15. Select **Use Depth map** and then select the depth render layer from the list box.

16. In the **Focal depth** box, enter the value you wrote down previously.

17. Use the preview to check if your area of interest is in focus. If it is blurry, try using 100 minus your original value for the focal depth. You can also move the slider until your focus area is sharp enough.

18. Click on **OK** to apply the effect.

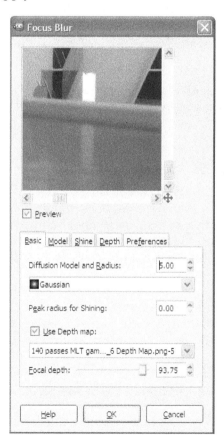

You can do this for any percentage value (1-100) to blur different areas of the image. You can see in my image (the following one) that the balustrade has been blurred and the stairs in the background are sharp.

 Apply some of the blur effect to the depth map image first; this occasionally gives a better effect.

Lighting effects

What about some of the lighting effects you can add at the postprocessing stage? Let's not leave those out. Some exceptional artists can render a scene with just plain ambient light and then add all the other lighting using image editing software afterwards. Although you may not always use it, you may want to learn how to as part of your toolbox. For example, you may wish to put some shining dots to indicate ceiling lights.

Adding light effects in GIMP

We will add some bright point lights with radial lens flare to the image. This technique is often applied in night scenes and for street lighting.

1. Open your artificially lit render from *Chapter 8, Photorealistic Rendering*.

2. Go to **Supernova** under **Filters | Light and Shadow**.

3. Click on the magnifying glass icon to zoom in with the preview image.

4. Click on a spot where you want the center of a new light to be.

5. Adjust **Color**, **Radius**, and **Spokes**, as you can see in the following screenshot:

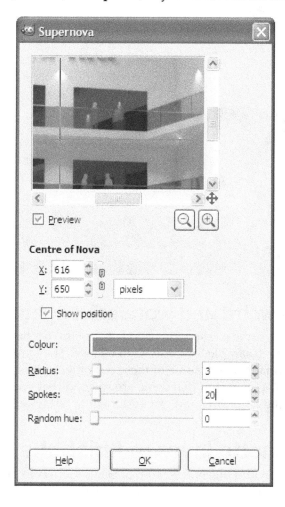

6. Blue is used to create the impression of a different color temperature for the new light points, as if these were halogen spots between compact fluorescent downlights.

7. I've set **Radius** and **Spokes** at **5** and **100**, respectively, for the light you can see on the right of the preview image. However, I've reduced the values for the current light because it's at a shallow angle to the camera.

8. Repeat the preceding steps for each light bulb.

Here is the image with several of these supernova effects applied:

Discovering weird and wonderful lighting filters

GIMP has some great, some not so great, and some plain "far out" lighting effects that you have just got to sample for yourself to believe. They are found under **Filters | Light and Shadow**. Try some of these out on your image and see the effects you can get. You may find that some are so good that you can leave out some lights during the rendering and just add them in GIMP on your next project.

Using a vignette layer to finish the image

When you are happy with your image, all that is left to do is to draw the viewer's eye further into the image. This final process is the vignette, which is a posh word for a dark border. You have already learned all the skills you need for this in *Chapter 7, Non-photoreal Visuals with SketchUp*. It was slightly different in that case because you used a white border to let the image fade out at the edges. With photoreal images, you will darken the edges slightly instead.

Fading out the edges with a vignette

To draw the eye to the areas of the image you wish to focus on, parts of it need to be lit more than others. The edges, especially, should be darker than the center. The following is an exaggerated image showing where the vignette could be used:

1. Open your night-time rendering in GIMP.

2. Create a new layer. For **Layer Fill Type**, select **Transparency**. This is your vignette layer.

3. Select the **Paintbrush** tool.

4. Click on **Foreground – Background** (circled in the following screenshot) to get the colors back to black and white, if necessary.

5. Select a fuzzy circle brush and increase the scale to get a bigger one.

6. Start at the edges of the image and apply black paint all around.

7. Change the brush **Opacity** to **50** percent and gradually come in from the edge where you want slightly more light.

8. Repeat with the setting still at 50 percent to overlay your paintbrush strokes, as you can see from the exaggerated image.

9. You can use a 20 percent opacity brush if you need to fine-tune it.

10. Remember, work fast because you can change this at any time. Simply click the eraser and paint over the areas you need to alter. Set the eraser at 50 percent if you need a less definite effect.

11. Because you've done this really roughly, use the Gaussian Blur filter on the vignette layer with a high radius value (20-100 pixels) to smoothen things out a little.

12. Now, lower the **Layer Opacity** until you have a more subtle effect (I've used 30 percent).

With these steps, you added a final flourish to help draw the viewer's eye to the picture. This was achieved with a simple darkened overlay. Using this process, you can expose or hide certain areas of the composition. Here is a side-by-side comparison of the two images:

This is the end of the part related to image enhancements. You have learned how to give your image that little extra touch that makes all the difference!

Part 2 – compositing multiple images

In the second half of this chapter, we will explore compositing multiple images. You may have already learned a lot of the skills needed here in *Chapter 7, Non-photoreal Visuals with SketchUp*, so you're already half way there! The following few pages will equip you to stitch together finished images from different component parts.

Using a mask render for windows

You will repeatedly find this trick useful as you progress with your postprocessing skills. We will be going through just one application of this, but there are all sorts of other uses you will discover yourself. Remember in *Chapter 8, Photorealistic Rendering*, you created an image from the render's alpha channel. You'll put this to good use now.

1. Open your daylight scene from the last chapter in GIMP.

2. Go to **File** | **Open as Layer**, select the alpha channel image, and click on **OK**.

3. Repeat this with a sky image or even a holiday snap with a great-looking sky with some clouds.

4. Select the sky image layer and use **Move** to position the portion of the sky over the windows. You may need to resize the layer first by using **Layer** | **Scale Layer**.

5. Select the alpha channel render in the **Layers** pallet. Now, go to **Select** | **All**.

6. Go to **Edit** | **Copy**.

7. Right-click on the sky layer and select **Add Layer Mask** | **Add** and click on **Add**.

8. Now, click on the layer mask that just appeared in the **Layers** pallet.

9. Go to **Edit** | **Paste**.

10. Select the pasted item in the **Layer** pallet, then right-click and select **Anchor**.

    You have now copied the alpha channel render into the layer mask associated with the sky layer. But it still looks wrong! That's because you need to invert the mask.

11. Select the mask, then click on **Invert** under **Colors**.

12. Now, set the sky layer to **Multiply**.

Here is the image and layer stack you should end up with:

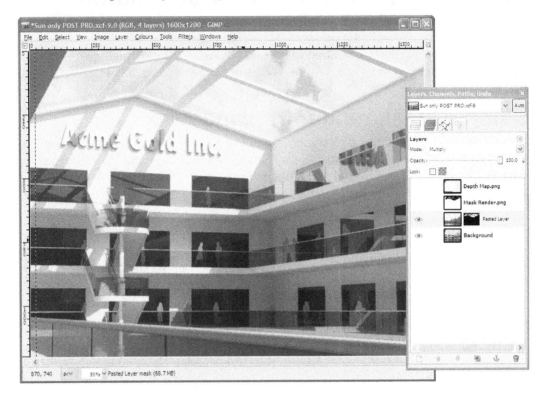

You produced an alpha channel render in Thea, which was completely black. The only part that was left white was the portion visible through the windows. You assigned this image to the mask channel of a sky image, so that only the sky portion showed through. This sky layer was set to **Multiply**, so that both the sky and the reflection in the glass would show together.

This technique is great when you don't have a sky or background image in an indoor render. You just add it later in GIMP.

SketchUp window reflections without rendering

You can take your SketchUp image and instantly add sky reflections to your windows without rendering! Take a look at the following image. Apart from my badly applied brick texture, can you distinguish it from a render?

I didn't think you would. So, follow these steps to learn the trick:

1. Open a SketchUp scene and zoom in to a window looking from a low angle, like the one shown in the following screenshot.

2. Export a colored view in your preferred style.

3. Using the same view, click on the shaded view button.

4. In the **Styles** pallet, turn off **Display Edges** and **Profiles**.

5. In the **Shadow Settings** pallet change **Light** to **0** and **Dark** to **100**. You can see the results here:

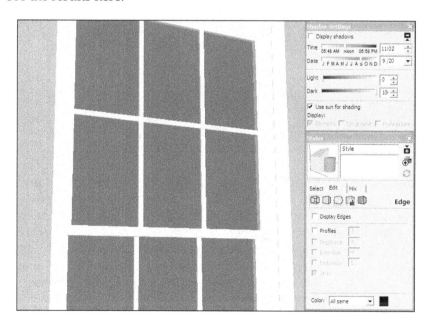

6. You will now have an image with flat colors like in the preceding one. Export this, making sure you haven't changed the view.

7. In GIMP, open the images as layers, as before.

8. Click on the flat colors image layer.

9. Select the **Select by Color** tool from the main tool pallet.

10. Click somewhere on the window. This will select only areas with the color of the window glazing.

11. Insert a sky image as before and create a layer mask for this new layer.

12. Select **Selection** and click on **Add**.

13. Adjust the opacity of the sky layer and mask out areas you don't need, like I've done with the lower sash of the window here.

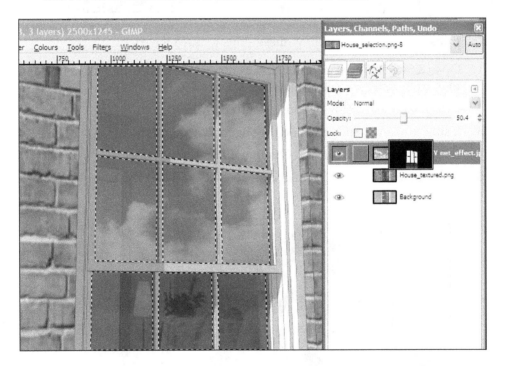

You can now use this technique to selectively replace, enhance, or blur any part of your SketchUp scene. Use the **Fuzzy Select** tool (*Magic Wand*) or the **Select by Color** tool in combination with a SketchUp flat color layer to select areas of your image and blur, darken, lighten, sharpen, or delete areas of your main image. Now, reuse the same selection technique to overlay parts of your scene with other images or textures. How many uses for this technique can you find to enhance your image? Enhancing doesn't just mean cleaning up; this can also be used to grunge up or add variation to textured surfaces.

Using paths to mask photos

If you have set up your scene using Match Photo, and want to insert a building into an existing image, you're going to need to do some masking in GIMP to separate the foreground and background from the render. You should be able to mask the outline of your building using a mask render, so that there is no problem inserting a background. The foreground may be trickier as you will see now.

I want to take this serene picture and insert a riverside hut. This is where I'm planning to retire once everyone knows how to use SketchUp!

Like all strapped-for-time architects, I'm simply going to download a design from the 3D Warehouse. Here it is rendered on a plain background:

I've rotated the view by eye in SketchUp to vaguely match the photo, using *Alt +
Tab* (*Cmd + Tab* on Mac) to switch between applications. I couldn't use Match Photo
because there are no right angles in the image. When I get it about right by trial and
error, I can try to match the sun and shadows and export the image for rendering.

OK, so you are in GIMP now with both images open as layers, just like you
did before.

1. Turn down the opacity on the hut layer and use the **Move** tool to place it
   (see the following screenshot).

2. Select the **Scale Tool** to size it. Hold *Ctrl* (*Cmd* on the Mac) to maintain the
   aspect ratio correct.

3. Select the background using the **Select by Color Tool** and hit *Delete*.

4. You now need to copy the photo layer and move it to the top of the layer stack
   (for the foreground elements).

5. Click the **Duplicate Layer** button and move the new layer to the top of the list.

6. Right-click and click on **Add** under **Add Layer Mask | Selection**.

7. Go to **Select | None**.

8. Click on the **Layer Mask**. Then click on the little **Double Arrow** in the main layer pallet to swap from black to white.

9. Click on the **Paintbrush** tool and select a rough brush. Make sure the opacity is set to 100 percent.

10. Paint in bits of grass (or whatever you need in your image) into the foreground, as you can see here:

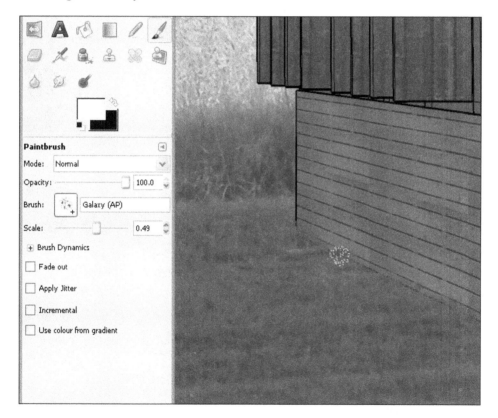

11. Turn off the hut layer.

12. Select the **Paths Tool**.

13. Click around the tree and use *Ctrl* + scroll to zoom in.

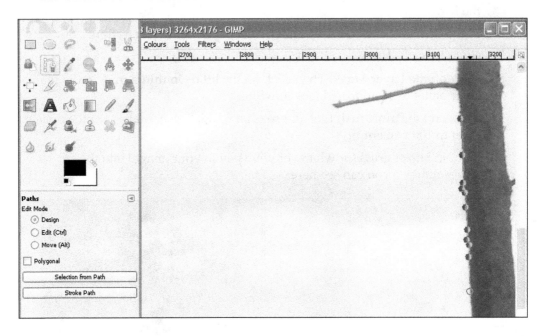

14. When you've finished clicking all round the tree, right-click and then go to **Select | From Path.**

15. Click on **Layer Mask**.

16. Select the **Bucket Fill Tool** icon and fill the selection with white.

17. Turn on the hut layer, so you can see the result.

18. Use **Burn Tool** to darken the edges of your foreground objects if you need to.

19. Go to **Select | None**.

20. Use **Colors | Brightness-Contrast** on the hut layer to match the image better.

21. Save the image in GIMP (*.xcf) format if you plan to work on it some more later on.

22. Go to **Image | Flatten Image** and save it as the final PNG file.
    Here's the result:

You just created what's called a clipping path around the area of the tree trunk that overlaid the hut. You then turned this path into a selection and filled the selection with white in the layer mask. This made the area of the layer visible again. This is the basic method of clipping and masking any foreground or background elements in your scene. Paths are very versatile, and it is worth reading more about paths on websites dedicated to GIMP or Photoshop. You can start with `www.gimp.org/tutorials`.

Summary

In this chapter, you have learned how to double your skills as a rendering artist. You have learned how to take renderings and native SketchUp images and add some seasoning. In particular, you will keep coming back to compositing photos and renderings into one image and tweaking levels to give realistic lighting. Creating the depth of field effects and adding reflection to windows can also be used in many scenes to make them look more realistic.

These are some of the main skills a 3D artist needs to get to grips with, and along the way, you picked up the skills to use these tools and methods in many other ways too. You have now graduated from SketchUp Architectural Visualization School! In the next chapter, you will learn how to storyboard and create flythrough animations.

10
Animations

In this chapter, you are going to learn the basic skills you need to produce animated walkthroughs and flyovers. SketchUp is an ideal piece of software to produce these types of animations. In fact, the film industry uses SketchUp as a previsualization tool. They work out the basic shots, camera angles, timing, and so on within SketchUp before they shoot it for real. And that's how we're going to use it too!

In this chapter, we will cover the following topics:

- What to include in an animation
- How to create a simple walkthrough in SketchUp
- Using paths for a smooth flythrough
- Stitching animated sequences together into a video
- Photoreal animated renders
- Video compositing, file types, and compression settings

Using the same principles for stills and animation

Creating movie sequences for architectural visualization requires a slightly different but related mindset to still images. That's because an animated sequence shows more of the scene than what is visible in a single image. For example, you might see the back of a building, which you wouldn't have bothered modeling for a still image; however, now you have to model it. All the principles that you have already learned in *Chapter 3, Composing the Scene*, are applicable here. The following is a recap:

- If you can't see it, don't model it!
- If it's in the background, make it low poly or a 2D cutout
- Use interesting and unique camera angles

However, this time, all of these principles have to be kept in mind for a duration of 30 seconds, 5 minutes, or even a feature length presentation, which is made up of many views of the model. This can quickly become an overwhelming premise. So, we need to break it down into bite-size chunks that are easy to handle. Just like you do every day with other design projects, you are now going to break down your animation into individual scenes, shot by shot.

Making a start – sketching it out

Even if you already have a fully detailed model that you can quite happily view from any angle, you need to start by making a plan of what you want to see in your animation. Well actually, that's not completely correct. Why would the client want to see what you want to see? So, from now on, we must start by considering the needs of the client or audience and only think in terms of their expectations.

Most of this thinking has also been covered in *Chapter 6, Entourage the SketchUp Way*, because it's entourage (people, cars, and trees) that tell the audience, "This could be you in this scene!" and "Wouldn't you enjoy this environment?"

Writing out the itinerary

If you were to visit the quaint English village of Bourton-on-the-Water, what would be the absolute "must-sees" of your trip? How do you plan out your itinerary? Whether you opt for a vacation trip or an animation sequence, there's a method of planning that's completely easy and foolproof. You can do this when you're on the train or eating your cornflakes:

1. Take a large sheet of paper (A3 size or 11 x 17 inches).
2. Start at the center of the page and write down a feature of the building you're planning to "sell" to your audience.
3. Rotate the page randomly and write another feature somewhere in a blank space.
4. Do this repeatedly.
5. Go completely crazy and write down whatever pops into your head (such as a dishwasher or great drainage or south facing).
6. When you have filled the page, collect them all up in a list.

7. Put three columns down on the right-hand side, each labeled **Quality**, **Desirability**, and blank.

   It doesn't matter if you spelled desirability wrong. That's the point of the exercise: no wrong answers. Don't worry about spelling or getting the best stuff down. Just get the flow going.

8. When you're done, give each point a rating anywhere between 1 to 5 in the **Quality** column for how good this part of this particular development is.

9. Now, do a valley fold (z-fold) to hide the first column.

10. In the **Desirability** column, give each item a rating between 1 and 5 for how desirable such a building feature is to your audience. You need to separate this rating from your particular building and your personal preferences. Rate it purely on how your audience would view this feature in any building.

11. When you're done, multiply the first and second column and put the total in the third column.

Unknowingly, you have just written the itinerary for your animation. Easy, wasn't it? Ok, you probably don't think you've achieved much, but you have. By using this method, you were forced to be dispassionate about your design or model. You were also forced to distinguish between features that you personally like and features that appeal to your intended audience (your clients). What you have in the third column is a definitive rating of the impact of each feature on your audience. Go ahead and label it **Impact** now to replace the blank heading there.

Generating the storyboard

You are now ready to sketch out the **storyboard** because you now know what to include in your animation and what to leave out. Take a pink marker and highlight everything that scores 20 or 25. These are your primary features. Take an orange marker and highlight elements with a score between 12 and 16, and take a yellow marker to highlight items that are rated at 9. Nines are just about tolerable.

What you now have is a color-coded scene allocation system. While deciding what to put into your animation, you should get as many of the pink marks in as many times as you can. You should get the oranges in the rest of the time. Also, you should use the yellows to pad the content out where necessary and give an overall context to the presentation. Anything you've not colored will actually detract from the presentation and stop people from buying the property. Don't model it, and try to avoid it in your presentation.

Dealing with detractions

As you've discovered, anything in your list that didn't get colored could easily detract your audience from the main features of your presentation. So, these areas should be minimized if possible, but what do you do if they are a central feature and have to be included for context (or honesty)? What, for example, about the electricity enclosure, the bin store, or the plant room? Here are a few ways to deal with this problem:

- Leave the noncritical areas blank and untextured, giving only the context but no details
- Cover or mask with entourage
- Leave areas unfocussed in the background
- Use viewing angles that obscure these features

Your efforts in minimizing bad features should be equal to those spent in promoting good ones. You should aim at showing the development in its best light and greatest potential.

The storyboard

Now that you have decided what needs to be included and what needs to be left out, decide how much time needs to be allocated to each feature, and what the camera views should be. Do the following steps on paper with sketches.

1. Split up your list into scenes, including wide views and close-up views.
2. Decide how long the whole animation should last. Add a couple of seconds for cutting later.
3. Decide if you are going to travel from one scene to the next, blend between scenes (in video editing software), or create a hard cut.
4. Work out how long to spend on each scene and each transition between scenes.
5. Create a rough sketch for the start of each scene.
6. Scan them into your computer.

[The following steps shown are specific to Windows Movie Maker but are similar to all basic video editing applications (Adobe Premiere Elements, Final Cut Express, iMovie, or similar).]

7. In Windows Movie Maker (or similar), import each picture.
8. In **Import pictures**, press and hold *Ctrl* to select more than one image, and then click on the **Import** button.

9. The pictures will open in the **Collections** area.

10. Drag them one by one onto **Storyboard** in the sequence you want.

11. Click on **Show Timeline**.

12. Drag the edge of each image out to the correct length for the shot.

13. Click on **Play** on the preview viewer.

14. Keep adding scene sketches and edit the timing until you have achieved a smooth animation flow.

15. Add a voice track or music to the **Audio** channel if you want. To do this, you can:

    1. Click on **Import audio or music**.

    2. Navigate to the file and then click on **Import**.

    3. Drag it onto the storyboard as before.

16. Remember to save the project.

You just storyboarded your whole animation so that you know exactly what you need to model and where it will show in the video. You did this in Movie Maker or similar, creating place markers so that you can easily import your movie clips later. This saves an enormous amount of time in the long run because you will only model, texture, animate, and render what you're going to see, not what will be left on the cutting room floor. If you already have your SketchUp scene completed, you can take screenshots from that instead of sketching out the scenes on paper.

When you are investing a lot of time into a project such as an animation, it's vital to get a second or third opinion early on. Use your rough movie sketch to talk it through with a colleague, tutor, or clued in friend. It's important to do this at this early stage before you spend a large amount of time on detailing and animating the scenes.

You're now at a stage where you can apply the techniques of *Chapter 3, Composing the Scene*, and compose each of your scenes.

Animating in SketchUp

Now comes the real fun bit! We're going to look at options to create animations out of SketchUp. And don't forget—whatever you animate in SketchUp can be turned into a render later. So, SketchUp is a previsualization tool for rendering as well as a visualization tool in itself.

Creating a simple walkthrough

To get a feel for the animation process, we will start with a basic scene:

1. Create the simple scene illustrated here in SketchUp. The tallest object is about 2 m (6.5 ft) in height.

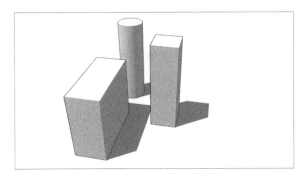

2. Texture all the faces differently so that you can recognize where you are at any given point in time.

3. Now, go to **Camera | Look Around**.

4. Type in the height in the **Eye Height** field as 1.7 m and hit *Enter* (see the inset in the following screenshot):

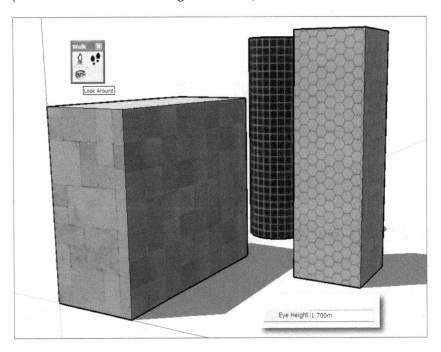

Your viewpoint will drop down to a height of 1.7 m, and the cursor will change to an eye symbol.

5. You can now look around the scene at a fixed position by holding down the left mouse button and moving the mouse.

6. This can be the start of your walkthrough. Go to **View | Animation | Add Scene**.

    We're going to walk in between the boxes and look at the backside of the boxes that we can't see.

7. Go to **Camera | Walk**. The cursor changes to a footprints icon.

8. Click on the screen and hold down the left mouse button. Now, move the mouse up on the screen. You start to walk forward! Move the mouse from side-to-side to steer.

9. Walk in between the boxes.

10. Add another scene.

11. Use the **Look Around** function to turn on the spot and look directly at the box to the right. Add another scene.

12. To see how you've done, go to **View | Animation | Play**.

You set up a simple scene and told SketchUp you wanted to view it from the eye level. Using the SketchUp **Walkthrough** tools, you simulated a person walking through your SketchUp model. This, in itself, is a highly effective presentation tool. You used the **Look Around** tool to change your view without altering the eye height or camera position. It's important to use these tools to change views rather than your usual **Pan** and **Orbit** tools in order to maintain a consistent eye height. You then created scenes to act like key frames for the animation.

Use your laptop for real-time walkthroughs

The walkthrough tools you've seen right here are really useful for helping people visualize a design. There's nothing better than interacting with an environment and seeing it as you would in real life. Why not take your laptop to meetings and allow people to see your models first hand?

Animation settings

When you reviewed your animation, you will notice that the animation pauses on the first frame, then flies quickly in between the boxes, pauses again, and then rotates the camera around. Go to **View | Animation | Settings** to change the settings that control the speed of scene transitions and scene delays. Go there now for a look.

The animation settings dialog box looks like this:

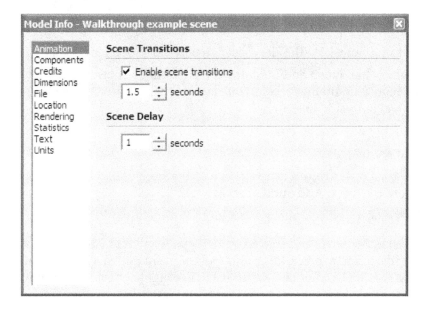

You will see that there are very few settings here, and it's not possible to control individual scene timings. That's a pity in one way, but it does help keep everything simple. We will look at how to control individual scene timings using a plugin a little later in this chapter. Here's what each setting does:

Function	What it does	Uses
Enable scene transitions	This allows travel from one scene to the next scene	Uncheck this to operate as a slideshow without transitions
Transition time	This controls the time it takes to travel from one scene to the next scene (speed)	Enter a number (seconds)
Scene delay	This sets the time for which the animation pauses at each scene	Set it to zero to go directly from one transition to the next without pausing

Getting the timing right

For now, you're going to add some intermediate steps to your walkthrough to smooth out the movement and also to slow things down a little.

1. Still in the settings dialog box, change the **Scene Transitions** field to **2** seconds.

2. Change the value in the **Scene Delay** field to **0**.

3. Close the dialog box.

4. Click on **Scene 1**.

5. Walk halfway between **Scene 1** and **Scene 2**.

6. Right-click on **Scene 1** and select **Add Scene**. You will see **Scene 4** appear between **Scene 1** and **Scene 2**.

7. Play the animation again and note the difference.

8. Click on the new scene tab to go back to **Scene 4** and now move your position or view direction, and then update **Scene 4** (right-click on the scene tab and select **Update**).

9. Play the animation again and repeat until you get a smooth timing and transition between scenes.

10. Now, create further scenes as you walk around the back of the cylinder and back through to where you started.

11. Click on each scene tab to view, edit, and update, as necessary.

You just learned how to adjust animation properties and create a regularly paced animated walkthrough. You set up the scenes and were able to go back and tweak each one to get the desired effect. You will have noticed that the animation can still be a little jerky, and we still want to alter individual transition timings. Thankfully, there's a plugin for this, and we're going to look at that now.

Adding individual timing to scenes

As promised earlier, we will now look at a plugin that allows you to control the timings of each scene individually. Unfortunately, this plugin is not available via the plugins store, so you have to download and install it manually.

1. Download the `scenes_transition_times.rb` file from `http://morisdov.googlepages.com`. Don't get distracted by the other cool plugins on the site!

2. Drop the file in your `Plugins` folder and restart SketchUp.

3. Go to **Plugins | Scenes Transition Times**.

4. The plugin dialog shows a timing option for each scene in your file.

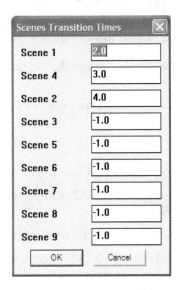

5. Type in values (in seconds) for each scene transition (the value -1.0 leaves the scene at the global default value set in the animation settings).

6. Play the animation again to see the difference.

7. Now, find the scene where you are turning your head to look at the box. Type in 4 as the transition time for this scene.

8. Play the animation again to see the difference.

You installed a plugin that allows scene transitions to be adjusted individually. You then increased the scene transition time to 4 seconds when you turn to look at the box beside you. You may have worked out that the value goes in the box relating to the scene after the one you need to edit.

Note that the animation is still jerky. This may be good enough for your current project, especially if you stitch together different scenes into a collage of moving views in your video editing software. You just cut out the dodgy transitions. However, for an altogether smoother animation, there are some further techniques that you can employ.

The Flightpath animation

The usual way of creating a flyover presentation in rendering software such as 3D Studio Max is to create a travel path. The camera is then attached to this path and told how fast to travel along it, where to point, and when. This is exactly what you can do in SketchUp too. This method is usually preferable over the walkthrough you've already looked at because:

- The travel is smooth, not jerky
- The speed of travel is constant
- There is greater control over where you go and what you look at
- Scenes are created automatically

To prepare for the next step, you need to download and install the following plugins:

- The `Flightpath.rb` plugin by Rick Wilson from `http://www.smustard.com/script/flightpath`
- The `BezierSpline` plugin by Fredo6 from the SketchUcation Plugin Store.

Smooth transitions

You're going to simulate an aircraft flying between tall buildings. This will teach you all the advanced skills you need for your architectural video, although you might be working on a smaller scale with a single building or site. We are going to use a 3D Warehouse city rather than a specific project, so you can practice all you like and not worry about getting it right for a client.

1. Download the `Rocane 2020` model from the 3D Warehouse. This is a highly detailed inner city model complete with bridge, sidewalk, and trees.

2. To speed up navigation, you can switch off the layers for trees and hide other elements. Keep only the roads and buildings.

3. Start by going to **Plan View** and switch to the monochrome view style. Also, turn off shadows. This will speed up manipulating and viewing the model and animation.

4. From your new **Bezier Spline** toolbar (**View** | **Toolbars** | **BZ_Toolbar**), select **Catmul-Spline**. This type is a bit easier to control because the curve goes through the control points.

5. Draw the path you want on the plan view by setting control points at roughly the same distance along the path, as shown in the following screenshot:

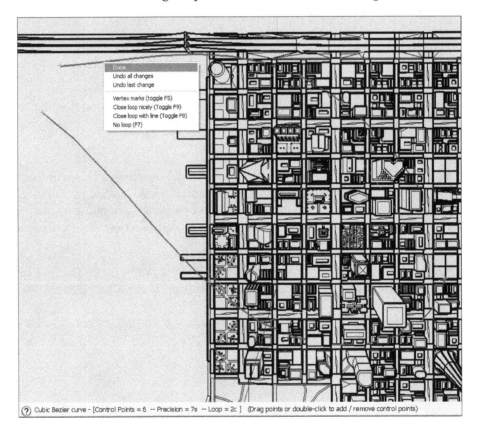

6. Set the last control point, then right-click and select **Done and Switch to Edition**

7. Adjust the control points of the curve to make sure the path is not passing through any of the tall buildings.

8. Double-click to finish your editing.

9. Orbit your view as you can see in the following screenshot, and then move the path up off the ground along the blue axis.

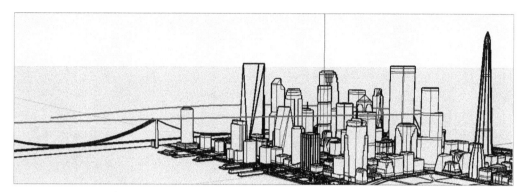

10. Now set the view style and shadows exactly as you want them.

11. Unhide anything you want to see in the animation.

12. Delete any existing scenes.

13. Save the model. This is important because you can't easily reverse the Flightpath operations.

14. Now, go to **View | Animation | Settings** and reduce the value in **Scene Delay** to **0**.

15. Select the path.

16. Right-click and select **Flightpath** from the context menu.

17. Enter the speed you want for your camera in meters per second. 88 meters per second is around 60 miles per hour (the speed of a fast car). I'm going for 500 m/s.

18. Click on **OK**. The script will create new scenes for viewpoints distributed along the path. The camera will look along the path to the next viewpoint.

19. You can review your animation by navigating to **View | Animation | Play**.

20. Go to **File | Export | Animation**. In Windows, also select the **Video** option.

21. Keep the file format at **Compressed with H.264 (*.mp4)**.

22. Click on the **Options** button. The export options dialog appears:

Export Options

Resolution: | 480p SD |

Aspect Ratio: | 16:9 Wide |

Frame Size (W × H): | 854 | × | 480 |

| Preview Frame Size |

Frame Rate: | 10 | ▼ | frames/second

| Restore Defaults |

☐ Loop to starting scene
☑ Anti-alias rendering
☐ Transparent background

| Cancel | | OK |

23. Set the value in the **Resolution** field to **480p SD**. This corresponds to a frame size of 854 x 480.

 If you want any other aspect ratio than 16:9, you first have to set **Resolution** to **Custom**.

24. Reduce the frame rate to **10** for a quick test animation.

25. Uncheck the **Loop to starting scene** option.

26. Click on **OK** to accept the options.

27. Set the filename and export the animation.

The animation will be exported as an MP4 movie file. If you need to make path adjustments after you view the animation, re-open your saved SketchUp file. Then, use the Bezier Curve tools to edit the path, followed by the Flightpath tool to create a new set of scenes.

You created a 3D curved path for the camera to follow. The Flightpath plugin creates scenes for each step in the path and sets the transition speed between scenes to keep the flight speed constant. You entered a speed in meters per second to control this. You now have a camera path converted to scenes, which you can edit individually. This is really great because you can fine-tune what the camera does every step of the way!

Fine-tuning with CameraControls

Now it's your turn to add some real panache to finish off your flythrough! Install the camera plugin `CameraControls.rb` by Rick Wilson, available at `http://www.smustard.com/script/CameraControls`.

This plugin is a little more difficult to install because you need to create a new folder in your `Plugins` folder. The details are in the `readme.txt` file, which you get when you download it. This plugin gives you fine control over the camera's pan, roll, and tilt effects and allows you to set values for these at each step of the animation.

Currently the `CameraControls.rb` plugin only works for PC, not Mac. However, if you're a Mac user, you can still achieve these camera effects manually. The plugin is just there to give tighter control over the values.

Camera pan, roll, and tilt

Add camera effects to each scene along your path using the `CameraControls` plugin. Here are some examples of what you can do with pan, roll, and tilt. Remember to update each scene after your changes.

Effect	Example of effect	Method
Pan	Focus on a building as you go past it to simulate a passenger looking out of the window	Use the pan slider to keep the camera trained on a building through several scenes
Tilt	When you want to simulate lift as the car or motorcycle sets off or brakes	Increase or decrease the tilt value on one scene
Roll	When you want to bank to the side like an aircraft does	Add progressively higher values of the roll effect to adjacent scenes

Let's put it together

Now that you've got the skills to create animated scenes in SketchUp, it's time to put it all together. Using the skills you have learned, render out a couple more simple animated camera shots. Refer to *Chapter 3, Composing the Scene*, to get some more ideas on viewpoints and camera focal settings. I'm trying the following with our city scene:

- Travel along the bridge approaching the city:

- Top-down flyover emphasizing the height of buildings:

- Slow travel along a road looking up at the sky:

- Some close up shots:

- Moving shadows or night shots:

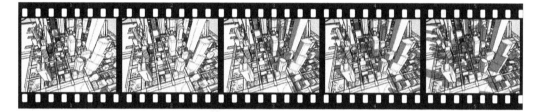

- Free-fall spinning camera:

- Different SketchUp styles (Monochrome, Sketchy, Blueprint, and so on):

All this will then be mixed in with the main flythrough sequence. The beauty of this is that the audience gets a constantly fresh, changing perspective, rather than a monotonous flyover. These scenes are interspersed to create this variety. They're also used to mask over the bits of your flythrough that you don't particularly want to see.

Interesting details and viewpoints

So it's your turn now to grab the mouse, zoom in to the SketchUp model, and capture some really interesting viewpoints, camera angles, and perspectives.

Make each of these no more than a couple of scenes long and restrict them to a few seconds each. The whole idea here is variety. Start with a saved copy of the model before you add the flythrough scenes. Save each mini animation as a separate .skp file for easy access later.

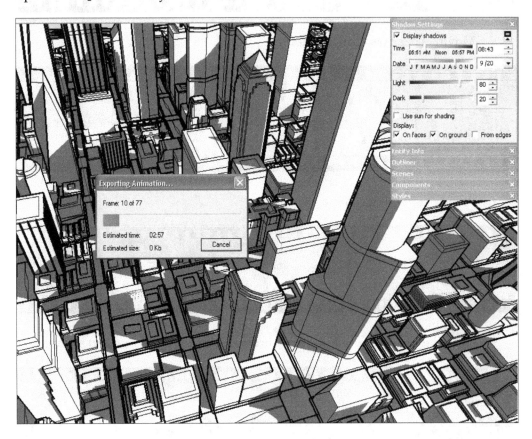

Authoring video sequences

So you've got a bunch of clips. These may or may not relate to the storyboard you set up at the start—it doesn't matter. You're just practicing. What you need to do now is put your SketchUp animations together.

To combine the short clips we will use a video editing software. Most of them are similar in nature and you can use any one of them to reproduce the following steps:

1. Open Windows Movie Maker (or a similar program to edit video sequences).
2. Go to **File | Import into Collections**.
3. Drag the main flythrough clip onto the timeline.

   You're now going to insert the short clips into the main flythrough.

4. Move the slider (see the next screenshot) to where you want to cut.

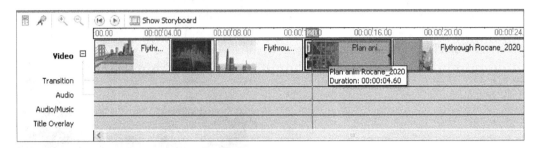

5. Click on the **Cut** button (circled in the next screenshot).

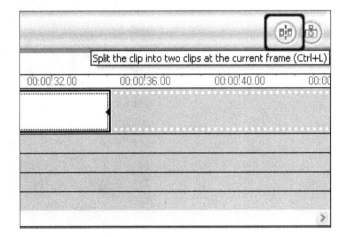

6. You can cut further on if you want to remove a section or leave it if you want to come back to where you left it.

7. Select the section and hit *Delete*.

8. Import one of your smaller clips and drag it into the space you created.

9. Adjust the start and end by clicking on and dragging the ends of the clip on the timeline.

Now that you've produced your low-resolution, quick mock-up and tweaked it to perfection, you're ready to go and render the final footage at a higher resolution in SketchUp, or photoreal in an external renderer. Thea imports the scene, sun, and camera movements exactly as they were in SketchUp, so you have done all the hard work already.

High-resolution animation from SketchUp

If you're aiming for a SketchUp sketchy movie, you now need to export the full resolution animation:

1. Go back to SketchUp, make any last edits if needed, and save your file.

2. Go to **Animation** under **File | Export**.

3. Select a location to save your file.

4. Use the following export options:

   ° Use the file format ***.mp4 compressed with H.264**

   ° Set the resolution to **1080p Full HD**

   ° Adjust the aspect ratio to **16:9 Wide**

   ° Set the frame rate to **24 frames per second**

   ° Do not loop back to the starting scene

5. Export the animation.

6. Review the final clip and repeat the preceding steps for all your animation scenes if you are satisfied with the quality.

Saving individual frames for an animation

When you use SketchUp to export directly to a compressed MP4 movie you rely on the quality of the built-in video encoder. In some cases, this may not be good enough and you have to export to individual image frames instead and use an external encoder such as VirtualDub to create the movie sequence. It is also a more robust and flexible method to create the animation. If the render you've left going overnight bombs out at the last frame or there is a power cut, you can still retrieve all the frames rendered up to that point. With a single animation file as export result you would have lost everything.

You can also check the progress of the animation immediately by opening the animation folder and taking a look at the frames as they are produced. You don't have to wait to the end of a four-hour render to discover that the lighting was wrong after all!

Animating with Thea

Thea does not export directly to a video, but produces the source frames as individual images. This will take up considerable space on your hard drive until you can convert them to a movie file. So try this first for one of the short clips you set up earlier. Also, the rendering of each frame will take much longer than that in SketchUp, so you don't want to use a sequence that will render for a week before you can see the results.

1. Prepare your scene for export to Thea as you learned in *Chapter 8, Photorealistic Rendering*.

2. Open the **Thea Tool** window and set up your export options.

In SketchUp, the render time is not affected too much by the resolution. In Thea, the render time for each image depends directly on the resolution. So choose the lowest resolution you can get away with. For a high-quality animation, this should be at least 1280 x 720 pixels (720p HD) at 25 frames per second.

3. Now open the **Thea Rendering Window** and select the **Rendering** tab.

4. For a walkthrough animation, select **Adaptive (BSD)** as the render mode and choose a render preset. The **Medium**, or even **Basic**, quality mode may be sufficient for an animation where you won't dwell too long on a single image.

5. Switch to the **Animation** tab.

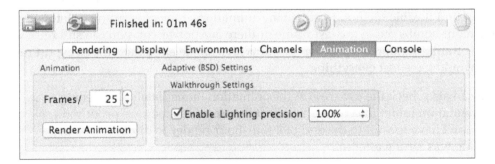

6. Adjust the frame rate to **25 frames per second** if necessary.

7. Check the box next to **Enable Lighting precision**. You can use this option to speed up the lighting calculation for a walkthrough animation where no other objects move. A value less than **100%** will reduce the calculation time, but may lead to inconsistent lighting between the frames. If you want really smooth lighting, you can also increase the value to up to **400%**.

8. When you are done, click on **Render Animation**.

9. Select a directory for the frames and the base name and file format for the images. The images will be saved with a number corresponding to the frame (such as `cityscene_0001.png`).

10. The rendering will start. You can follow the render progress in more detail on the **Console** tab.

How long will my animation take to render?

The render time of a single frame times the frame rate times the number of seconds in the animation.

So, at 2 minutes per frame and 25 frames per second, a 5 second animation will render for 2 x 25 x 5 = 250 minutes. It is not unusual to allow the computer a day or two to render even a short animation.

You used Thea to automatically render the animation frames generated by SketchUp. The frames are saved as JPEG or PNG files in the folder, which you specified when exporting the animation. Other formats such as TIFF or HDRI and even additional channels are also possible, but you should only use these when you plan to perform the postprocessing of the individual frames in a professional video-editing application. The frame resolution and aspect ratio were set to HD video to ensure good quality on modern TVs and the Web. Of course, if you particularly need to go full **High Definition** (**HD**), you need to raise this to 1920 pixels wide x 1080 pixels high. Think carefully before you do this because it greatly increases render time.

You're now ready to stitch all this together into your final video.

Compositing in VirtualDub

VirtualDub basically creates animations from still images and has loads of other image filters too. In just a couple of steps, you are going to take the individual frames saved from Thea or SketchUp and turn them into an uncompressed AVI video.

> **Animation on the Mac**
>
> VirtualDub is a Windows-only application. To do the same job on a Mac, download the free app Zeitraffer from the Apple App Store. This small application let's you select a folder with numbered images and save them as a QuickTime or MPEG-4 video, with optional resizing and frame rate adjustment. That's all we need for this step.

Creating an animation from still images

Follow these steps to turn your images into a video:

1. To open VirtualDub, double-click on the `VirtualDub.exe` file (or shortcut).

2. In VirtualDub, go to **File| Open Video File**.

3. Navigate to the folder where you saved the image frames and click on the first image.

4. Click on **Open**. The images will be loaded in sequence.

5. Click on the **Play** button on the left to preview the animation.

6. Go to **Video | Framerate** and change the frame rate to 25 if necessary.

7. You should now have a 720p HD video at 25 frames per second. This will give you the most flexibility in what you want to use the video clip for.

8. If you're going to further edit the video or export it to an HD video for the Web, skip ahead to step 16 for editing levels.

9. If you want to resize the video, go to **Video | Filters**.

10. Click on the **Add** button.

11. Select resize from the menu and click on **OK**.

12. You can now resize for any standard you wish. For example, 720 x 480 is the NTSC standard, so enter 720 as the width under **New size** (the height will be calculated automatically). Under **Framing options**, select **Letterbox/crop to size** and enter 720 in the first field and 480 in the second as the target size. This will resize each frame and add a black bar at the top and bottom to fill the screen.

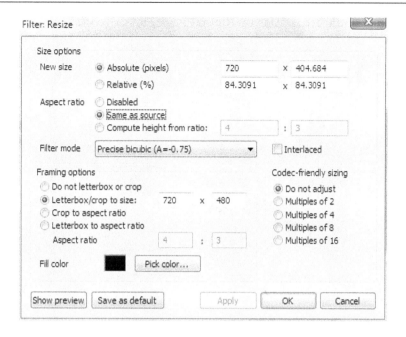

13. If the end use for this is a PAL TV screen (for example, for a DVD in the UK), use 768 as the new width and 768 and 576 as the target size.

14. Use the **Show preview** button to check the effect on the image. In our example, the image will show black bars at the top and bottom because the input aspect ratio of 16:9 is larger than that of the output format.

15. Click on **OK**.

16. To edit the levels just like you did with your still image in *Chapter 9*, *Postproduction in GIMP*, click on the **Add** button in the **Filters** dialog box again.

17. Select **Levels** from the menu and click on **OK**.

18. Click on **Show preview**.

19. Click on **Sample video...**. VirtualDub will analyze all images and show a histogram for the whole sequence.

20. Move the little arrows as you did in *Chapter 9, Postproduction in GIMP,* until you're happy with the preview image (see the following screenshot).

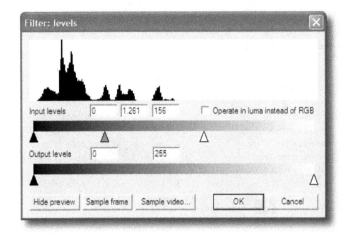

21. Click on **OK**.

22. Now go to **File | Save as AVI**. VirtualDub will take the individual frames, apply your filters, and export them as an AVI animation (see the next screenshot).

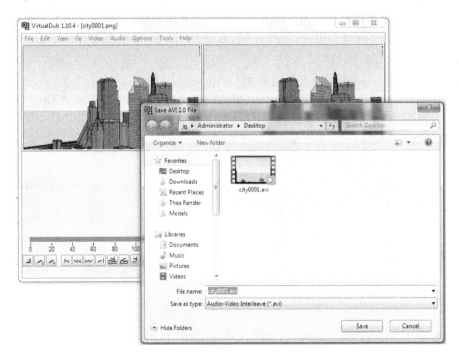

VirtualDub has taken the individual frames and stitched them together into an AVI file. This can be played using a standard viewer on your computer or edited as part of your video sequence in Windows Movie Maker or similar. When you save the AVI animation, the file is not compressed, allowing you to use it in video editing software without losing further quality. If you had saved it straight from SketchUp as an AVI, it would have already been compressed and you would lose quality through further editing.

Creating the final video composition

You now have photoreal clips from Thea and/or non-photoreal clips from SketchUp, which need to be stitched together into your final presentation. You will have already created a Windows Movie Maker project (or similar) with SketchUp preview animations or scanned images. You now need to convert this into the final production. This is just a matter of replacing the sketches or low-resolution animations with your high-resolution clips, then exporting to the correct format. Just follow the steps outlined here. Remember to use only uncompressed AVI files for this, not MP4 files.

1. Open your project in your favorite video editing software.

2. Hover over a clip in the timeline or storyboard. Read the clip length.

3. Insert your new final production clip next to it and adjust it to match the length of the adjacent clip (if you trimmed it before).

4. Click on the low-resolution clip and hit *Delete*.

5. When you have replaced all the clips like this, you have a high-resolution version of your video presentation.

6. If you like, add scene transitions by dragging them into the slots in your storyboard view.

7. Export the final movie to your hard drive. If your video editing software supports it, you can export directly to a *.mp4 video. If not, just create a *.avi or *.mov video with the highest quality settings you have available. Make sure you have sufficient disk space!

You just used your rough storyboard video project as a skeleton to build up the final high-quality presentation video. By replacing each existing preview sketch, you made sure that the final video has the same timing and content as the preview. Then you created the final video file that can be viewed with a video player such as VLC.

Did you notice that the video you have exported has a huge file size? This may not be a problem if you burn it to DVD, but many clients will want to show this video online via streaming services such as YouTube. So what now? Let's use a video encoder to create a compressed version of the movie with a much smaller file size.

Compressing for online streaming services

The following steps will allow you to upload your video to YouTube and other video-sharing sites. The frame rate and video size you set earlier is the recommended size for HD videos on YouTube. The video you prepare for upload should be of very high quality and good resolution because the streaming service will use it as a master copy to generate the video streams that the users will see. This process will reduce the quality a bit so your uploaded video should be as good as it can be.

Creating an MP4 video with HandBrake

To create the MP4 video clip, use the AVI file from Movie Maker and convert it into the recommended format for YouTube:

1. Open the HandBrake application.

2. In the toolbar at the top, click on the **Source** button.

3. Select **Open File**.

4. Open the AVI file you just saved from your video editing software.

5. Under **Destination**, select a directory and filename for the compressed video. Set the filename extension to `.mp4`.

6. Under **Output Settings**, select **Mp4** in the **Container** field and check the option for **Web Optimized**.

7. Select the **Video** tab in the lower half.

8. Set the options there as shown in the following screenshot:

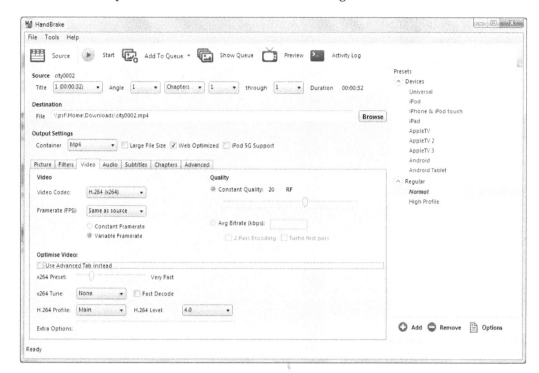

9. Note that the **x264** preset slider is in the left half of the range. This influences the encoding speed and the video quality. Faster speeds reduce the video quality.

10. Also, note the setting for **Quality**: **Constant Quality**. It is set to **20** and here a lower value means higher quality. The value of 20 is a good starting point. For some videos, you may have to decrease this value to 16 to reduce visual artifacts from the encoding process.

11. Click on the green **Start** button to start the encoding process.

12. When it's done, open the new file in a video player such as VLC to check the quality.

This file is now ready for upload to a web host such as YouTube or Vimeo. You can watch the video on their home page or just use their streaming server and embed a link to the video on your own website. After you have uploaded your video to YouTube, select the options you require and copy and paste the URL code from the **Embed** textbox into your website or blog as you can see here:

You just compressed your video to the MPEG-4 format with the H.264 compression codec and uploaded it to a streaming service website. This is immensely good news for the following reasons:

- H.264 allowed you to compress the video with little reduction in quality.

- MP4 is a web-optimized streaming format that can be viewed over the Internet.

- The video can be shared with anyone with an Internet connection. Just e-mail the YouTube link or the address of your website with the embedded video.

Summary

In this chapter, you learned how to create flyovers and walkthroughs. You found out how to set up the camera to follow a path and tweak individual views along the path. You then discovered how to put clips together into an overall presentation. Some skills you picked up in this chapter were:

- Planning your animations the easy way
- Plugins you need to achieve smooth animations
- How to render photoreal frames for an animation
- How to best prepare videos for viewing on the Internet

All that knowledge will set you on the path to happily produce SketchUp animations for architectural visualizations. As you have seen, it's not hard to generate great results with SketchUp and a few other video-editing and conversion programs. Of course, if you find yourself creating animations regularly, you can take these skills and apply them to video compositing applications that are industry standard, such as After Effects or Nuke, or try an open source alternative such as Blender 3D.

Now that you know how to animate your projects, we will be looking at professional presentation of 2D still images with LayOut in the next chapter.

11
Presenting Visuals in LayOut

This chapter is all about presentation. Think about the types of visuals you've created so far: the many different media, styles, viewpoints, and angles on your building. Do these individual images speak for themselves? Do they individually have both context and focus? Usually, the answer to this will be "no", because it takes several images to create an overall impression and communicate your design intent. You may already be skilled at displaying visuals as posters, on websites or in presentations, but you may not yet have looked into LayOut. This chapter is a brief introduction to it.

In this chapter, you will discover how to:

- Display plans and elevations
- Import SketchUp models and rendered images
- Add dimensions and text
- Set up a CAD style border
- Create PowerPoint style presentations
- Print to scale and control line weights

LayOut comes with SketchUp Pro or you can try it free for eight hours when you install a trial version. The free trial should easily be long enough to try out the practice sections found in this chapter.

Getting started with LayOut

You will find that many things in LayOut remind you of SketchUp tools, so you should feel right at home. It's designed to interact closely with SketchUp. Some areas of LayOut, such as dimensioning, are an exciting development as they extend SketchUp's reach into the domain where CAD programs reside. The following screenshot is an overview of the available tools:

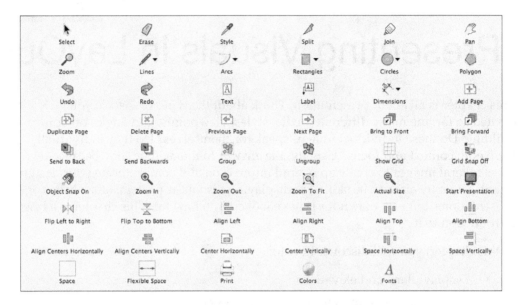

You will notice that some of the tools — such as the **Circle** tool — have a small triangle next to them. These buttons are used to access multiple similar tools such as **Circle** and **Ellipse** or **Rectangle** and **Rounded** in **Rectangles**. Just click on the triangle to see the available options.

Creating a custom page border

For our first steps in LayOut, let's customize one of the preinstalled page border templates and turn it into a customized architectural drawing sheet set. You can then save it and use it for future projects.

1. Open LayOut by double-clicking on the program icon.

2. When you start without an existing document, you first have to select a standard page size and template for your project. Click on the **+** icon next to **Title block** and select **Simple**, then select **A3 Landscape** (or **Tabloid Landscape** depending on your local convention) as shown in the following screenshot:

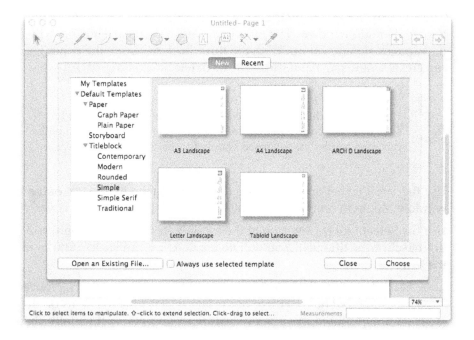

3. Click on **Choose**. The main LayOut window opens with the page that has a simple border in the main window.

4. On Windows, you will find the pallets arranged on the right-hand side of the main Window. On Mac, the pallets are independent of the main window but should show up on the right edge of your screen. Click on the title bars named **Pages** and **Layers** to expand the pages and layers pallet. You can see both the pallets in the following screenshot:

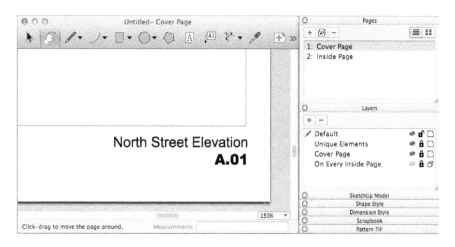

5. Click on **Cover Page** or **Inside Page** in the **Pages** pallet to switch between the two in the main window. The template you selected earlier came with both these pages already set up. With the three buttons above the pages list, you can create a new page and duplicate or delete an existing page.

 Unlike in SketchUp, where the pallets are often moved around or switched off, LayOut pallets are best left where they are. Each pallet can be expanded or collapsed simply by clicking on the title bar.

6. Use the scroll wheel of your mouse to pan and zoom in and out of the main window. Zoom in on the text on the bottom-right corner of the cover page.

7. Use the **Select** tool (arrow icon at the top-left corner of the screen) and double-click the title text. You will notice that you can't select and modify the text.

8. Look at the **Layers** pallet. The template has four existing layers. Notice you have a lock symbol next to three of the layers? This means items on that layer cannot be edited. It's a safety feature to stop you accidentally changing elements that you want to keep static.

9. Click on **Cover Page** in the **Pages** pallet to select the first page, then select the layer **Cover Page** in the **Layers** pallet and click on the lock symbol. The padlock symbol opens (see the next screenshot).

10. You can now edit the title and any other existing element on the **Cover Page** layer. Do not modify any text between the <...> signs. These symbols identify **Auto-Text** fields and have a special meaning in Layout (see the *Using Auto-Text* section). Also don't forget to add a nice company logo.

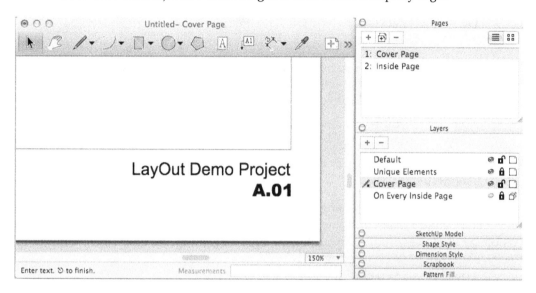

11. When you are done with the changes to your border, click on the lock again to protect the elements on this layer against further accidental changes.

12. Repeat the changes on the page **Inside Page** with the layer **On Every Inside Page**. You can then duplicate this page with your personalized information for any new page you need in your project.

You selected a standard template to start your project. It already included a front page and an inside page. Both pages have different page borders set up on dedicated layers. This allows you to keep them locked, so their content is not changed accidentally. As you have seen, you can edit any of the text you want once the corresponding layer is unlocked.

Using Auto-Text

LayOut 2014 introduced a new feature called **Auto-Text**. With Auto-Text, you can place a keyword in your text field that gets replaced into context-specific text such as the page number or the date on which the document is saved. You can use this feature wherever you need dynamic text components (such as a page number) or want to use the same text consistently in several places (such as a project number or client information).

When you start your LayOut document from an updated template, you will already find fields for general information such as client details. You can use the existing fields as a form of checklist for all the information that needs to be updated at the setup of a presentation document. You can also define your own fields.

1. Go to **File | Document Setup...**.
2. Select the **Auto-Text** entry to the left.
3. Go through the list and update any general information about your project. Changing a value here will update it everywhere in the document where the **Auto-Text** field has been used.
4. To place an **Auto-Text** field in your document, position the cursor in the correct location in a text box.
5. Select the menu entry **Text | Insert Auto-Text** and select the desired field to place it on the page.

Now, it's a simple matter of changing the text you find in the **Auto-Text** fields to reflect your project. Also, add lines and rectangles to the title block or border to customize it. Make sure you are adding or removing elements on the correct layer for the page you're on by clicking on it in the **Layers** pallet. The current layer you're drawing on shows a pencil icon next to it.

Have a go at this now, and when you're finished, set the bottom three layers back to the locked state again. Then click on **File | Save As Template...** and enter the name of your new template. You can now choose this template whenever you start a new LayOut presentation.

Displaying SketchUp models in LayOut

Any view or scene in SketchUp can be viewed within LayOut. You don't need to export any images or files to do this. LayOut links to your SketchUp file directly, so every change you make to your model in SketchUp will be visible in LayOut. This is great because similar to animation storyboarding in the previous chapter, you can set up dummy views in LayOut based on a rough SketchUp model. Once set up, you know exactly what views you have to detail in SketchUp, and you can check your progress through LayOut. It's just like a page with windows into your model.

Preparing SketchUp scenes for LayOut

Before you jump right into LayOut, you should prepare your SketchUp model for the use in LayOut. Generally, you should set up the following scenes and styles corresponding to the views you want to show on your LayOut pages:

- One or more **Hero Shots**: These are perspectives of the building that show dominant architectural features, perhaps even glorify them. You can use sketchy or artistic styles for these views, too.

- Traditional **Elevations** of the building facades: Use a parallel projection and clean line styles without line extensions or profiles. You can use a black and white style or shaded as you want but don't let the colors and textures detract you from the geometry.

- **Sectional Views**: Use a parallel projection and enable section cuts.

- **Plan View**: This is a top-down view with parallel projection and section cut. You may need several of these, one for each floor.

When you set up views and perspectives, keep in mind that the aspect ratio of your view in LayOut can be different from your SketchUp screen. Think where you want to use this view and what's the best size for it on the page, not in SketchUp.

You should use one style for one type of view and similar styles for views that will appear on the same page. This will keep the appearance of your LayOut project consistent. For some projects—especially those in early design stages—a convincing artistic style is more important than to convey all the details of the model.

For this chapter, we will use the `Crissy Airfield House` model from the 3D Warehouse as an example again. After you have imported the component from the 3D Warehouse, rotate the model to align it with the global SketchUp coordinate system. This will make setting up the views easier.

Aligning the view to the model

Some models have more than four elevations or are rotated against the SketchUp coordinate system. If this is the case for your model, you can't just use the predefined **Top**, **Left**, and other views to show a building facade because these are aligned to the global coordinate system of the scene.

To align the view with the building facade, perform the following steps:

1. In SketchUp, select a face of the model that's parallel to the facade you want to show.

2. With the face selected, right-click on it and select **Align View**.

3. Go to **Camera | Parallel Projection** and then set up a scene (by navigating to **View | Animation | Add Scene**).

Go through your list of planned views and create scene tabs for each camera setup and corresponding style. When you have created all the scenes and styles, save the SketchUp file. You are now ready to return to LayOut.

Display a SketchUp 3D view

With suitable scenes set up in SketchUp, presenting the model in LayOut becomes very easy. To do this, perform the following steps:

1. In LayOut, create a new layer called `SketchUp Model` and make it the active layer. Also, check that the layers used for your border elements are locked.

2. Select the **Cover Page** in the **Pages** pallet.

3. Go to **File | Insert...**, then navigate to your SketchUp model and click on **Open**.

4. A **viewport** appears on your page with a view of your SketchUp model shown in it. Don't worry if this is not the view you want for the front page.

5. Click on a corner of the viewport rectangle and stretch it to fill the page. Note that you can snap to the corners and edges of the border as you can see in the following screenshot:

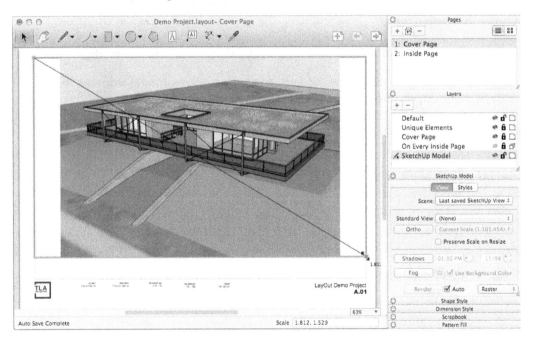

6. The view will resize to fill the window.

7. Right-click on the window and navigate to **Scenes | Hero Shot** in the context menu (or whatever you named the view for your cover page).

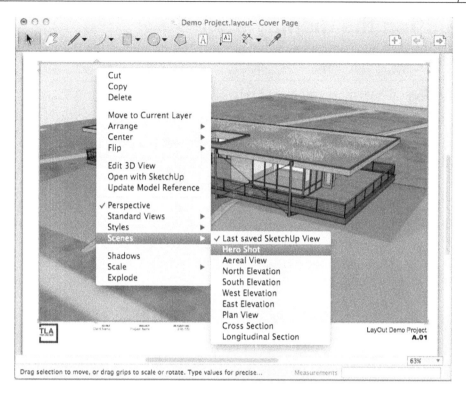

8. The view will update to show your hero shot.

9. If you find that the view is not quite right, double-click on the viewport. This activates the viewport for 3D editing.

10. You can now orbit, pan, and zoom the model just like in SketchUp.
To switch between the view tools, right-click on the viewport and select **Camera Tools** from the context menu.

11. To end your view adjustments, hit the *Esc* key or click on the white area next to the viewport window.

You have just inserted your SketchUp model on a page in LayOut. You adjusted the view as you would in SketchUp, but now you can see exactly what it will look like on the page when it is printed out. This is a fundamentally different way of working compared to other 2D layout applications such as CorelDraw, Inkscape, or Pagemaker because the images on display remain a fully editable 3D model.

Adjusting the display style

Not only can you change the viewpoint, but you can also overwrite the scene style options in each LayOut window as follows:

1. Select the viewport you want to change.

2. Click on the header bar of the **SketchUp Model** pallet to open it.

3. Under the **View** tab, you will find the following options:

   ° **Scene**: Select one of the scenes you set up in SketchUp

   ° **Standard View**: Pick one of the default views (**Top**, **Left**, and so on)

   ° **Ortho** and **Scale**: When you use an orthographic (parallel) projection, LayOut will size the image to the given scale. Perspective views don't use this setting.

   ° **Shadows**: This enables the display of shadows and adjusts the time of day.

   ° **Fog**: This enables fog settings.

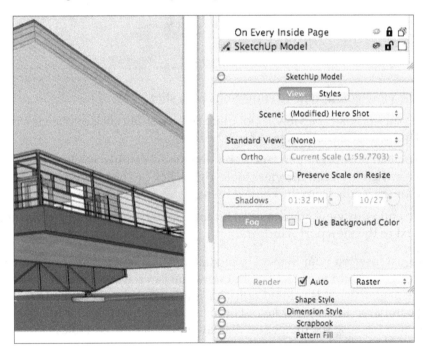

4. Our view is on the north side of the building, so the shadow settings won't help us much. However, we can use a slightly colored fog to add a bit of drama to our image (see the previous screenshot).

5. Note that the **Scene** drop-down menu now has a **(Modified)** prefix. This indicates that you have made changes to the scene that was saved in the SketchUp file.

6. To return to your original settings, just select the original scene from the drop-down list.

Using SketchUp styles

Choosing a different style is just as you would do it in SketchUp:

1. Select the **Styles** tab at the top of the pallet.

2. Choose the style you want from the available SketchUp styles. Use the drop-down menu above the list (the small house icon) to select styles from another collection as shown in the following screenshot:

3. Also, note the **Line Weight** box at the bottom of the list. This defines the thickness of SketchUp edges in the viewport.

4. Again, use the *Esc* key or click on the area outside the viewport when you want to stop editing.

Creating multiple views in LayOut

You're now ready to set up the internal pages of your presentation. For a real project, you should plan carefully what to show. You already gained all the skills for planning your scenes at the start of *Chapter 3, Composing the Scene*. Now, let's create multiple views in LayOut:

1. Click on the SketchUp view you inserted into the cover page.

2. Then, go to **Edit | Copy** (or right-click on the view and select **Copy** from the context menu).

3. Select the **Inside Page** in the pages pallet, then right-click on **Inside Page** and select **Duplicate**. This keeps an empty copy as a template for further pages.

4. Right-click on the copy and select **Rename**. Give it a name that describes the content (for example, Elevations).

5. You can drag the new page above the template **Inside Page**.

6. With the new page selected, right-click on the main LayOut window and select **Paste** from the context menu. A copy of the view from the cover appears on the page.

7. Resize it using the corner grips. A little less than a quarter of the page should do.

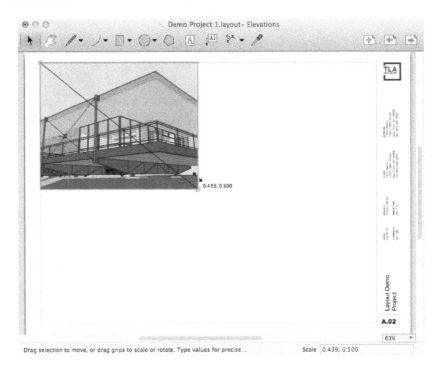

8. Right-click on the viewport and select **Scene | East Elevation** (**East Elevation** is one of the scenes I have set up in SketchUp).

9. Open the **SketchUp Model** pallet.

10. Notice that this view is set up as an **Ortho** projection with a given **Current Scale** of roughly **1:81**.

11. Pick a scale of **1:100** from the drop-down menu. If you are more at home with imperial scales, you can also use **1/8" = 1'-0"**. The scene displayed in the viewport will shrink by a small amount.

12. Make sure that the option to **Preserve Scale on Resize** is checked for the viewport. You should now have a page and settings like those in the following screenshot:

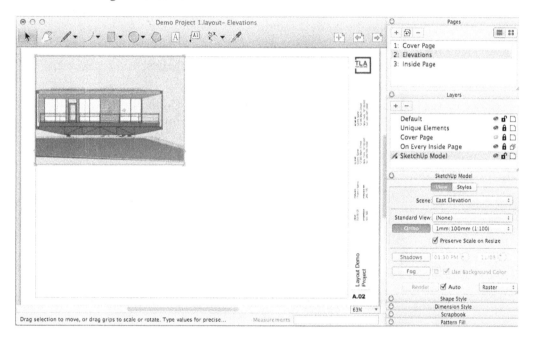

13. The view cuts a bit of off the building at the left edge. To correct this, right-click on the viewport and select **Edit 3D View**. The outline of the viewport will change and you will see the mouse cursor change to the **Orbit** tool icon.

14. Right-click again on the viewport and select **Camera Tools | Pan**. The mouse cursor changes to the **Hand** icon.

15. Now, center the building in the viewport with the **Pan** tool.

16. Hit the *Esc* key to end the 3D view edit session.

Arranging the viewports

With the following steps, we create new viewports quickly and fill the page with views of the model:

1. Use copy and paste to create two new copies of this viewport: one to the right-hand side of the viewport (for the scene `West Elevation`) and one below the viewport (for `North Elevation`).

2. Resize the `North Elevation` viewport to span the whole page.

3. Right-click on each of the views and select the corresponding scene from the **Scenes** context menu.

4. Adjust the scale after you have selected a new scene. All viewports should be set to `1:100` (or `1/8" = 1'-0"`). You can also right-click and access the viewport scale via the context menu.

5. Use **Edit 3D View | Camera Tools | Pan** again to align the east and west elevation vertically. You can draw a horizontal line first as a reference. Zoom in closer for finer adjustments.

6. Now is a good time to save your LayOut project. Go to **File | Save As** and choose a name and location related to your project.

7. Your finished page should look like this:

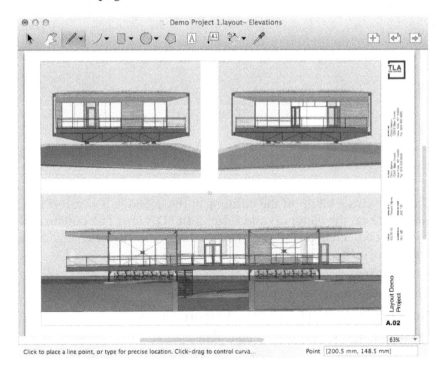

You have set up an orthographic view and adjusted its size on the paper to a standard architectural scale. Copying this view made it easy to create equally sized viewports. The existing scenes in the SketchUp file allowed you to quickly change from one view to another so that all you needed to do was adjust the alignment of the views on the page.

Annotations in LayOut

Now that you have your views arranged, you need to give them a title so that your clients can understand what they are looking at. You could just use the **Text** tool and perhaps add few graphic lines like you can see in the page border, but LayOut has much better options to add standard elements such as drawing references: the **scrapbook**.

A scrapbook is a collection of drawing elements that you can add to your own project just by dragging it onto your page. You can then customize the element for your particular need, for example, by changing some text.

Using scrapbooks

LayOut already has a few scrapbooks with standard elements set up. We will use these to add drawing references to the viewports:

1. Before you add any new elements, create a new layer named
   Annotations.

2. Open the **Scrapbook** pallet.

3. Select **TB-Simple | Drafting Symbols 1** from the drop-down list in the pallet.

4. Click-and-drag one of the drawing reference symbols from the list onto your page. You can see the available symbols in the following screenshot:.

5. The new symbol is a group of text and line elements. Double-click on the group to be able to edit the parts.

6. Double-click on the text **Drawing Description** and change it to East Elevation.

7. Change the **Scale** text to 1:100 (or 1/8"=1'-0" as appropriate).

8. Finally, change the reference number from 0 to 1.

9. Copy and paste the modified group. It will be inserted on top of the original.

10. Move the copy to the West Elevation viewport. Note that LayOut also uses inference snapping when you move an object vertically or horizontally.

11. Adjust the text and drawing reference for the new elevation.

12. Repeat for the North Elevation.

There, you're done. Scrapbook symbols give you a quick way to add decorative or annotative elements without having to draw them from scratch in each document.

Editing scrapbooks

You may have noticed the small **Edit...** button in the top-right corner of the **Scrapbook** pallet. When you click on it, a new LayOut window will open with the list of symbols as a page. Scrapbooks are only LayOut documents that are saved in one of the paths defined in the **Preferences | Folders | Scrapbooks** setting.

Displaying SketchUp sections

There is currently no function to create building sections only in LayOut, so you need to create sectional views in SketchUp first. Once you add a scene with an active section plane to the SketchUp model, it will be available in LayOut as a scene in the viewport menu.

This process is not different from setting up any other view but we can do better. To create clean lines and solid fills for our section elements, we will use SketchUp to create lines that we can then import to LayOut as vector objects. These will always be rendered at maximum quality regardless of the setting of the main SketchUp view.

This technique has been presented by Nick Sonder at a SketchUp Bootcamp and documented in several videos on YouTube. If you want to see more about this and his incredibly detailed LayOut drawings, just search for `Nick Sonder Process` on YouTube.

Creating section line work

To prepare the line work, we need to go back to SketchUp and set up a section plane through our model:

1. Set up a scene in SketchUp that contains an active section plane and arrange an orthogonal view of the section cut. We are using a plan view of the building as example.

2. Set up a new viewport in your LayOut document with this scene as explained in the steps in the previous sections.

3. Go back to SketchUp and select the section plane.

4. Right-click on the section plane and select **Create Group from Slice**.

5. SketchUp will create a new group with lines for every face that is cut by the section plane.

6. You may have to disable the section plane now to be able to see the newly created group.

7. Select the new group now. Start editing the lines to fill solid elements such as walls with a surface, and remove details that you don't want to see in your LayOut presentation.

8. Finally, assign a dark or bright color to the group, whichever works better for the style of your section (we use a bright red for illustration). You can see the resulting geometry in the following screenshot, moved above the section plane for easy editing:

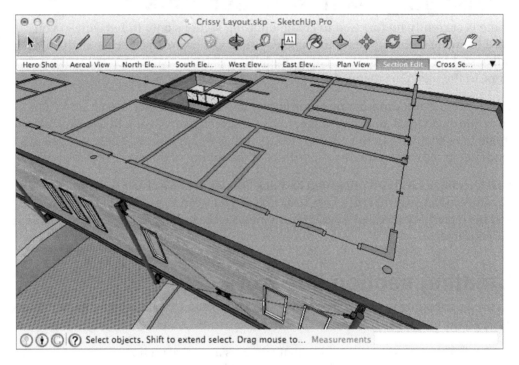

9. Select the section lines group, right-click on it, and select **Copy**.

10. Change back to the LayOut application and select the page with the viewport for your section view.

11. Create a new layer called SectionLines and make it active.

12. Lock the layer with your existing viewports (**SketchUp Model** in our case) to avoid any changes to the view setup.

13. Now go to **File** | **Paste**.

14. The geometry you copied in SketchUp will be inserted as a new SketchUp model with its own viewport. You can apply the same modifications and transformations to this viewport that you can apply to an external SketchUp model, including perspective changes and scaling.

15. Adjust the scale of the new viewport to match your underlying view. You can see the result in the following screenshot:

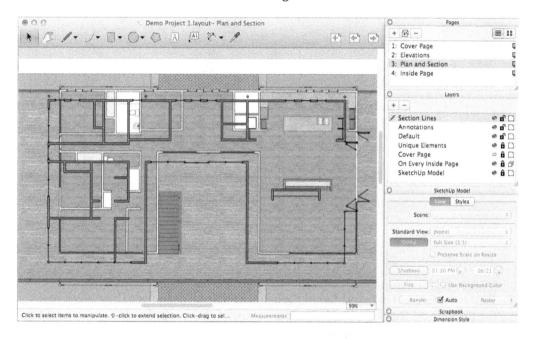

16. Now, move the new view with the lines in place above the old (shaded) section view.

17. The last thing to do for this viewport is to set the render mode at the bottom right of the **SketchUp Model** pallet to **Vector** for a crisp outline of the lines and polygons.

Now, all this looks like a lot of work for a section that you can just as well get for free from a SketchUp scene with section planes enabled. The benefit is that the vector-rendered section lines will always come out crisp regardless of the quality of the other views. It will also help with dimensioning because you can snap the dimension lines precisely to the section geometry.

Dimensions

Adding dimensions is pretty much self-explanatory. Just click on the **Dimensions** button and snap to the end points of the building. In the following screenshot, a few horizontal dimensions have been placed in the drawing:

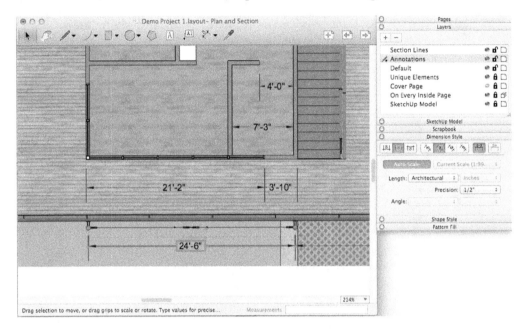

Use the **Dimension**, **Text**, and **Label** tools now on your drawing. They work just like the dimension tools in SketchUp or any other CAD program. You may find that sometimes the dimension displayed by LayOut is not correct. This is usually because the dimension line will snap to points in 3D space and LayOut calculates the 3D distance between the points and not the 2D distance that you expect. In that case, switch off the layer with your SketchUp viewports and snap the dimensions to the section lines we created in the previous section.

When your initial dimension line doesn't look quite right, use the options in the **Dimension Style** pallet to adjust the appearance. You can also move the position of the dimension line after you have placed it on the drawing.

Slideshows and presentations

LayOut is a cross between CAD, vector graphics software, and PowerPoint. If you set up multiple pages in LayOut, they can be viewed as a slideshow just like a presentation in PowerPoint (but without the scene animations you get in SketchUp) or printed as a portfolio of pictures.

Creating a presentation

With the following simple steps, you can quickly create a slideshow presentation of your model:

1. Start a new file in LayOut by navigating to **File | New**.

2. Select a plain paper template in landscape format.

3. Add elements to the page that you want to see on every slide of your presentation, such as a logo or page counter. Use **Auto-Text** for page numbers.

4. Insert a SketchUp model on the first page as before.

5. In the **Pages** pallet, click on the **Duplicate** button.

6. Modify the viewport perspective or style, and add text or other elements.

7. Repeat the steps 5 and 6 for all of your slides.

8. To view your slides, go to **View | Start Presentation**.

9. You can use the left and right mouse buttons or the arrow keys on your computer to go forward and backwards between the slides.

10. While you show the presentation, you can also use the mouse to add notes and markup to your slides. When you finish the presentation, you will be asked if you want to save these markups to the file.

Adding further elements to enhance LayOut pages

By inserting background images, adding shapes, and controlling the view order of each element, you can build up interesting page layouts.

The order of elements is defined via the layer stack. Elements on the same layer can be arranged with the **Arrange** menu. Just select an element and go to **Arrange | Bring Forward / Send Backward** as you need.

For some SketchUp styles, LayOut automatically clips the background, which allows the elements on another layer to show through. You need to have the **Background** option in the **SketchUp Model | Styles** pallet deselected to make this work.

You can use LayOut to arrange several views of your SketchUp model, along with photos, renderings, or a non-photoreal output that you modified in GIMP. Each page can now be shown as a slide, or exported as a PDF or individual images.

Exporting and printing

You can export your whole project or only individual pages as PDF, JPEG, or PNG images. PDF is usually a good choice because it combines vector quality markup with raster images at varied resolutions. PNG or JPEG should only be used when PDF is not possible or when you want to edit the exported image further in GIMP.

Exporting a PDF document from LayOut

Before you export your document, set the render quality according to your needs and the intended use of the document. Always follow these steps just to make sure you have the right option selected:

1. To start the export, go to **File | Export**.

2. Make sure that your output format is set to **PDF**.

3. Click on the **Options** button.

4. The important option here is the **Output Quality** drop-down menu. It will affect the file size but also the resolution of the rendered SketchUp views. Choose **Low** or **Medium** if you are placing the PDF document on the web or sending it via e-mail and **High** if you want to print from it.

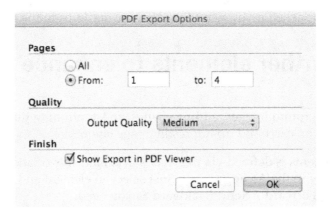

5. Pick a filename and location and click on the **Save** button.

6. Your PDF file will be created. If you export more than one page, you will get a single PDF document with multiple pages.

7. Depending on the **Finish** option (see the preceding screenshot), the PDF will open in your viewer once it has been created.

Export to print

If you have a high-quality color printer in your office, you can print out your creations directly from LayOut. Before you do so, change the output quality to get the best results:

1. Go to **File | Document Setup...**.
2. Select the **Paper** options.
3. Under **Rendering Resolution**, set the **Output Quality** drop-down menu to **High**.
4. Click on **Close**.
5. For each SketchUp viewport, you can also set the render method from **Raster** to **Vector** or **Hybrid** independently.
   - **Raster**: This method renders the view exactly as in SketchUp using pixels.
   - **Vector**: This method uses lines and color fills. It is better for lines or solid-colored surfaces, but it won't retain sketchy line styles or textures.
   - **Hybrid**: This method is a bit of both, so it can produce the best image quality but takes longer to process.
6. Finally, you can go to **File | Print** and click on the **Print** button.

Summary

In this chapter, you have briefly experienced the capabilities of the LayOut application, which comes with SketchUp Pro. You can use it to set up drawings from a SketchUp model or compose a 2D collage out of various source images.

You've learned how to create custom drawing borders to give your documents a professional appearance and how to use SketchUp scenes and styles to show your 3D model on paper. You set the viewport scale of your SketchUp model to an accurate value and added text and dimensions. You also looked at the preparation of slideshows for output on a projector and how to arrange a mix of SketchUp views, renders, and other images.

I hope this chapter has given you a feel for LayOut and that you will continue to use it for your future projects. You are now fully equipped to ride on the crest of SketchUp's wave and produce and present powerful images on the screen and on paper.

In the next chapter, we will go beyond SketchUp and look at some current technologies to create animations quickly or prepare interactive 3D environments for your clients.

12
Interactive Visualization

So far, you have learned how to create visuals and animations from SketchUp or an external renderer. These fulfill more or less the role of the traditional architectural drawing. We even used GIMP to make our renderings look more like hand drawings! However, progress in computer graphics and processing speed has not only made photoreal rendering accessible to everyone, but it has also opened up new ways of storing and presenting the information that is embedded in a digital image.

In this chapter, we explore a few new technologies that will allow you to interact with your rendering or 3D environment in real time. In particular, we will look at the following options:

- The **Relight** feature that's built into Thea Studio
- **LumenRT** by e-on software (www.lumenrt.com)

You already have Thea Studio installed and can download a trial version of LumenRT from the website. Be warned that the download is almost 2 GB in size. The trial is fully featured for 14 days, but limited in the content that comes with the applications. You will also find that the output quality is limited, and there are notes and watermarks to indicate that you are not using a licensed product.

Lighting animation with Thea Relight

At first, we will take a look at a feature that is part of Thea Studio: Relight. With Relight, you can modify the distribution of light in your image after the rendering is complete. This means that you can create combinations of lighting levels and colors and even create an animation from a single, rendered image. The major benefit here is that the new settings can be applied immediately and don't require a new image to be rendered.

Preparing the SketchUp scene

To work with Relight, we need a scene that contains a few light sources. We can return to our gallery scene from *Chapter 1, Quick Start Tutorial*, and simply add a few spotlights and a striplight using the Thea plugin. To illustrate the positions and directions of the spots, I have added a tracklight component from the 3D Warehouse. In the following screenshot, you can see the scene with the new elements:

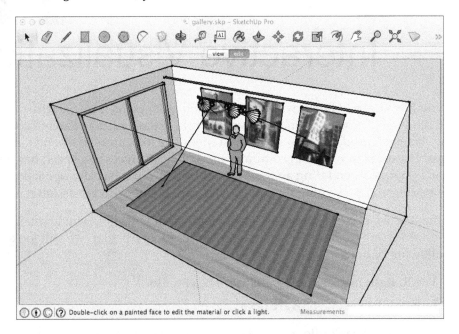

In our example, the spotlights have the default values for the hotspot and falloff. Only the light intensity is set to 100 Watt for each light source. The striplight is created as a rectangle with a light-emitting material. The light intensity here is also set to 100 Watt. It is not important to find the perfect balance for the light fixtures now. Just give them enough power to have a noticeable effect on the scene. You should keep the light color to the default white, though.

 You can download the SketchUp file of this scene from the download section of this book at www.packtpub.com/support.

Exporting to Thea Studio

We want to open our scene in Thea Studio, so we have to export it to a `*.scn.thea` file first. To do this, perform the following steps:

1. Create a new folder on your hard drive to hold all of the files for the scene. Using a dedicated export folder keeps all the necessary files together.

2. In SketchUp, set up the view you want to export, save it as a scene, and make it your current view.

3. Open the **Thea Tools** window and set up the aspect ratio and resolution for your image. In the end, we will create an animation from this image, so don't go crazy with the resolution.

4. Disable the options for **Use Sky** and **Use Sun**. We only want the spots and area light in the scene.

5. Go to the **Tools** tab and click on the **Export model as Thea Scene** button.

6. Select the folder you just created and give your scene a name for the export, such as `gallery_relight.scn.thea`. The main scene file and associated files (such as our image textures) will be saved in the new folder.

7. Open the Thea Studio application. It should be enough to double-click on the `gallery_relight.scn.thea` file that was just created. Thea Studio will open with a 3D preview of the scene, as shown in the following screenshot:

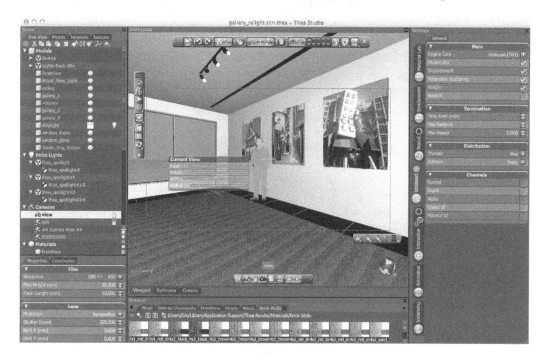

8. On the left-hand side of the screen, you will find a **Scene** outline of the objects. If you don't have the correct view displayed in the 3D window, search for your scene in this list under **Cameras** and double-click on it to set the right camera angle.

9. Below the 3D view, you find tabs for **Viewport** and **Darkroom**. Switch to the **Darkroom** tab now.

10. The lower part of the **Darkroom** screen shows the **Display** settings that you are familiar with from the SketchUp plugin. Adjust **ISO** (800), **Shutter Speed** (125), and **f-number** (2.8) for an interior scene with artificial lighting.

11. On the right-hand side of the screen, you see the **Settings** window with vertical tabs. Click on the **Unbiased** tab. The options for the unbiased render engine will be shown.

12. Under the **Main** settings, you will find the **Relight** option. Activate it.

13. Now, just hit the **Start** button to begin the render. You have to use the unbiased render method to produce an image that is usable for Relight.

Using Relight

Let the image render for a while. When it has reached a quality that you are happy with, you can stop the rendering process. The raw rendering will look like the example in the following screenshot:

You will notice that overall it's not very well lit, and the spotlights create very visible patches on the wall. Don't worry; we can fix this in a second with Relight.

Switch to the **Relight** tab (next to the **Display** tab). You will see the Relight controls, below the image, as in the following screenshot:

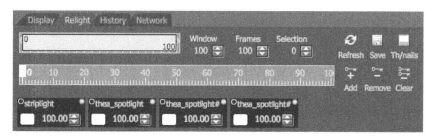

The controls are arranged in the following three groups:

- Frame selection (horizontally at the top)
- Key frame buttons and other actions to the right
- A list of light sources in the scene at the bottom (one **striplight** source and three **thea_spotlights** sources in our case)

You can click on the **Th/nails** button in the second group to switch the display of light sources from a simple list to small thumbnails with each light's distribution. There is also a small rectangle with a light color and an indicator of the light intensity. So far, they are all white and set to 100. Using these controls, you can now adjust the impact that each light has on the final scene.

Go ahead and test a few variations. Change the intensity of each light or click on the white rectangle to change the color in a color-picker dialog box. Don't forget to click on **Refresh** after each change, or you won't see the main image updated.

Creating a Relight animation

When you have experimented with the effects of each light source, it's time to create an animation where we will fade each light in and out and finally settle for a balanced composite of all the lights:

1. Set the **Frames** value in the first group to 500. This will define the length of our animation (about 20 seconds at 25 frames per second).

2. The top scale now shows a shorter bright bar. This gives you the position of the lower frames window relative to the whole animation. Make sure it's positioned all the way to the left.

3. In the **Frames** window, move the key frame indicator to `frame 0`.

4. Set all the lights to zero output and click on **Refresh**. Now, the image is completely dark.

5. Click on the **Add** button to add the first key frame for the animation.

6. Move the indicator to `frame 50` and increase the light output of the **striplight** to `100`. Don't forget to refresh to see the selected state.

7. Create another key frame.

8. Move on to `frame 100` and add another key frame with all the lights dark again.

9. Repeat this for each light at a step of 50 frames. As you can see in the following screenshot, you can also change the color of the light during the animation:

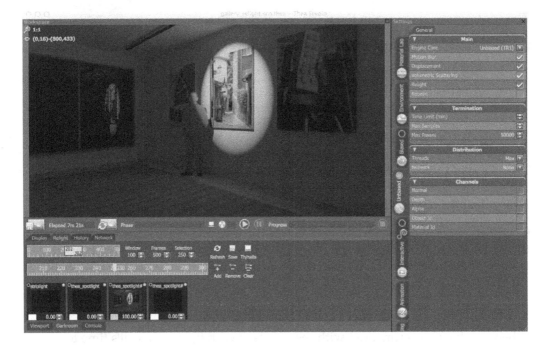

10. At `frame 400`, you should have all your lights back at `0`.

11. Now, add a last frame at the position `500` where the intensity of each light is well balanced in the scene. I think increasing the striplight to `300` and reducing the spots to `80` makes the image brighter and removes the visibility of the spots on the wall.

12. Create a new folder to hold all the frames of the animation.

13. Now, click on the **Save** button and select to export the whole sequence.

14. Choose the new folder as the location and pick a filename. The images will be created with the frame number appended to the filename, for example, `relight_animation0001.png`.

Now, the animation frames will be created. Each frame will show a different fraction of the light so that the animation will look like a continuous dimming of each light. The main advantage of creating the frames using Relight is the time that is required to calculate all the images. It only takes a second or two for each frame depending on your image size and computer hardware.

After all the images have been done, you can use the tools we introduced in *Chapter 10, Animations*, to convert the images into a video clip. Since the whole scene is static except for the lights, you can easily slow down the frame rate of the animation without visible artifacts. You can do this to achieve a more compact animation file with slower rendering times.

Changing materials with Colimo

Thea has another feature that will surprise you: an interface to **Colimo** by Motiva (`www.motivacg.com/en/colimo`). With this software, you can exchange materials in an image after it has been rendered, just like you did with individual lights in Relight.

Before you render, you enable the option for materials to be editable in Colimo, then you render the image. At first, the image will have no colors or textures on the designated materials; however, when you export it to Colimo, you are able to assign colors, textures, and surface characteristics with immediate feedback.

This is not just a simple change to a specific color in the image that you could also manage with GIMP or Photoshop tools. The change gets applied to all areas of the image that were affected by the original material, such as reflections or refractions in a translucent object. You should go and check some of the YouTube videos that the developers have published to get an idea of its potential and how much time you can save when you want to test various combinations of materials in a scene.

Immersive environment with LumenRT

In this section, we will look at a product that generates interactive 3D environments from a SketchUp scene. Thanks to the advances in computer graphics—and also to the success of video games—there are now a number of new software products available that can convert a SketchUp or CAD 3D model into a photoreal environment with textures and natural lighting. Some of these are even based on video game rendering systems (the game engine), while others are dedicated to high-quality visualizations.

LumenRT is published by e-on software, famous for its *digital nature* line of products to create and render natural environments and vegetation. LumenRT is available for Windows and Mac, and you can download a trial version and sample projects from `www.lumenrt.com/download`. Like all software that uses the advanced features of your graphics card to perform calculations, LumenRT requires a recent graphics card with current drivers. You can find the detailed requirements on its website.

Using the LumenRT plugin in SketchUp

When you install LumenRT, it will install a plugin for SketchUp on your system. When you restart SketchUp afterwards, you will find a new toolbar and submenu in the **Plugins** menu. The following screenshot shows the contents of the **Plugins** menu:

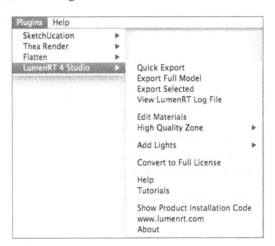

As you can see from the previous screenshot, there are three export options (**Quick Export**, **Export Full Model**, and **Export Selected**). The export to LumenRT also includes a conversion process called "baking" that can take a few minutes, especially if you have a complex and detailed model. During setup and for tests, you don't always want to wait so long. In that case, you can just use the **Quick Export** option, which produces lower quality exports within a shorter time.

You can also find menu entries to **Edit Materials** and **Add Lights** (spotlights and point lights). These tools work like their counterparts in Thea or other rendering applications, where they create special material properties or entities that are not available in SketchUp. The installer has also copied a number of special LumenRT components into the SketchUp component library folder. You can access these via the standard SketchUp **Components** window.

As a test scene, we will use the **Crissy Airfield** scene from the 3D Warehouse again. I have removed the walkway and turned the model by 180 degrees to have the balconies facing south. This will give us nicer shadows in the scene. Again, you can download the modified scene from Packt Publishing's support website for this book.

Editing materials

When you have a scene modeled and textured in SketchUp, you can add further properties to the materials to make them look more realistic using the following steps:

1. Navigate to **Plugins | LumenRT 4 Studio | Edit Materials**.

2. The LumenRT material editor window opens, which can be seen in the following screenshot:

3. Select a material via the drop-down list or use the eyedropper button to pick a material from the SketchUp scene.

4. Set the appropriate material type and then assign the desired values for specularity, bump, and so on.

For typical opaque materials, material type **Standard** is used. The other available material types are **Varnished**, **Metallic**, **Glass**, and **Water**. They offer the usual advanced options for specularity and other values that you already know about. In the preceding screenshot, you can see that I have selected the material type **Metallic** for the **Structural Steel** material in SketchUp. The material type **Water** is special; it creates an animated water surface that produces caustic refraction patterns. LumenRT will also assign a specific material type if the material name contains keywords such as "glass" or "brick".

Adding digital nature components

To add more realism to the scene, you can add optimized components to the scene that get translated by LumenRT to highly detailed models of plants, vehicles, people, or animals. Some of these are even animated to perform certain movements or move with the wind. Be careful with the animated characters, though. Sometimes, the added realism is just enough to make the characters look even more artificial. To add components, perform the following steps:

1. To find the components, open the SketchUp **Components** window.

2. Click on the small house symbol and choose the **LumenRT 4 Studio** collection.

3. The collection is organized into **Animals**, **Characters**, **Plants**, and **Vehicles**. Choose the **Plants** folder.

4. The trial installation of LumenRT only has a limited set of components. Pick one of the available plants and place it into the scene, just like any other SketchUp component. The following screenshot shows the **Plants** collection in the **Components** window:

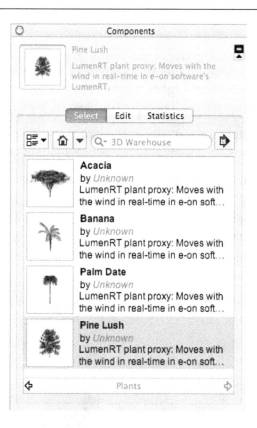

5. To add more variety, you can scale and rotate a component in the scene. The modifications will be picked up by LumenRT during the export and applied to the high-resolution model.

6. Add a few more plants to the scene to give it a bit of context (see the next screenshot for an example).

Adding lights

You can add point lights and spotlights to your scene to add illumination for night-time renderings. Just select the **Add LumenRT Point Light** or **Add LumenRT Spot Light** option from the **Add Lights** submenu to place a new light in the scene. There are no options to set for the lights via the SketchUp interface.

If you already have components in your scene that mark the position of the lights, add the necessary lighting information to the component instances, as follows:

1. Select one of the components that you want to modify.

2. Now, navigate to **Plugins | LumenRT 4 Studio | Add Lights | Point Light / Spot Light from Component**. This option is not available when no component instance is selected.

3. During the export, the plugin will create a light source for each instance of this component in the scene.

The following screenshot shows our scene with several plant components surrounding the building:

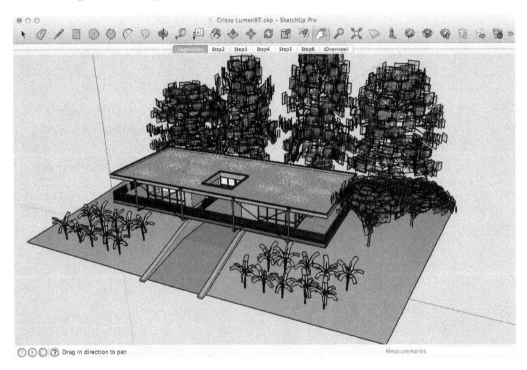

Exporting the scene

With the scene setup complete, create your first LiveCube using the following steps:

1. Go to **Plugins | LumenRT 4 Studio | Export Full Model**. The export dialog window appears (see the following screenshot).

2. Leave the **Adjustable time of day** option checked.

3. Under **SKY** and **HORIZON**, choose a preset environment for your scene. The trial version only offers one option, so we will leave it at the default.

4. The **LIGHTING QUALITY** field sets the options used to calculate the lighting environment during the baking phase. This option has a large impact on the rendering time, so for the first export, choose **Draft** or **Standard**.

5. Click on the spanner symbol to access further options for the scene export.

6. Choose **Grass** for the **PEDESTAL** option. The pedestal is an area that surrounds the model. You can think of it as the ground plane.

7. **Smooth Motion** defines how much interpolation is used for the calculation of a camera path from an animation that was set up in SketchUp. Higher values provide a smoother transition between the scenes.

8. Leave the remaining options checked. They are mostly relevant for larger models.

9. Click on **OK** to close the **Options** window.

10. Back in the main export window, click on the large **Start** button to begin the export.

11. Check the SketchUp status bar for the progress of the export. It will give you the count of the processed entities and of how many still need to be exported.

After the export phase, the LumenRT baker application will start and begin to convert the exported geometry into a LiveCube. Depending on the settings of your lighting quality and the complexity of your model, this process can take anything from a few minutes to hours. With a quality setting of **Standard** and a model the size of our example, you should be done within 5 to 10 minutes.

The finished LiveCube will be saved in a new folder at the path `Documents/e-on software/LumenRT 4 Studio/[scene name]`. Should LumenRT crash during exploration, you can find the LiveCube in this folder and start it up again.

Navigating the LiveCube

When the LiveCube baking is done, it will open on the screen, and you can start exploring your photoreal environment. If you had an animation set up in SketchUp, it will be included in the LiveCube, and by default, it will start to loop through the animation path. Note that the following screenshot does not show a precalculated animation movie but a live rendering of camera movement through the scene:

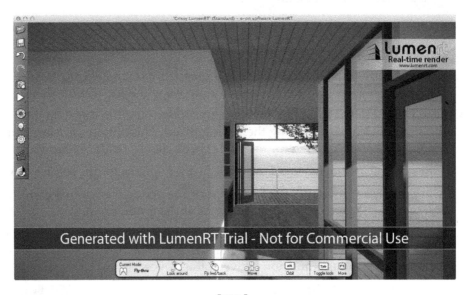

If you have any experience with first person video games, you should be able to navigate around the LiveCube with ease. The following are three different modes to move around the scene; you can switch between them via the function keys on your keyboard:

- **Animation** (*F2*): This mode is only available if you set up a key frame animation in SketchUp or LumenRT.

- **Walk-Thru** (*F3*): Click the left mouse button to move forward and move the mouse to indicate the direction. Your viewpoint will be fixed to 1.6 m above the ground, but you can walk up inclined surfaces or steps. *PageUp* and *PageDown* will help you move vertically.

- **Fly-Thru** (*F4*): In this mode, you can use the left, middle, and right mouse buttons to locate, zoom, and pan in the scene. The movement is similar to the navigation in a CAD application.

In the default setting, a small ribbon shows the mouse button and key functions related to the current mode. To activate an extended menu, press the *F1* key. Experiment with the movement modes and explore your model in 3D. While you are moving through the scene, you can modify the shadow settings with the *G* and *H* keys. These will change the time of day, and so, the shadow, intensity, and color of the daylight.

LiveCube tools and settings

You will notice that LumenRT does not have any menu options or visible buttons. To access the available scene settings and tool options, press the *Tab* key. The main menu will appear at the left edge of the window. The following is a screenshot of the main menu:

At the top of the column, you will find two icons—**Load** and **Save**—to load and save the LiveCube settings. Note that the settings file does not contain the whole LiveCube data but only the changeable options.

The next two icons are **Undo** and **Redo** and work as expected.

Exporting images

When you discover a stunning view of your project while walking around, you will obviously want to share it. To create a rendering for your current view of the LiveCube, perform the following steps:

1. Right-click on the **Camera** icon (only for the first image, to set the export options).

2. The **Photo Options** window opens, as shown in the following screenshot:

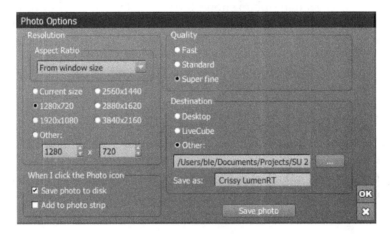

3. Set **Aspect Ratio**, **Resolution**, and **Quality** as per your needs. Although creating an image is much faster than with a traditional renderer, it will still take several seconds for a large image of high quality to be saved to disk.

4. Set the destination folder with the folder location and image filename. Each new image will be created with the name given in the **Save as** field and a number appended to it (for example, Crissy LumenRT001.jpg).

5. Click on **OK** to close this window.

6. Now, left-click on the **Camera** icon. This will save a new image to the destination folder. Alternatively, you can also use the *F6* key.

7. Move around in the scene a bit, and when you have found another good view, just left-click again; a new image will be saved in the same folder.

Continue to walk through your scene and create as many new images as you like. You can map out all the angles and vantage points of your model and document any good locations in an image.

 Note the options under **When I click the Photo icon**. You can save a new image to your hard drive and add the image to a **Photo strip**. This second option is an alternative way of creating a key frame animation.

Creating an animation

The simplest way of creating an animation is to set it up in SketchUp as a sequence of scenes. These will be imported as key frames into LumenRT, and you can have the animation sequence start as soon as you open the LiveCube. Once you are in the application, you will have more control over the key frames than in SketchUp. To edit or create a new clip, open up the **Timeline Editor** via the **clapperboard** symbol in the toolbar, as shown in the following screenshot:

The **Timeline** window is displayed below the current view of the scene. At the top, you'll find one tab for **Movie Editor** and one for each animation sequence (called "clip") that you have set up. You can create new clips with the **+** symbol next to the tabs.

Editing an animation sequence

If you used the **Photo strip** option while creating the snapshots, you will also find a tab called **Photo Strip** that contains all the images that you took as key frames for the sequence. The images may not have been taken in order, or the time interval between them may not be conducive to a smooth animation. Either way, some editing is in order.

1. Click on the tab for your clip to show the sequence of images in the editor.

2. The orange bar at the top indicates the length of the sequence in seconds. The triangular marker above the line is your current position, while the square markers below indicate the position of each key frame.

3. You can move your position along the line by dragging the triangle along the time scale.

4. If you need to change the sequence of the images, just click on an image that is not in the right place and drag it across to the correct location.

5. Click on the key frame markers and drag them along to change the time between the previous or following key frame. LumenRT will try to keep a steady animation speed by inserting key frames based on the distance in camera positions. Larger steps will be assigned more time.

6. During the setup of your clip, new frames will be added at the end of the animation.

7. If you see that you are missing a frame, you can also insert a new frame by moving the current frame indicator to the desired position. You will see a small camera symbol appear between the two frame thumbnails. Click on this symbol to add an intermediate frame to the clip.

8. At any time, you can click on the triangular **Start** button to the left of the timeline to play back the animation.

Editing a movie

The first tab is called **Movie Editor**. It is very similar to the clip editor, but instead of key frames, it shows entire clips. Here, you can arrange the individual clips that you have created into a complete movie. You can also import static images and add transitions between the clips. In short, it is a simple version of Movie Maker built right into LumenRT.

Exporting a video

So far, the animation sequence is only available within the LiveCube. To export the movie sequence, you just set it up as a standard video clip that everyone can play back. Click on the **Play Movie** button in the task bar to the left of the scene window. You will see the following movie export options:

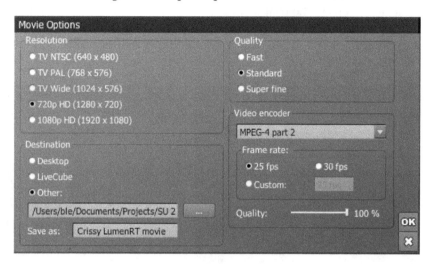

You have preset standard video resolutions to choose from as well as frame rate and image quality. When you pick the video encoder, remember that you can always use HandBrake to convert the video from LumenRT to your desired format, for example, if you want to use H.264 compression.

Choose the destination and name for the video file and click on **OK**. The export of the movie will start, and a pop up window will show the current frame. You will notice immediately that it takes only seconds to calculate each frame. Nevertheless, if you are working on a particularly long animation, you should still consider a test animation with **Quality** set to Fast and a low resolution. It will finish within a fraction of the time, and you can review the entire project and make changes.

When the export has been completed, you can open up the movie in a video player to check the quality and overall appearance.

Publishing the LiveCube

The last—and most compelling—feature of LumenRT is the ability to create a standalone application that enables everyone with a computer to navigate and explore the 3D scene without the need for any other installed software. To do this, you need LiveCube Publisher, which is a separate application from LumenRT that needs a dedicated license. The trial includes a time-limited version of the Publisher and also adds a watermark to the generated LiveCube. The following screenshot shows the options available for the export that define the appearance and behavior of the LiveCube:

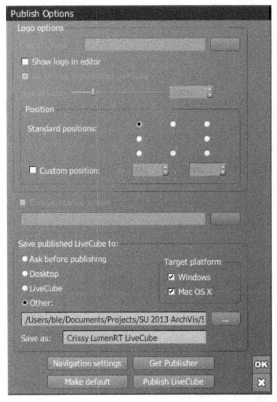
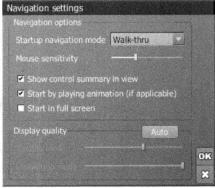

1. To access the **Publish Options** window, press the **Publish** icon in the toolbar.

2. If you are using the trial version, you will get a nagging message to buy the full product license before the trial is over.

3. Most of the options cover branding of the final LiveCube, such as the choice and position of a logo or startup screen.

4. You can choose to generate a LiveCube for Windows, Mac OS X, or both.

5. Define the location and filename of the finished LiveCube.

6. Click on the button for the **Navigation settings**.

7. Here, you can define under **Startup navigation mode** if the LiveCube will start with an animation (if available) or in the **Walk-thru** or **Fly-thru** mode.

8. The other options are good defaults. Always keep in mind that your clients may never have used a LiveCube before and need guidance on how to interact with the 3D environment.

9. Click on **OK** to close the **Navigation settings** window.

10. Finally, click on **Publish LiveCube** to generate the standalone version of your 3D scene.

11. Wait for the message that the process was successful.

Now, you can pick up your published LiveCube in the folder that you specified and distribute it to your clients. The files may be quite large, so you should have a good file sharing solution in place. Be sure to contact them later for feedback to learn more about the way your clients and colleagues interact with the 3D scene. This is a new technology, and we all have to learn how to use it to communicate our designs most effectively.

Summary

You have now seen—and hopefully experienced firsthand by following our examples—how important planning the right view and scene setup is for the impression you want to make. You learned simple and fast techniques for SketchUp and GIMP that can change the appearance of your rendered images dramatically.

You used Thea to render photoreal images from SketchUp scenes and created animations and LayOut presentations to present your project. In this last chapter, we have completed our tour of visualization technologies with a quick introduction to interactive 3D environments.

We hope you enjoyed the topics in this book and that you will be able to use this knowledge to create mesmerizing architectural visualizations for your project.

Choosing a Rendering Software

On your way to become a pro rendering artist, you will have to make the decision about which rendering application you are going to use. While most artists keep testing new software when it becomes available, they stick to one specific package for the majority of their work and invest significant time and money in education and upgrades. To give you some means of evaluation of the currently available technologies, we have provided this short list of criteria for rendering applications.

What should I look for in a renderer?

In general, you should look for the following features in a photorealistic rendering software:

- Rendering quality
- Integration with SketchUp
- Advanced materials and lighting
- Training and support
- Data exchange
- Other considerations

I've chosen these criteria — and their order — based on the general rendering and workflow requirements. You may find that you have other specific requirements that are not listed here. In this case, feel free to amend this overview according to your needs. Always remember that your individual workflow requires a matching solution that may not meet other criteria but is nevertheless the best option for you.

Rendering quality

Of course, the most important aspect of a rendered image is the final quality. You don't want to spend hours of setup and rendering time and then, just get a mediocre image rendered.

Many elements influence the rendering quality, but a good global illumination model has, by far, the biggest impact on the appearance of the scene. Unfortunately, this is also not an easy-to-spot element in an image, but a rather subtle quality to the distribution of indirect light. It's easy to miss good global illumination when it is done right, but you will notice it immediately when the indirect light is done wrong or missing altogether.

Ideally, it should also work out of the box without the need to study and understand all the features of the renderer. Unbiased rendering engines provide this at the cost of long rendering times. To achieve faster renderings (for example, for an animation), biased rendering engines are better but require a significant amount of learning before they produce images that are as good.

Interoperability with SketchUp

In general, you should look for a renderer that works within SketchUp and also generates a quick view of your scene without any additional steps. This allows you to set up a workflow with a quick feedback loop. For this, it is also important to know how secondary SketchUp features such as shadow settings or the component hierarchy are supported and how render-specific information is maintained in the SketchUp scene. After all, you don't want to repeat the same light and material setup each time you reopen a SketchUp file.

Sometimes, an integrated renderer can be as much of a drawback as a benefit, because you can't carry on modeling when SketchUp is locked in a rendering cycle for hours! Also, an external renderer usually handles imports of other file formats better. So, what you should look out for is a standalone render application with a SketchUp plugin or one that supports SketchUp's native `*.skp` format really well. Most up-to-date plugins should work with SketchUp Maker, but some older versions may require a Pro license (usually for the `*.obj` export feature).

Training and support

The most effective learning material that you can find is a free demo version. Nothing gives you an idea about the workflow and features of a renderer better than actually using it. A demo version should allow you access to all the features, although you will find that frequently advanced features are disabled after a period of use. The longer you can use the software before you have to make a decision to buy it, the better.

Once you start rendering regularly, you will become more and more aware that rendering is more about time than quality. Once you have the quality settings sorted out (and you will), the amount of readily available content (materials, entourage, and render templates) that you can download and use in your own projects can become a significant factor so that you can produce renders quickly, efficiently, and on schedule. You should look for active user forums with many example materials and scenes but also for commercial 3D content providers and how their material can be used in your software. The dominant file formats in this market are `*.3ds`, `*.max`, and `*.obj`.

The time required to learn new software may also be an issue. User forums and online documentation can be of great help, but they require that you invest your own time to read and follow the threads and tutorials. Online or on-site training offers by experts can help you speed up the learning process and may be worth the investment for your company.

Other considerations

Once you are creating your own renderings, you will find that the final image is never the product of a single application; you use SketchUp to set up the scene, perhaps, with the help of a few specialist plugins. Third-party content may need to be converted before you can use it in SketchUp or directly in your renderer. You may use a specific HDRI environment in the project and need to edit the HDR images first. Then, you have several postproduction steps before the raw rendered image is finished. Connectivity to other supporting software is the key for a productive workflow and can very well decide the suitability of a renderer.

For your everyday work, you will also wish for good hardware support—and good hardware in the first place. Consumer graphics cards have reached an incredible level of complexity, and more and more developers of professional graphics applications try to utilize these resources to speed up the rendering process. This can give your workflow a great boost, and even give you instantaneous feedback. To achieve the best results, you have to choose both hardware and software carefully. There are competing technologies on the market, and your rendering requirements could dictate both hardware and software to use.

On the subject of hardware support, a network-rendering feature may also be of interest, especially when you consider the creation of animated content. After you have accomplished the scene setup on your workstation, the rendering of large images or individual frames of an animation can be distributed to powerful (but noisy) server systems to speed up the rendering process—if the rendering software supports it. Today, you can also find online services that offer network rendering in a cloud environment. These services save you the cost for rendering hardware and licenses.

Are you outgrowing Thea Render?

If you have used Thea to follow the examples in the book, you may wonder why you should choose a different rendering application when Thea can provide all of the features that you need to create photoreal renderings. In fact, there is no immediate need for you to use anything else, and this is exactly the reason why I picked Thea as the rendering software for this book.

With Thea Render you get the following features:

- It provides easy-rendering modes for beginners but lets you tweak the render settings to improve the rendering time or achieve advanced effects as you become more experienced

- At the beginning, you can download a number of high-quality materials from the website and experiment with the settings in the material lab when you have the need for more specialized materials

- You can use the existing sun and sky models to create realistic lighting conditions or use HDRI images for specific atmospheres

- There are advanced features (such as Relight or the Colimo interface) that can be useful for the presentation and evaluation of design options

- You have the choice of using it entirely from SketchUp or as a standalone product with Thea Studio

I think that with these features, Thea Render has the common requirements of a rendering application well covered. However, other features are not present, and if you consider projects that require some of the following functionality, you should look at other packages:

- Real-time rendering for interactive presentations

- Physics and particle animations (for example, weather or crowd animation)

- Advanced animation features such as inverse kinematics

The following table can serve as a quick reference guide for you and will answer some of your questions. It is not exhaustive, and our selection is more an overview of available technologies and features, than a representation of the current market in rendering software.

The following table guides you with the specifications of different rendering software:

Rendering Software for SketchUp						
Category	Photorealistic Rendering					
Name	Indigo	iRender nXt	Thea	Maxwell	SU Podium	V-Ray
Platform	Win, Mac	Win	Win, Mac, Linux	Win, Mac, Linux	Win, Mac	Win, Mac
SketchUp integration	plugin	plugin	plugin stand alone	plugin stand alone	plugin	plugin
SketchUp features						
scenes/cameras	yes	yes	yes	yes	yes	yes
animation	no	yes	yes	yes	no	yes
proxy support	yes	yes	yes	yes	no	yes
shadow settings	yes	yes	yes	yes	yes	yes
textures	yes	yes	yes	yes	yes	yes
Render features						
unbiased/biased	yes/no	no/yes	yes/yes	yes/no	no/yes	yes/yes
GPU support	yes	no	yes	yes	no	yes
IBL support	yes	yes	yes	yes	no	yes
HDR output	yes	no	yes (EXR)	yes (Studio)	yes	yes
pp channels	no	no	yes	yes (Studio)	no	yes
Support						
user forum	+	-	+	+	-	+
resources	o	-	o	+	o	+
training	-	-	-	+	-	+
Purchase						
website	indigorenderer.com	renderplus.com	thearender.com	maxwellrender.com	suplugins.com	chaosgroup.com
trial version	yes	30-day	yes	yes	30-day	yes
price	EUR 595	$499	EUR 245	$99/$775	$198	$800
Comment						hardware

Rendering Software for SketchUp

	free		realtime		
	Luxrender	Kerkythea	Lumen RT	Lumion 3D	Podium Walker
	Win, Mac, Linux	Win only	Win, Mac	Win	Win, Mac
	plugin (beta)	exporter	exporter	DAE export	plugin
	yes	yes	(yes)	no	(yes)
	no	no	yes	yes	yes
	yes	no	no	no	no
	yes	yes	no	no	no
	yes	yes	yes	yes	yes
	yes/no	yes/no	--	--	--
	yes	no	yes	yes	no
	yes	no	no	no	no
	yes	no	no	no	no
	yes	yes	no	no	no
	o	+	-	+	-
	o	+	+	+	o
	-	-	-	o	-
	luxrender.net	kerkythea.net	e-onsoftware.com	lumion3d.com	suplugins.com
	--	--	limited	yes	yes
	free	free	$795/$1495	$2999/$1499	$99

Index

U

unbiased rendering process 38
uncanny valley 207
unwanted image noise
  removing 302-304

V

Value Control Box (VCB) 10, 85
vegetation
  about 208
  automatic veggie maker 209
  non photoreal sketchy trees 208
vehicles 209
video
  exporting 403
video sequences
  authoring 347, 348
video sequences, authoring
  animation, with Thea 350, 351
  high-resolution animation, from SketchUp
    349
  individual frames, saving for animation
    349
view
  aligning, to model 367
  setting up 21
viewpoints 346
viewports
  about 368
  arranging 374
vignette layer
  creating 232, 233
  used, for finishing image 316
Vimeo 55
VirtualDub
  about 55, 56, 351
  URL, for latest stable release 56
virtual light switch
  creating 282
visibility 16
visuals
  sketching 61, 62
Vue 209

W

Walkthrough tools 335
white board capture feature 164
window modeling
  about 28-30
  painting, with digital photos 31, 32
  rendered image, saving 38
  SketchUp materials, enhancing 34-36
  test rendering, performing 33, 34
windows
  mask render, using for 319, 320

Y

YouTube 55

Z

Zoom Extents tool 12
Zoom tool 12

Thank you for buying

SketchUp 2014 for Architectural Visualization
Second Edition

About Packt Publishing

Packt, pronounced 'packed', published its first book "*Mastering phpMyAdmin for Effective MySQL Management*" in April 2004 and subsequently continued to specialize in publishing highly focused books on specific technologies and solutions.

Our books and publications share the experiences of your fellow IT professionals in adapting and customizing today's systems, applications, and frameworks. Our solution based books give you the knowledge and power to customize the software and technologies you're using to get the job done. Packt books are more specific and less general than the IT books you have seen in the past. Our unique business model allows us to bring you more focused information, giving you more of what you need to know, and less of what you don't.

Packt is a modern, yet unique publishing company, which focuses on producing quality, cutting-edge books for communities of developers, administrators, and newbies alike. For more information, please visit our website: www.packtpub.com.

Writing for Packt

We welcome all inquiries from people who are interested in authoring. Book proposals should be sent to author@packtpub.com. If your book idea is still at an early stage and you would like to discuss it first before writing a formal book proposal, contact us; one of our commissioning editors will get in touch with you.

We're not just looking for published authors; if you have strong technical skills but no writing experience, our experienced editors can help you develop a writing career, or simply get some additional reward for your expertise.

Unity for Architectural Visualization

ISBN: 978-1-78355-906-0   Paperback: 144 pages

Transform your architectural design into an interactive real-time experience using Unity

1. Simple instructions to help you set up an interactive and real-time scene.

2. Excellent tips on making your presentations attractive by creating interactive designs.

3. Most important features of computer games covered, to develop compelling, interactive scenes for so-called "serious games".

Getting Started with Lumion 3D

ISBN: 978-1-84969-949-5   Paperback: 134 pages

Create a professional architectural visualization in minutes using Lumion 3D

1. A beginner's guide to architectural visualization.

2. Tips and tricks for modeling, texturing, and rendering using Lumion 3D.

3. Add a special touch to your images with Photoshop.

Please check **www.PacktPub.com** for information on our titles

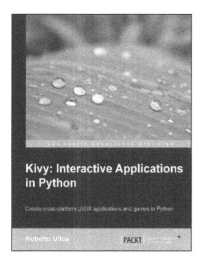

Kivy: Interactive Applications in Python

ISBN: 978-1-78328-159-6   Paperback: 138 pages

Create cross-platform UI/UX applications and games in Python

1. Use Kivy to implement apps and games in Python that run on multiple platforms.

2. Discover how to build a User Interface (UI) through the Kivy Language.

3. Glue the UI components with the logic of the applications through events and the powerful Kivy properties.

SketchBook Pro Digital Painting Essentials

ISBN: 978-1-84969-820-7   Paperback: 112 pages

Create stunning professional grade artwork using SketchBook Pro

1. Discover tricks and techniques that will help you make the most out of Sketchbook Pro.

2. Packed with practical examples that help you create expressive sketches ranging from cartoons to portraits.

3. A step-by-step guide packed with supporting imagery.

Please check **www.PacktPub.com** for information on our titles

www.ingramcontent.com/pod-product-compliance
Lightning Source LLC
Chambersburg PA
CBHW082116070326
40690CB00049B/2856